*Memoirs and
Confessions
of a
County
Planning Officer*

Frank Tindall, born 1919, died 1998.
Photograph taken by Jessie Ann Matthew in our garden at Ford House after these
Memoirs were completed in 1997.

Memoirs and Confessions

of a

County Planning Officer

FRANK TINDALL

the Pantile Press

First Published in 1998
by The Pantile Press
Ford House, Ford, Midlothian, EH37 5RE

ISBN 0 9534013 0 8

The following organisations and people have kindly granted permission for the
reproduction of photographs in this book:
The Royal Commission on the Ancient and Historical Monuments of Scotland,
East Lothian District Council,
John Dewar, Patricia Macdonald, Russell Turner,
Jim Catherwood, Ian Fullerton.

Typeset and designed by Kenneth Wilson, Cockburnspath, Berwickshire.
Printed in the Republic of Slovenia by Gorenjski Tisk
Printing and Publishing Co.

DEDICATION

These Memoirs are dedicated to my wife Mary who shares with me many of the memories, both pleasant and aggravating. She has brought her considerable architectural and personal sensitivity to help me throughout my career.

ACKNOWLEDGEMENTS

I am indebted to Councillor Pat O'Brien, Convenor of East Lothian County Council, for the Foreword and for permission to use the drawings and photographs from my days as County Planning Officer. I am also indebted to the Earl of Wemyss and March, K.T., LL.D., D.Univ., J.P. for agreeing to write an Appreciation of the book.

I was very lucky to have two talented photographers, Tom Scott, sadly now dead, and John Dewar, whose family lived in Gullane and who was up in the air photographing significant developments as they occurred. Their plates have been supplemented by Ian Fullerton of my County staff and Jim Catherwood of my Regional staff, to both of whom I am also very grateful. Jim Catherwood also assisted greatly with the editing.

I am greatly indebted to Stephanie Wolfe-Murray who gave us much good advice and encouragement, to Ken Wilson who designed the book, Lydia Skinner, and many others who helped. Lastly, again, to Mary who took on the laborious task of typing and retyping these memoirs and for that I am extremely grateful.

FOREWORD

East Lothian owes an enormous debt of gratitude to Frank Tindall. It is now nearly twenty five years since he left East Lothian County Council, but his influence has remained strong through two changes of local government.

Frank became County Planning Officer in 1950. He was one of a new passionate breed enthused by the pioneering work of Sir Patrick Geddes and Sir Frank Mears. They had supported a philosophy that preferred conservation to redevelopment and that valued all aspects of vernacular architecture and craftsmanship. To him we owe the conservation of some of the magnificent farm steadings and doocots of East Lothian. Thanks to him we retain some of the finest traditional villages in Scotland. Because of him the first town centre refurbishment scheme in Scotland was initiated in Haddington, and copied so often since. As a result of his determination so much was saved— Prestongrange beam engine, the Gullane dunes, Mitchell's Close in Haddington.

For a man of Frank's vision, it would never be enough to merely act as a planning regulator. He wanted to inspire and educate the people of East Lothian to appreciate their heritage of history, buildings, landscape and countryside. He introduced the county ranger service, he set up the first local nature reserve in Scotland at Aberlady, he established the Haddington to Longniddry Railway Walk, and he installed a range of open-air information boards full of insights into architecture and natural history.

Frank left East Lothian in 1975 to become Director of Physical Planning with the new Lothian Regional Council, but his legacy still informs so much of what we do, as councillors and officials. Since his retirement, he has retained all of his enthusiasm and continues to do great hands-on work with bodies such as the Lothian Buildings Preservation Trust, responsible for the recent magnificent restoration of the ruined Bankton House. How much poorer East Lothian would be without him.

Pat O'Brien
Convener
East Lothian Council   3 February 1998

AN APPRECIATION
By The Earl of Wemyss and March, K.T., LLD., D.Univ., J.P.

This work, which contains many references to things which have interested me in the past, is fascinating, informative and, withal, most pleasantly readable. I cannot praise it too highly.

When East Lothian County Council in 1950 sought for a Planning Officer, Frank Tindall was the only applicant for the job, and of course he got it. What a good thing that was! Had there been other applicants, one of them might have been preferred, perversely, by the authority; and then think what we would have missed.

It saddens me greatly that I must write these few paragraphs so soon after attending Frank's funeral service in the glorious old church of Crichton in Midlothian, not far from Ford, where he and Mary live. Lying in a remote and rather desolate area, and recently declared redundant by The Church of Scotland, it has now become Crichton Collegiate Church.

The first occasion when I saw a good deal of Frank was the Public Inquiry in 1953 in Haddington, when he, as County Planning Officer, was engaged in putting forward a Development Plan (in those days this was supposed to happen every fifth year) to which The National Trust for Scotland, of which I was then Chairman, objected, because it involved the demolition of some attractive old buildings in Tranent, Prestonpans, and above all in Haddington itself. This was confrontation indeed!

After it was all over, but before the result came out, my late wife and I went by sea, in cold, stormy weather, to Norway—"tae Norroway o'er the faem" as one of our old Scots ballads puts it. Inspired by that I wrote a ballad myself all about the Inquiry, in which Frank Tindall had his due place. Nearly forty-five years later I can be glad that I gave him at least a word of praise "Frank Tindall's the skilliest planner e'er cam frae Inglis land." He deserved that.

Of course, the last thing he wanted was to destroy East Lothian's heritage of lovely old buildings or any part of it; and indeed, largely through him, Haddington became known as one of the best preserved and most attractive examples of 18th and 19th Century burghal architecture in Scotland.

Frank Tindall went to Norway too. He was always keen to find out new things. He also went to Russia. Some regarded this as proof that he was a communist, and some of his students got the same idea. This was, of course, nonsense. He was indeed an enlightened socialist who linked and balanced preservation—keeping the good things we have—with conservation—using them properly and improving them.

Let us remember his hard and productive work on the "Countryside in 1970" Conference, when he was Secretary of the Scottish Study Group, and produced much good material which led directly to the Countryside (Scotland) Act, 1970. Let us also remember all the little plaques with thistles on them which he had affixed to buildings just before East Lothian County Council gave over to the Region and District (1975). we have a few of these here at Gosford, but they do not appear on the house itself, nor on churches; all of these are too obvious. What a splendid idea to leave them off buildings where there is no need to prove they are old and interesting!

Frank felt that the industrial heritage also should be cared for, before anyone else noticed it was there. In many ways he went beyond the strictures of his job for the good, although no doubt more died-in-the- wool planners often despaired of him.

I would make a reply to Frank's question at the end of this great work where he says "It is for others to judge whether I left East Lothian a more contented, prosperous and beautiful place than I found it."

My reply is Yes, obviously! both by what you have caused to happen and by what you have prevented from happening.

Wemyss

5 June '98

CONTENTS

PLATES

PREFACE

The Halcyon Days of Town Planning
Arrangement of the Memoirs

The Halcyon Days of Town Planning
County Planning Officers have rarely published their memoirs and little
has been written about the halcyon days of town planning in the post-
war years. Then, for the first time, the County Councils were charged
with the duty to survey all aspects of life in their counties, prepare
development plans for them and control all developments so that they
contributed to the realisation of these plans. The Town and Country
Planning Acts, 1947 also gave them compulsory powers to implement
their plans.

Few County Planning Officers have had such a beautiful county
in their care as East Lothian—a small county of 700 square miles lying
east of Edinburgh with a population in 1952 of 52,000 and a landscape
and a building tradition of great distinction, which has endeared it to
many people. It represented a microcosm of Scottish post-war
problems—declining basic industries, rural depopulation, an eroding
coastline and decaying burghs. It called for positive action both to
conserve and develop and these memoirs are the story of this endeavour.

They are written twenty years after I left East Lothian to take up
the post of Director of Physical Planning in the Lothian Regional
Council, and no doubt they have a golden glow. But they are firmly
based on published documents that cover the twenty five years: the
County Survey and Development Plan 1953; the two Annual Reports
of 1961 and 1962/3; and the Record of Policy and Achievements, 1974.
I have also refreshed my memory by re-reading the many reports I
made to the County Planning Committee. What I have not done is to
research through Committee minutes and other obfuscations that
controlled our daily lives. To this extent they are Memoirs and not a
Record

Since 1975 planning and development have become fragmented
and local government devalued and starved of money. Things have
moved on, as those now in my former position keep telling me.
Enterprise Companies, Housing Associations, Scottish Natural Heritage,
Tourist Boards and other state quangos have taken over. Town and
Country Planning has taken a more regulatory role and become bogged
down on one level by legal processes and on another by vast feasibility

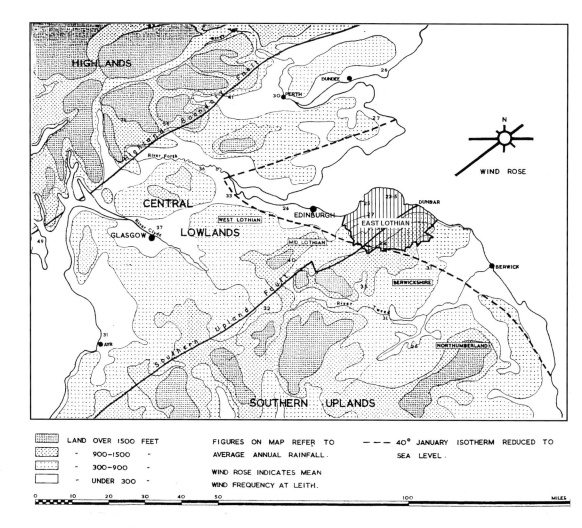

Plate I   The Regional Setting

The first illustration in the County Survey Report showed the geographic factors influencing the County. The end papers give a more detailed view of the County with its roads, railways and place names. The County did not include Musselburgh to the west, but did include the head waters of the Bothwell Water in the Lammermuirs now in the Borders.

studies. However with the re-establishment of Unitary Authorities in 1996 and the Labour Party's undertaking to empower once again Local Authorities, things may change again and my experience of 1950-1975 may be of value.

Arrangement

In these memoirs I first describe the planning problems of East Lothian as I found them in 1950 in its four very distinct parts. These were as set out in the County Survey Report and I include the subsequent action to overcome them. Secondly, I go through the County Development Plan 1953 and show how its policies had worked out on the ground by 1975. Then I tell of how things were achieved, starting with the Haddington Story and going on to describe how we created 2,974 jobs, rescued historic buildings, made 22 miles of coastal lands available to the public, cleared derelict land and carried out our other functions. I introduce the characters I met on the way, David Spence, the legendary John Muir and the young Richard Adams. I do not forget to mention where we tried and failed.

It was these activities and the escapades they led to which brought excitement and satisfaction to my work, to that of my loyal staff and eventually, I think, to that of the Councillors, who, as the years went by, increasingly trusted me with the care of the County.

1

THE BACKGROUND

My Appointment • Sir Frank Mears
The Geddes Philosophy • My First Four Staff • My Marriage
Councillors and Chairmen

My Appointment

When I came for interview by the East Lothian County Council in the late spring of 1950 I found myself the only applicant for the job of County Planning Officer. Sir Frank Mears, who was their planning consultant, had advised the Councillors to set up their own planning department to carry out the new functions required of them under the Act. I was not perhaps the type of person they were looking for. I had graduated in history at Cambridge University in 1940, I had the Diploma with Distinction from the School of Planning, London in 1948 and had spent two years with Berthold Lubetkin working on the social and economic aspects of the Master Plan for the New Town of Peterlee in County Durham. I had resigned with Lubetkin and the rest of the Master Plan team. My only experience of local government was two years as an elected Councillor for Egham Rural District on my demobilisation after four years service in the Middle East, the Sudan and Italy with the Eighth Army. I had also spent a year as an unpaid trainee in the Ministry of Town and Country Planning whose offices were in the old apartment block on the corner of St James' Square, London—learning experience—as it would now be called. But what an experience: with Sir William Holford, head of the department, Professor Gordon Stephenson, and Sir Colin Buchanan, in whose room I sat. In the drawing room/draughting office there were Sir Peter Shepheard, John Early, Donald Reay, Bill Compton, James Macaulay, Ian Warwick, Peter Joseph—to name but a few. During my time there they were chiefly concerned with the production of the *"Manual for the Redevelopment of Town Centres"* and with approving, after much modification, plans for rebuilding bombed city centres. All this was hardly relevant experience for East Lothian.

However the Councillors had not much option. They had left it rather late in taking the advice of Sir Frank Mears. Planners with local government experience were all placed in jobs and at that time there were only eighteen qualified town planners working in Scotland, most in the Department of Health for Scotland. Now there are eighteen hundred. Several counties had entrusted their planning to road surveyors and it had been the intention of East Lothian to hand responsibility to their newly appointed County Architect, Duncan Livingstone, who had a planning qualification, once the business of satisfying the Department of Health with a Survey and Development Plan was over.

The only concern that the Committee expressed over my appointment was how long this young graduate bachelor would stay. I remember assuring them that I would stay long enough to make it worthwhile for us both. I stayed twenty-five years.

Sir Frank Mears

I had the support of Sir Frank Mears, who was the son-in-law of Sir Patrick Geddes and provided the architectural studies to illustrate many of Sir Patrick's visions. I very much admired the fine rendered drawings of the new University Buildings for Jerusalem based on Geddes' integrated/inter-related faculties which hung in his office in Queen Street, Edinburgh. He had a flourishing architectural practice in the 1920s and 30s and some of his attractive houses can be seen in Gullane. They all had high slated roofs with dormer windows to light the bedrooms within the long combs. Green Craig at Kilspindie, now a hotel, is his most accessible house built out on the southern point of Shell Bay. During the 1930s he kept the flag flying for town planning in Scotland with small practical schemes such as one for North Berwick Harbour. In the late 1930s he became planning consultant for several counties and was appointed by the Secretary of State to lead the wartime Survey and Plan for Central and South-East Scotland, which complemented the Clyde Valley Plan led by Sir Patrick Abercrombie— each being based on a river valley, the Forth and the Clyde, as Geddes would have done. His Plan was a truly inspiring and Geddesian volume, but I found it of little practical help in preparing the County's Development Plan.

Mears was a slight man with a full grey moustache who wore old tweed clothes. On one occasion when my wife was about to take him home, she inquired why he had never owned a car and he replied that he had no need as there were always plenty of people willing to drive him. I remember a very typical incident when he had spotted a book he wanted in an antiquarian bookshop, of which there were many in the Edinburgh of the 1950s. He did not like the asking price and sent the office boy, not known to the bookseller, to acquire it for less some days later. He was a very wise, very canny old man much loved by his office and all who came in touch with him. Lady Mears, who survived him, was a magnificent virile woman, a landscape architect, who was

6

Plate II   Portrait of Sir Frank Mears, 1880 - 1953.

I had great difficulty in finding any photograph of Sir Frank but this pastel portrait of
him in his academic robes by James Cowie, RSA, reflects both his interest in the Royal
Scottish Academy, of which he was the President from 1933 to 1944, and his interest
in improving bridge design.

undertaking canoe trips well into her eighties. I regret I never came to know her well.

Sir Frank Mears left for New Zealand in the autumn of 1952 and died there and I was then on my own. He left me two gifts which proved of inestimable value. One was two shoe-boxes of old postcards which I constantly referred to when in doubt as to the answer to a conservation problem; the other, a complete set of drawings to 1/8 inch scale of the elevations of both sides of the High Street in Haddington. Curiously the two ends were omitted. They had been measured by his office at the beginning of the war after the shock of the first bomb in Scotland which was jettisoned over Haddington, demolishing a building on the south side of Market Street which is still a vacant site. Sir Frank was determined that the Haddington High Street facades should be rebuilt if they suffered total damage. Later we supplemented them with floor plans showing how the buildings could be adapted and improved, and the elevations were later used as the base drawing for the co-ordinated colour scheme of 1962. A similar prescience enabled the old square in the Warsaw Ghetto to be faithfully rebuilt after the war.

The Geddes Philosophy

Sir Patrick Geddes, 1854-1932, was a scientist, botanist and sociologist, and had laid down the philosophy of town planning in the cryptic words "Survey—Analysis—Plan leading to Action" which still guide us today. Before him, planning had been largely concentrated on urban design— fine beaux-arts layouts for town centres and housing estates. He introduced social surveys and the consideration of economic factors, and plans that could be implemented by many small realistic actions rather than one great dictatorial sweep.

I had read much of his writing during my years in Cambridge when my special subject was the period 1293-1301, which saw the growth of towns taking over from the feudal system. It was this study and my participation in the Cambridge University Research Branch for the Preservation of Rural England which had set me on a town planning career.

When I left for the Middle East in 1941 I arranged for the McAllisters, then working for the Town and Country Planning Association in London, to send me new publications dealing with the rebuilding of Britain after the war. Through their kindness I received the Uthwart and Scott Reports dealing with "Compensation and Betterment", and "Rural Affairs" respectively and many other books that filled my haversack leaving no room for the field-marshal's baton. A heavyweight was the "Middlesborough Survey and Plan" by Max Locke which took social survey further than any other wartime plans and was a seminal document as far as I was concerned.

Plate III Portrait of Sir Patrick Geddes, 1854-1932
Botanist, Sociologist and Town Planner. Photographed about 1920.

The first five months of my appointment I worked from Sir Frank Mears' office and lived in part of a seventeenth century condemned tenement flat in St James' Court, overlooking Princes Street Gardens. My companions were a stationery embosser and a potter but I was the only one to sleep there. As this was illegal, it was a stipulation of George Scott-Moncrieff, a writer, who lent it to me that I did not open or clean the windows and so, frustratingly, I only saw the magnificent view across the New Town to Fife through an ever thickening mat of cobwebs.

Under Sir Frank's gentle guidance and with the help of his colleagues, Robert Naismith, later to write the well researched books *"The Story of Scotland's Towns"* and *"Scottish Vernacular Building"*, and Miss Comrie, I reported on planning applications and got to know the County.

One abiding lesson he taught me was not to get upset when the Planning Committee failed to accept our advice. He described it as blood letting. The Committee had to have their own way but later they would come round to accept our good advice. This lesson was borne out in Prestonpans where the Town Council was determined to clear away all their old eighteenth century High Street which before the First World War had made Prestonpans as picturesque as Crail. No argument would stop them, but when it came to rebuilding they accepted that it must be done in stone.

My First Four Staff

By September 1950 the County Council had cleared and allocated to me a room in County Buildings under the Sheriff Court in the north-east corner facing Court Street. I had acquired furniture and four members of staff: a planning assistant, Neroli Wilkins, a New Zealander from the School of Planning, two draughtsmen, George Alexander from the Ordnance Survey, very useful at the first vital step of bringing the maps up to date, the other, John McNeil from the Burgh Surveyor's office in Tranent and Joyce Sheerin, our typist. We all worked in that one room for many years, the draughtsmen by the two windows onto Court Street, the typist by the door acting as receptionist and myself at a desk in the far back corner.

My Marriage

It was that same autumn that I got engaged to Mary Miller, an architect and planner, whom I first met at the School of Planning. She says her first impression of me was as Major Tindall, wearing a waistcoat and carrying an umbrella, which she considered most unsuitable wear for a student; and mine of her as the first girl I had seen wearing the "New Look", a long brown suit acquired in Canada while in Britain clothes were still rationed. Our love affair developed during that last student year and we both went to work at Peterlee. She, too, resigned with Lubetkin and all the Master Plan team and having pointed me towards East Lothian, which she knew from her war-time work in the Department of Health for Scotland, she took a senior planning job with Kent County Council. However by the autumn we both realised that we could not live apart: I proposed to her on the banks of Loch Lomond and we decided to marry on 10 March 1951 in London. Since then she only ever practised as a town planner through me and I owe to her all the architectural sensitivity that I came to have. She continued practising architecture from the house and has left a number of beautiful restorations throughout the County. Of course I could never recommend her, or later my son Benjamin who also became an architect. They both complain that they have suffered from negative nepotism.

After Sir Frank Mears died I had to settle down on my own and finish the County Survey and Development Plan which were to guide development until the re-organisation of local government in 1975. By then I had a very very able chief planning assistant, Graham Duncan, and we agreed one holiday weekend that I would apply for the job of Director of Physical Planning with the newly created Lothian Regional Council and he would apply for the Director of Planning with the East Lothian District Council. This luckily worked out. I had always realised that East Lothian's future depended on developments in the Edinburgh City Region and so was able to have some influence on the development of the County during the rest of my working life, until 1983.

Councillors and Chairmen

Perhaps I should comment here that East Lothian County Council had a majority of independent members, but followed a socialist policy. This suited me fine. However I found that it was a little exacting, as I had to continually remind members when deciding cases not only of their policy but the reasons for it. Even then their decisions were often very erratic and it was my job to try to find a thread of consistency to satisfy the public.

I never had a very close relationship with the succession of Chairmen of the County Planning Committee. The Marquis of Tweeddale held himself very aloof and was of an older generation. Mr Gilbert, the Provost of North Berwick for many years and a prominent garage and motor dealer, was a very fair man and knew a good job when he saw one, but had little imagination and was greatly bound up in North Berwick affairs. George McNeil, the labour Provost of Tranent who ran a plasterer's business was a more active and thoughtful man with whom I got on best. He was later elected to the Lothian Regional Council. Perhaps the two people I remember best were Lady Broun-

Lindsay of Colstoun who provided me with a lot of support, although she would not allow me to plant sycamore (a wonderful tree for coastal areas) because she saw all its bad features in her woods. The other was Baillie Toal of Prestonpans, a fine old miner who often came to lunch after committee meetings before I drove him home.

It was very different and easier in the Regional Council where the Councillors spent more time on their Council business and where there was a dining room in which we met more frequently. The Councillors were organised in strong political groups and I had to work with both Labour and Tory majorities. One knew where one was when advising them and I could carry out the ruling group's policy with certainty, not continually changing as the independent members grouped and regrouped on individual issues. I am glad to say that in the Regional Planning and Development Committee the debates were not highly political and a considerable effort was made by the successive chairmen to keep it that way.

2

THE FOUR PARTS OF THE COUNTY AND THEIR PROBLEMS IN 1951

THE MINING AREA.
Prestongrange and Other Collieries • Mining Towns and Villages
Housing Land • Open-Cast Coal • Employment for Women

THE CENTRAL AREA.
Rural Depopulation • Flooding of the River Tyne
Mineral Resources • Limestone

THE HILLFOOT AREA.
Demographic Survey • Village Spheres of Influence
Hill Land Use • Gully Erosion

THE COASTAL AREA.
A String of Villages • Land for Private Housing • Port Seton
Longniddry • Aberlady • Gullane • Dirleton • North Berwick
Whitekirk • Dunbar

COASTAL CONSERVATION
Seton Camp • Longniddry Foreshore • Gosford • Aberlady Bay
Gullane Bay • Yellowcraig • Tantallon Castle • Tyninghame
Barns Ness • Coastal Lands • Skateraw • Thorntonloch

My wife and I, like many other couples at that time, spent our first six months in lodgings. We used our free time getting to know the County and developed a great affection for it. East Lothian lies to the east of the City of Edinburgh, bounded on the north by the Firth of Forth, to the east by the cold North Sea, to the south by a curving line along the top of the Lammermuir Hills and to the west by a meandering line separating it from Midlothian. This was altered in the reorganisation of local government in 1975 and the Burgh of Musselburgh was taken into East Lothian giving it a shared boundary with Edinburgh. It has a dry and temperate climate and this with its fertile soil and proximity to the City led to both the earliest agricultural improvements and to the earliest small scale industrial development, based on the workings of the shallow coal seams to provide cheap fuel.

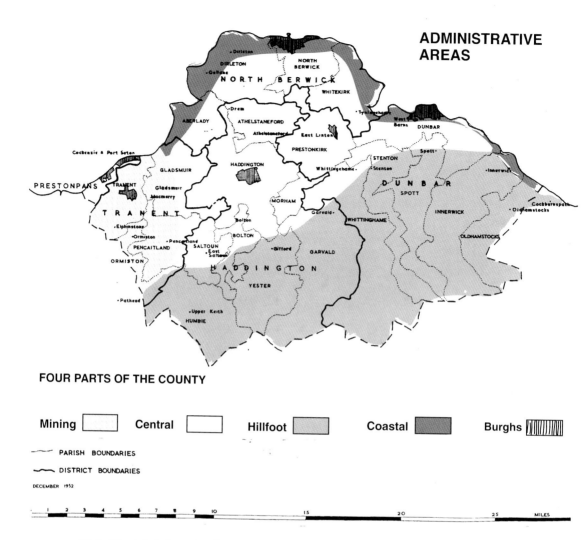

ADMINISTRATIVE
AREAS

FOUR PARTS OF THE COUNTY

Mining [ ]   Central [ ]   Hillfoot [ ]   Coastal [ ]   Burghs [||||||]

- - - - PARISH BOUNDARIES

─── DISTRICT BOUNDARIES

DECEMBER 1952

1 2 3 4 5 6 7 8 9 10   15   20   25   MILES

Plate IV   Administrative Areas

The Survey Report contained this map showing the Seven Burghs and the Four Districts into which the County was divided. Each had an elected Council and small staff who were consulted at all stages of plan preparation. Superimposed are the four areas we used in describing the County and identifying its problems.

In the 1950s it had four very distinct parts which were dealt with in separate chapters of the Survey Report, each printed on differently coloured paper. It became County Planning Policy to unite these four areas and now, 46 years later, they are much less distinct and all look to Haddington as the County Town. However I will describe the County planning problems as set out in the Survey Report in its four parts, and will bring them up to date to show the results of our planning endeavours and so make it more recognisable to the current reader—so many have been the changes.

THE MINING AREA

In the west of the County the limestone coal seams of the Midlothian basin outcrop in a great curve from Longniddry through Macmerry, Pencaitland, Ormiston and on to Pathhead in Midlothian.

Prestongrange and Other Collieries

In 1951 there were three large collieries, two on the coast at Prestongrange, employing 694 miners, and Prestonlinks, where Cockenzie Power Station now stands, employing 836 miners, and one at the Fleets, south of Tranent, employing 595 miners, where the Inveresk Research Station was built. Another prominent site which concerned us, although not a colliery, was the central washery for the Edinburgh Coal Company built alongside the mainline railway at Meadowmill with a large two-headed bing which has now been transformed into a handsome green pyramid, with playing fields where the coal stocking grounds once were. Both coastal collieries tipped their spoil into the sea off coastal bings. There was a dastardly proposal by the management at Prestongrange to build an aerial ropeway to tip directly into the sea off the Ox Rock, that raised the spectre of total despoliation of the coastline as coal and stones were washed along the shore, as had happened in County Durham. This had only been averted by the Town Clerk of Edinburgh serving an interdict on the National Coal Board. The coastal bing has since been grassed and planted up and provides a fine coastal open space although the coal harbour of Aitchison's Haven, later Morrison's Haven, has still to be dug out and reclaimed. The site of the Prestongrange Colliery is still marked by the great beam pumping engine and the Industrial Heritage Site of which more anon in Chapter 12. A similar grassy area marks the site of Prestonlinks Colliery, courtesy of the South of Scotland Electricity Board, but again more anon in Chapter 5.

There were four other smaller collieries, the most easterly, Glencairn, on the south-west edge of Longniddry. Such was the need for coal after the war that the National Coal Board sank four additional shallow drift mines, of which little trace now remains, to work pockets of coal in the Great Seam, the grand six foot thick seam of coal exploited from the twelfth century onwards.

In all 2,771 miners were employed in 1950. There was also a war-time report recommending the sinking of a major new colliery south of the Mid-Road, adjoining the railway at Prestonpans, to work the undersea coals in the Firth of Forth. Miners from the west of Scotland, where coal reserves were exhausted, were to be transferred to man the colliery. It was proposed to build a new town for them at Seton, south of Port Seton, and a compulsory purchase order had been served on the landowners. The proposal was dropped by the National Coal Board when the coal industry was nationalised in 1947. Instead, a colliery was built at Monktonhall with a 3,000 foot shaft to reach the bottom of the Midlothian coal basin. However right up to 1980 the National Coal Board pursued the idea of working the under-sea coals by sinking a man-riding shaft at the mouth of the River Esk and taking the coals to Monktonhall for processing and loading into wagons. But declining demand and problematic geological conditions put an end to this proposal.

Mining Towns and Villages

It was these mines and the miners who dominated life in the west of the County. Many settlements had houses built by the private coal owners—attractive groups remaining at East Wynd, Prestonpans and at Beech Terrace, Pencaitland to man the Woodhall pit, and at New Winton. The Labour Party had seen to it that the three Burgh Councils of Prestonpans, Cockenzie and Tranent, and the County Council at Preston, Macmerry, Ormiston and Elphinstone, exercised their powers under the Housing Acts to build new houses for them between the wars. In 1951 over 95% of the houses in Prestonpans were either Council or Coal Board houses to rent.

Prestonpans was a "wild place" with strife between Catholics and Protestants originating in the influx, in about 1900, of Irishmen to work the coastal collieries. Its people had little self esteem. For instance there was never a public telephone kiosk that was not vandalised.

In 1953 it still had remnants of its old industries: salt panning, although no longer evaporating sea water but purifying and packaging rock salt; soap making; and Fowler's Brewery was well known throughout Scotland for its "Wee heavy". The last pottery, Bellfields, had closed in 1939 and its premises were being used by a tyre retread firm. I am ashamed to say I never penetrated this building, or I would have found a bottle kiln, and even more ashamed of my successors who allowed it to be demolished. There is now a growing interest in Prestonpans pottery and I persuaded the Scottish Mining Museum to mount an exhibition in 1990 "*Pots from the Pans*" which showed a range of fine pottery, way beyond the brown ornamented teapot which is the general image. The salt works fared only a little better in that I sent out two draughtsmen to survey Mellis's extensive buildings with all their complicated flue structures for heating the cast-iron pans. I left a proposal for the eastern part next to our small Civic Square to be turned into a lock-fast museum with the key held by Ford the Bakers, but to no avail: it was all swept away for housing.

At Cockenzie and Port Seton old inhabitants remembered days before the collieries when Edinburgh folk took houses for the summer holidays—a tradition still perpetuated at Seton Sands Holiday Camp, and a swimming pool and promenade had been built in the 1930s to encourage this business. Cockenzie also had its coal-harbour built by Robert Stevenson in 1835 and then used for boat building. The County Council later bought it to safeguard this marginal industry. Port Seton had a fishing harbour built by Lord Wemyss in 1880 which, thanks be, still has a fishing fleet although it is away much of the year.

Tranent was the main town on the East Lothian coalfield and had developed a large Co-operative Society which took over the other smaller societies in the County—although the Prestonpans Co-operative Society held out a long time against them. They developed a large central butchery, bakery, creamery, boot repair, tailoring and funeral undertaking businesses in the town and owned several farms in the area to supply vegetables and graze their dairy herd. The large Co-operative emporiums attracted working people from throughout the County and its dividend payout nights were great social occasions. It was always said that the Tranent Town Council and the Board of the East Lothian Co-operative Society were the same team in different jerseys and the Town Council never had any difficulty in acquiring land for the expansion of the town.

The main planning problem was to identify stable ground for building as the area was both riddled with old coal workings at shallow depths and affected by current workings. There were countless stories of horse and carts disappearing as the pillars of coal holding up the surface collapsed or old shafts reopened. I went with the Burgh Surveyor of Tranent, Jimmy Walker, down into one of these old workings just 15 feet below the surface under a pre-fab housing scheme where a hole had opened up. It was a dark muddy place of criss-cross passageways, "stoop and room workings" as the miners called them, where coal was dug in a grid of criss-cross galleries leaving blocks of coal to support the roof. When the miners reached the limit of their lease they worked their way back shaving off further coal from the pillars, leaving them as small as they dared. It was these that had deteriorated through the action of water and air and mining at lower levels. We did not venture very far through these crumbling passages but in the past they had been a place of refuge for Tranent people on the approach of the English armies. When the County Council built the Tranent Town Centre where Well Wynd used to spill out onto the High Street and where the Library now is, we had to pump in weak concrete to fill these caverns to ensure support for the buildings.

The Survey Reports for the Burghs were each accompanied by a map showing the factors affecting development. They also showed areas of permanent danger due to old workings at shallow depths and areas affected by projected coal workings and the date, after settlement, when they could be deemed to be safe. They identified old shafts which

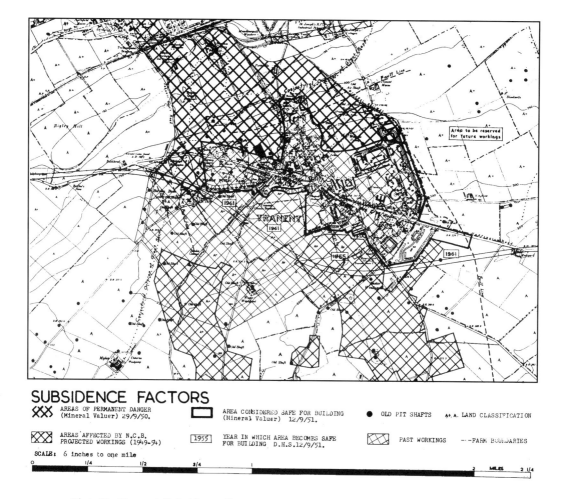

SUBSIDENCE FACTORS

✗✗✗	AREAS OF PERMANENT DANGER (Mineral Valuer) 29/9/50.	▭	AREA CONSIDERED SAFE FOR BUILDING (Mineral Valuer) 12/9/51.	● OLD PIT SHAFTS	A+, A. LAND CLASSIFICATION

| ✗✗✗ | AREAS AFFECTED BY N.C.B. PROJECTED WORKINGS (1949-54) | [1955] | YEAR IN WHICH AREA BECOMES SAFE FOR BUILDING D.H.S.12/9/51. | ⧄ PAST WORKINGS | ---FARM BOUNDARIES |

SCALE: 6 inches to one mile

0   1/4   1/2   3/4   1   2   MILES   2 1/4

Plate V   Tranent Subsidence Factors

Plan from the Survey Report showing the analysis that was carried out to delineate possible housing areas. Tranent was constricted to the north and it could only spread south, but as this was A+ agricultural land it was decided that housing should only be provided for local people and speculative housing should leap-frog the mining areas to build up Haddington as the County Town. The area to the east shown as reserved for future workings is the Blindwells Open-cast site.

were always a matter of concern since few had been properly filled and they were liable to collapse. They showed the agricultural classification of the land and the farm boundaries and in the case of Tranent the proposed southern bypass for the A1. It was these maps which showed the limitations on the development of these towns. The rule was adopted that council houses could only be permitted in the areas where there was ten fathoms (sixty feet) of good rock cover over the old workings and each site had to be drilled to establish this rock cover. Such housing could be no more than two storeys high in blocks of two.

Housing Land

As well as the stability of the land there was the question of how much was to be zoned for housing. Our main difficulty was to get information on the expected life of the collieries.

The officials of the National Coal Board were by and large the same men who had worked for the private coal companies and had inherited their tradition of secrecy, mystification and non-co-operation with the local authorities. I had experienced the same attitude in the Durham Coalfield and it was not until a new generation of mining engineers and managers had risen into responsible jobs in the industry that they began to co-operate and take a wider view of their national responsibilities. Still there was sufficient information for me to question and halt the large housing expansion for Ormiston proposed by the Housing Committee when I could show that the two local collieries, Limeylands and Tynemount, only had a short life. The planning system was beginning to bite.

The Housing Committee had always built on the basis of the length of the waiting lists of people wanting houses in each village. I was able to bring other considerations into the argument—future employment, the agricultural classification of land, subsidence danger and areas liable to flooding, the availability of drainage, water and electricity supplies. The Survey Report also recorded the increasing movement out of mining villages to work elsewhere and analysed the housing preferences as kept by the Housing Manager. It drew the conclusion that in all mining settlements the housing programme should be limited, while expanding social and other amenities so that they could continue to hold their current population. Part of this policy meant the building of houses for old people so that the existing family houses could be made available to young families who did not, therefore, need to move away. I suppose in much of this I was influenced by the memory of the deserted villages of West Durham but this policy of community consolidation has been an objective throughout my planning career.

Open-Cast Coal

While the National Coal Board Deep Mining officials were secretive, the Open-cast Executive were more forthcoming, being newer and dependent on receiving local planning approval for their workings. The Survey Report showed all areas they had prospected and where proven coal reserves existed. It was a political decision, before my time, that stopped the open-casting of a large area of high grade agricultural land south-east of Penston. It was argued that open-cast operations would reduce food supply and discourage farming, and should be on poorer land in Central Scotland and Fife. This policy was continued by the Lothian Regional Council after 1975 but with the proviso that open-cast coal reserves should not be sterilised but excavated in advance of other developments.

Employment for Women

The Survey Report also documented the poor employment position of women, who made up only some 20 per cent of all employed in 1948 in the Tranent Employment Exchange Area compared with 35 per cent in the Haddington Area. Their employment was also mainly in uncongenial work in agricultural field gangs. The case for new industry was clear, but not perhaps the role of the County Council in stimulating it. That had.to wait until the severe rundown of mining and agricultural employment in the early 1960s when the County Council were finally prepared to develop the old RAF technical site which lay south of the A1 at Macmerry. This was zoned in the County Development Plan 1953 as the central site for providing new industries for redundant miners, their womenfolk and agricultural workers.

THE CENTRAL AREA

The Central Area, the heartland of East Lothian, is a land of large prosperous arable farms, at that time with an average size of 450 acres, served by three market towns: Haddington, the tiny East Linton, and Dunbar, and a few pantiled villages. It is divided by the Garleton Hills into the coastal plain to the north and to the south the wooded landscape of the River Tyne Valley with its mixed arable and stock farms and its mansion houses and policies reaching to the foothills of the Lammermuirs. Through it runs the A1, the Great North Road, which on the County Surveyor's drawings was always titled the "London-Thurso Trunk Road". The main line railway to London runs through the coastal plain north of the Garleton foothills and crosses the Tyne into the wooded landscape at East Linton.

East Lothian is the County whose seventeenth century landowners pioneered the development of the first agricultural revolution in Scotland. It is the land of the Rennies, the great civil engineers, and of the Meikles, agricultural engineers and millwrights. It is the land of large "ferm-touns" each with a good slated farm house, up to twelve pantiled cottages and a large steading with six or eight cattle courts for over-wintering store cattle in order to get their invaluable dung for the corn crop. It is the land of 'smooth cultivation' as John Muir described it. It never ceases to astonish me how each spring the corn comes up in the straightest of lines within fields surrounded by the trimmest of hedges. It is a truly wonderful, smiling landscape. Nevertheless, by 1950 there were few farmers who, like their eighteenth century predecessors, saw it as a worthy objective to

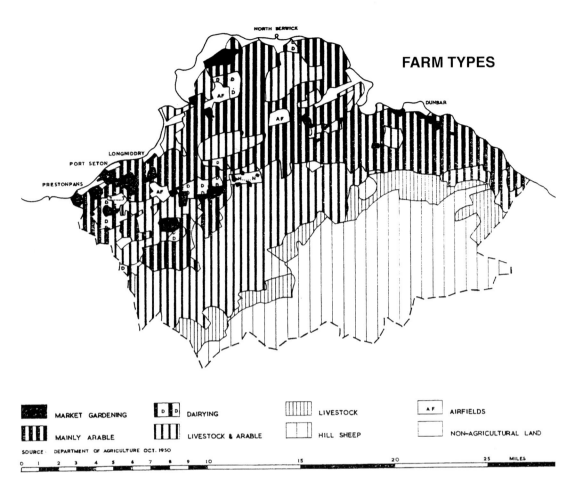

FARM TYPES

NORTH BERWICK

DUNBAR

LONGNIDDRY
PORT SETON
PRESTONPANS

| | MARKET GARDENING | | DAIRYING | | LIVESTOCK | A F | AIRFIELDS |
| | MAINLY ARABLE | | LIVESTOCK & ARABLE | | HILL SHEEP | | NON-AGRICULTURAL LAND |

SOURCE: DEPARTMENT OF AGRICULTURE OCT. 1950

0 1 2 3 4 5 6 7 8 9 10   15   20   25 MILES

Plate VI Farm Types

The intensity of cultivation is delineated with market gardening—which employed the largest number of people per acre—solid black, and narrowing bands of black showing the arable, livestock and hill sheep on the Lammermuirs. Also shown are the dairy farms, the three airfields, and the larger forestry plantations.

There were some twenty-seven maps and diagrams published in the Survey Report analysing all the physical and social features of the County. In all, with detailed maps, there were sixty-one drawings

increase the numbers they employed by developing new crops and new markets. The Chalmers Watsons, whose doctor father had established a dairy herd at Fenton Barns for the health-giving properties of fresh milk, were a notable exception, later developing a turkey business and then mushroom production. This was the farm where a distant relative of mine served a jovial apprenticeship as recorded in his diaries in the middle of the nineteenth century, when budding farmers came from all parts to study the advanced cultivation. Now the majority of farmers merely invest in more powerful machinery, reduce manpower and concentrate on cereal production with fieldwork largely done in the six to eight week period after the harvest by contractors.

The three planning problems examined in the Survey Report were firstly, measures to check the depopulation of the agricultural parishes; secondly, measures to prevent the recurrent flooding of the Tyne; and thirdly, the extent of the area's mineral resources.

Rural Depopulation

The continuing decline of population in the agricultural parishes which had started in the 1850s had quickened between 1931 and 1951 and plummeted when tractors superseded horses. It was clearly important that the County Council should take what steps it could to retain sufficient people on the land to work it. I was rather suspicious of the effects of the universal tied cottage system which was driving families off the land in England. But the farm cottages in the County were in the main well-built and had been much improved in the 1930s by the gentle persuasion of John Reid, the County Sanitary Inspector. They had water and sanitary facilities and I oversaw the spread of electricity to the remotest farms in the 1950s. The two-roomed cottages were being combined together to provide larger houses. There was little grievance on this score.

The rural villages were also well served with schools, halls, churches and, at that time, blacksmiths' forges and carpenters' shops. What they lacked was the middle class of ancient and retired families which characterise English village life and give rise to a much wider range of occupations and facilities. This was slowly altered by encouraging middle class people to restore houses in the villages and build on suitable sites in the countryside.

The answer to retaining agricultural workers lay in building up the burghs, so that their sons and daughters could get access to secondary education, and the employment and enjoyment no longer provided on the farms or in the villages, so that whole families did not migrate into the cities. The Haddington Story, Chapter Four, recounts how this was done. The other factor driving people off the land was that there was no ladder of advancement for ambitious farm workers through smaller tenanted farms. The Department of Agriculture for Scotland, not the County Councils as in England, had the responsibility for creating small holdings. A number of large farms had been divided up into five and ten acre holdings in the 1920s and 30s for the purpose of settling the unemployed on the land. Through time, the Department amalgamated some of these at the Boggs, Letham and elsewhere into larger more viable holdings. But nowhere did they consciously create a ladder of advancement for farm workers enabling them to get beyond the status of farm grieve or manager and today the situation is getting worse. Farms have got bigger and tenanted farms fewer. To be a farmer in East Lothian it is almost necessary to inherit or marry into a farm. This problem is still unresolved.

Flooding of the River Tyne

When I moved into East Lothian memory was still fresh of the catastrophic flood of 1948 when the River Tyne lapped at the doorstep of the Town House in Haddington. The Survey Report examined the river, its history of flooding and the sources of its pollution. In the 1950s most settlements and industries discharged through grossly overloaded septic tanks into the Tyne or its tributaries. It was the achievement of the Lothian River Purification Board, established in 1952, and a tribute to the energy of the County Sanitary Inspector, Jimmie Gibson, that this situation was transformed during my twenty-five years in East Lothian. The Tyne now supports good fish and bird life with salmon and kingfishers as far upstream as Pencaitland. However the Purification Board was not empowered to deal with flooding or to carry out engineering works on the rivers. It was quite difficult to persuade the Board to lengthen their marker boards to measure the optimum flood flows as well as the minimum flows which were their main concern.

This was to be a particular interest of mine after the recurrence of flooding in 1956 when both my home at Haddington and the old house at Ford, 11 miles upstream, which I had just bought, were under four feet of flood water. We mapped the extent of the flood plain along the Tyne and then made it County Planning Policy to refuse consent for any new buildings within it and also recommended that floor levels of restored or extended buildings should be one foot above the 1956 flood level. This was termed the 25 year flood, occurring four times a century. The previous one had occurred in 1931 and the subsequent one in 1984. There was also the catastrophic 100 year flood in 1948. Damage from flood water largely resulted from the build-up of trees and other debris behind bridges, raising the level until the force of water broke them and the whole bang lot went rushing downstream to block the next bridge. This was particularly notable in the 1948 flood when a succession of ten railway bridges on the main line were destroyed one after the other.

So in 1956 we plotted the fallen timber, overhanging trees, hen-houses and other obstructions on the flood plain and wrote to the owners asking them to clear them. We had no statutory powers to support this action, but we got a reasonable response and much clearance was carried out. Where there were no identifiable owners, as at Hailes, we organised volunteers to clear away the mess. This is an operation which should be repeated at regular intervals but it appears to have been all but forgotten and the River Tyne is again in a very dodgy state. The Lothian Regional Council did set up an Emergency Plan which gave advance warning of flooding on the Tyne and provided sandbags and succour. Forty years on, the Flood Prevention and Land Drainage Act 1997 placed a duty on local authorities to assess likely causes of flooding and maintain water courses.

Mineral Resources

The third matter the Survey Report examined was the mineral resources of the County. We identified and tried to protect those quarries formerly used for building stone which could be reopened if the demand ever arose, as indeed the Rattlebags Quarry was reopened to build the new Monastery at Nunraw. The hardrock quarries for road metal were the problem. The County Council itself was the main culprit, enlarging a small quarry at the foot of Traprain Law into a massive face which cut high into the eastern ramparts of the iron age hill-town, legendary capital of King Loth of Lothian. It became a progressively greater eyesore as a tarring plant and workshops were erected alongside it. It was not until I took my 50 page damning dossier on the quarry to the Regional Council in 1975, that it was eventually closed. Other messy road-stone quarries were closed down at Dirleton and in the Garleton Hills, but Bangley Quarry was permitted to expand.

Limestone

Limestone was a more interesting mineral with many disused lime kilns for burning lime. Two deposits were still being worked. That at East Saltoun was being quarried the traditional open-cast way by the Co-operative Wholesale Society who produced agricultural lime for "gooding the land". It ceased working in the 1960s, was filled with domestic refuse and is currently the subject of an environment improvement proposal. The other, at Oxwellmains, Dunbar, was mined by the Coltness Iron Company of Motherwell. This was a twenty feet high cavern with pillars of limestone holding up the sandstone roof and the limestone was being worked in benches. It was loaded onto wagons on the mainline railway and transported to Coatbridge for use in the steel smelters.

Labour practice was also old fashioned in that miners turned up when they wanted, filled as many tubs as they wanted and left when they had had enough. Several of them had a profitable sideline in collecting winkles from the sea-shore for the London markets and so their mining activity was determined by the tide tables.

It was this deposit that came casually to the notice of the Associated Portland Cement Manufacturers Ltd who had been scouring Scotland for a limestone deposit that would support a cement industry. Their development is described in Chapter Five but the magnificent old mine still exists below the bing of overburden rock west of their Works.

THE HILLFOOT AREA

The Hillfoot area lies across the Southern Upland Fault which, with its twin to the north, the Highland Boundary Fault, defines the Central Lowlands of Scotland. The County embraced not only the north face of the Lammermuirs, which terminate in a line of foothill villages where the hill burns enter the broad glacial plain, but also a considerable area of the flattish eroded top of the Lammermuir Hills including the upper valleys of the Whiteadder, the Faseny, the Bothwell and Monymusk rivers which all drain south and east through Berwickshire. It is a most confusing area where a walker without a compass can easily get lost. After the local government re-organisation in 1975 these upper valleys were transferred to the Borders Region. It holds a "granite basin" within its old silurian rocks which had supported much life in the Iron and Bronze Ages as shown by the remains of many forts and homesteads. In the 1950s it contained the small hamlet of four houses and a school, Kingside, which were demolished for the new Kingside Reservoir in the 1960s. Sir Frank Mears was very interested in the health of the hills and considered that it was vital for the County Council to maintain the hill population. In the immediate post-war period he had persuaded the County Council to build houses in the hill villages and even a pair at Kingside, which later became a letting nightmare for the Housing Manager.

We therefore undertook two special surveys. First, a social survey of the composition of the population on the farms and in the villages which served them, the so-called villages' spheres of influence. Second, a land-use survey of the hills to show their potential. These were beyond the requirements of the Department of Health for Scotland whose circulars and planning requirements were concentrated largely on urban problems. They gave us a great opportunity to get into the hills and gather fresh facts, not merely gleaning and correlating information from other sources.

Demographic Survey

The Social Survey proved relatively easy. We did not call at each house but found two knowledgeable people in each village—maybe the resident policeman, the district nurse, a farmer's wife or the schoolmaster who knew the families in the vicinity and could provide sufficiently accurate information for our purposes, although as a precaution we checked their information with other informants. We avoided the ministers who tended to know only their congregations. In this way we built up age and sex profiles for all the villages and people living in their sphere of influence in ten year age bands. We also got information on pre-school, school 5 to 15 and post-school 16 to 20 age groups. This information later proved most useful in examining school closures. These age-profiles were drawn up in the usual way and could be interpreted to show the different characteristics of each village but they all showed a disproportionately small 16 to 20 age-group with teenagers leaving home. The three village profiles of Humbie, Gifford and Garvald were all top heavy with older age groups exceeding younger ones. In Stenton and Spott it was the reverse but this was occasioned by the temporary presence of forestry workers both felling and planting trees. This showed the valuable part that the expansion of forestry could play in maintaining the village populations. A similar study was done as a check on Athelstaneford which showed a more robust profile.

Village Spheres of Influence

A phenomenon we found when plotting the village spheres of influence was that alternate villages were increasing their attraction at the expense of intermediate ones. Gifford, a most attractive planned village dating from 1720, was already attracting Edinburgh commuters, and was the largest and best equipped village with a population of 466. It was increasing its draw from Humbie and Garvald. Stenton similarly was drawing people from Spott and Whittingehame, and Innerwick people from Spott and Oldhamstocks. This led to the decision to build up these key villages with new schools at Gifford and Innerwick and to the fight to keep open the Stenton school. The intermediate villages were not written off. Where the schools were closed, as in Garvald, they were used to attract village industries, of which more anon, and as in Spott for a village hall. We instituted an active programme of directing inquirers to old properties needing restoration in all these villages but the County Council only built houses in the three key villages. All this helped to check depopulation and enliven life in the hill villages.

Hill Land Use

The other study we made was of land-use above the 800 foot contour and reaching to the County Boundary. As well as arable and pasture land this identified heather, woodland and devastated woodland which amounted to more than four fifths of all the woodland. It also identified marshy ground, gully and sheet erosion and shingle accumulations in the valleys as a result of the 1948 flood. The main existing woodland was in the Humbie area where arable cultivation reached well up to 1,100 feet, 300 feet higher than anywhere else, showing the ameliorating effect of woodland and shelter belts.

After the 1956 flood we tried to initiate a tree planting programme above 800 feet to counteract the Department of Agriculture's financed drainage and hill grazing improvement grants. These had resulted in a

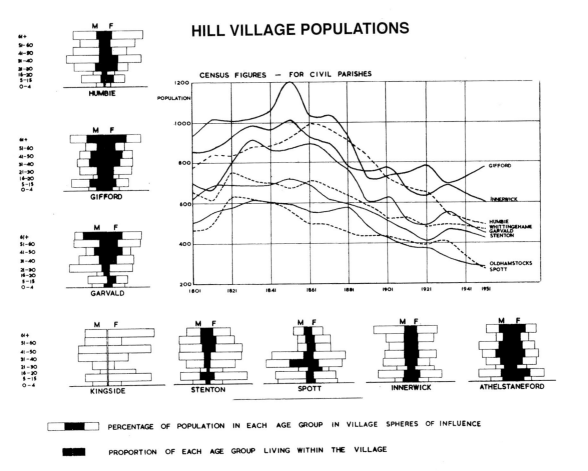

HILL VILLAGE POPULATIONS

CENSUS FIGURES — FOR CIVIL PARISHES

PERCENTAGE OF POPULATION IN EACH AGE GROUP IN VILLAGE SPHERES OF INFLUENCE

PROPORTION OF EACH AGE GROUP LIVING WITHIN THE VILLAGE

Plate VII   Hill Village Populations

The graph shows that the hill parish populations peaked between 1841 and 1861 and have steadily declined since then. The diagrams show the 10 year age groups both of the villages and of those living on the farms in their sphere of influence. They all tend to have more older people except for Stenton and Spott which at the time of the Survey had forestry workers. This illustrates a beneficial effect of afforestation.

far quicker run-off of water from the Hills, leading to flash floods on the tributaries which led into the River Tyne lower down. We hazarded the figure that for every one percent increase in the total woodland cover above 800 feet the peak flood level in Haddington would be reduced by one inch, and it is these unwelcome last inches that do the most damage. Increased tree planting would act as a sponge, delaying the run-off and improving the stock holding capacity of the hills. As the result of the survey we could show that there was a lot of waste land, either devastated woodland, bracken covered, or steep land, that was useless for agriculture. We held a big representative meeting in the Council Chambers in Haddington to put this message across to the landowners, farmers and others involved. The purpose was to encourage them to take up Forestry Commission grants and to persuade the Department of Agriculture to increase the proportion of woodland planting required as part of their approval of farm improvement grants. Unfortunately this initiative was sabotaged by the Department of Agriculture officials who denied that their hill drainage resulted in any increased flooding and by the landlords who said that due to cost they would only afforest accessible easy land and not the waste land we had identified. However the Abbot of Nunraw, Father Mulcahy, took our message and carried out extensive planting around the Abbey and on its Castle Moffat farm and the Forestry Commission co-operated by acquiring Pressmennan and several devastated woodlands in the Thornton area and along the Monymusk Water.

It was, however, always our policy that the smooth lines of the Lammermuirs should not be broken by plantations or crossed by electricity pylons but should keep its smooth heathery skyline. I could do nothing about the bright green patches which appeared on the northern face due to re-seeding in the agricultural expansion days of the 1960s, but am glad to see that most of these have now reverted to heather.

Gully Erosion

I was also concerned with the prominent erosion scars on the northern face of the Lammermuirs. We tried various practical experiments with the East Lothian Water Board to check this gully erosion which was filling the Hopes reservoir with shingle and debris. I had seen check

Plate VIII Flood Prevention

The drawing which was presented to the big meeting as a result of our survey of the upland catchments flowing into the Tyne. It showed the amount of drainage and reclamation going on and proposed on the one hand, and the felled woodland and wasteland suggested for replanting on the other, which would reduce the speed and intensity on the run-off. There was plenty of legwork involved in making this map and all to little effect.

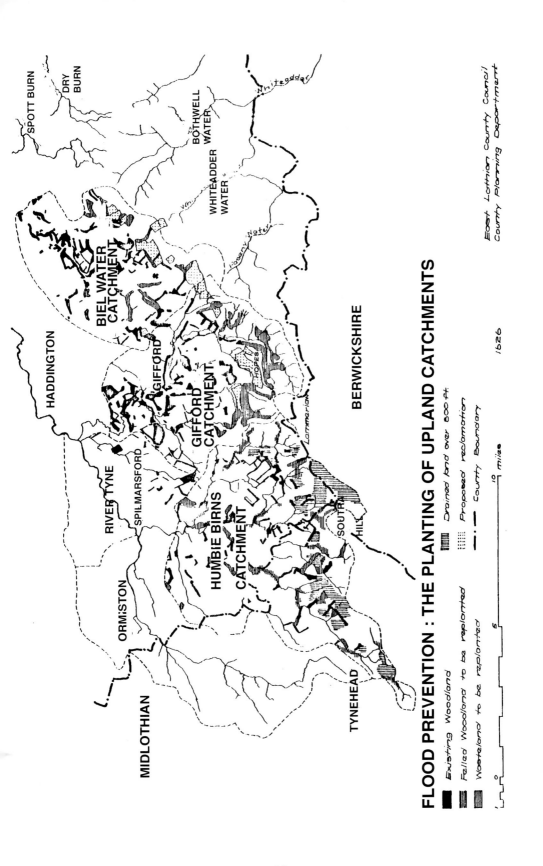

FLOOD PREVENTION : THE PLANTING OF UPLAND CATCHMENTS

SPOTT BURN

DRY BURN

BOTHWELL WATER

WHITEADDER WATER

Whiteadder

BIEL WATER CATCHMENT

HADDINGTON

GIFFORD

GIFFORD CATCHMENT

BERWICKSHIRE

RIVER TYNE

SPILMARSFORD

HUMBIE BIRNS CATCHMENT

SOUTH HILL

ORMISTON

MIDLOTHIAN

TYNEHEAD

Existing Woodland

Felled Woodland to be replanted

Wasteland to be replanted

Drained land over 800 ft

Proposed reclamation

County Boundary

East Lothian County Council
County Planning Department

1626

0   5   10 miles

29

Plate IX   Gully Erosion

Photograph (a) shows the problem of a typical deep erosion gully on the north face of the Lammermuirs with the loose rocky material cascading down to the Hopes Reservoir.

dams used in Switzerland.   These were erected high on the mountain streams to retain cloud bursts and so prevent them scouring the valleys. We did this by bringing willow hurdles up from Somerset and staking them at intervals across the gullies. They trapped the earth and gravel washed out of the higher ground and so slowly filled up the gullies which then could grass over. They were also fenced off, excluding the sheep and encouraging tree seedlings and other growth.

Much of this action was necessarily rather stretching the powers conferred on the County Council by the Planning Acts and I was constantly being asked by the County Clerk under what powers I was acting. Although some of the time I could justify it by saying I was implementing policy approved in the County Development Plan, much of the time I had to rely on a section of the Local Government Acts which enabled County Councils to carry out works for the good of their area. But the County Clerk did not think much of that argument.

THE COASTAL AREA
A String of Villages

East Lothian has the most beautiful and varied coastline, backed by

Photograph (b) of Crow Clough shows the answer with check dams in the stream bed and afforestation on the sides of the gully.

sand dunes and rock cliffs, and inland a string of villages and towns. Some of these were ancient such as Port Seton, a fishing village; Aberlady, the port of Haddington; Dirleton, a castle-toun; North Berwick, a royal burgh with a harbour, greatly expanded in Victorian times as a result of the golf craze; Whitekirk, a place of medieval pilgrimage, and Dunbar, another royal burgh of the thirteenth century with a harbour and castle of great strategic significance to the English armies invading Scotland. The other two intermediate villages were landlords' creations mainly of the late nineteenth century and early twentieth century, Longniddry and Gullane, based primarily on their golf courses.

Land for Private Housing

All these places had attracted both private and local authority house building between the wars. After the war the building of private houses had been limited by the Labour Government through the licensing of building materials to a fifth of the rate of local authority house building. In the period 1950-52 100 houses were built in Longniddry and Gullane and 23 in Aberlady. However there was a large pent-up demand from Edinburgh people and clearly the Development Plan had to make some provision for this, although we were not able to quantify it. The Regional Survey and Plan had drawn attention to the dangers of the spread and sprawl of uniform development along the coast as had happened in the south-east of England with which of course I was very familiar. On the other hand there was the increasing need to improve sewage disposal, which was uniformly discharged untreated at low water mark, and to maintain and develop the existing amenities. For this, not only was additional rateable value needed but also additional people.

The Survey Report analysed the character of each settlement, the capacity in their schools, sewers and other services, and the value of the agricultural land surrounding them. This produced an interesting rhythm with alternate places suggested for expansion and the limitation of the older villages in between. These were Aberlady and Dirleton, both of which had been earmarked for substantial development before the 1939-45 war.

Port Seton

Port Seton was limited to the south by good agricultural land and was the last of the string of places served by the B1348 road and there were good arguments why it should not be expanded eastward, ribboning along the coast. These arguments were not strong enough to prevent some expansion along the old links to the east after the 1970s—a Committee decision I very much regretted and has led recently to a massive further development to the south over the best of agricultural land.

Longniddry

Longniddry had a mainline railway station and was the first coastal place to be reached along the A198 from Edinburgh. It was clearly a very incomplete community and so was earmarked for development by private feuing. The main sites overlooking the golf course had already been developed during the 1930s but the back land was very suitable despite its agricultural value. The story of its development is told later.

Aberlady

Aberlady had not attracted much private development between the wars and was on the edge of the Local Nature Reserve at Aberlady Bay. The school was at capacity and it had an adequate range of shops, inns and halls. There was a need to concentrate the attention of people wishing to live there, not on new buildings but on the restoration of the old pantiled cottages. I remember the Committee refusing consent for the demolition of a listed single-end cottage, a one-roomed house, arguing that some single professional person would come along and restore it. It proved to be a very suitable house for an artist.

Plate X Dirleton Conservation Village

In the foreground the thirteenth century castle on its rocky outcrop with its round towers and the fifteenth century wing to the right. It shows the bowling green amongst yews to the left with the flower borders. Beyond, the triangular green bordered with former croft houses. The subsidiary triangular green leads to the seventeenth century church and the large manse in the trees. The Open Arms Hotel faces the beehive Doocot which we had floodlit off the street lighting cable and account!

Gullane

Gullane was also very suitable for development with plans to construct a new school and sewage works and with no agricultural limitations. Here the County Council promoted private housing development by acquiring and servicing the 24 acre site at Muirfield Park from the Hospital Board who were using the House as a children's convalescent home. They also built council houses in 'Little Korea', south of the railway station, so called, as it was built at the time of the Korean War but also reflecting its detached location.

Dirleton

Dirleton had sprung up beside its thirteenth century castle and was arranged round two triangular greens—one fronting the castle and the other fronting the church, a quite unusual arrangement for Scotland. There had been pre-war estate plans to vastly increase the size of the village, and there had been some recent developments such as the upgrading of a former guest house into the Open Arms Restaurant, the demolition of old single storey houses to make way for two storey council houses at Ruthven Terrace, and the building of a terrible bungalow with a horseshoe front door facing onto the Green. These showed how fragile the place was and how easily it could be spoilt. However it had a very dicky sewage system debouching onto the beach at Yellowcraig and this was adequate reason to check further residential or tourist developments in Dirleton.

North Berwick

North Berwick, the next in line, was however very suitable for residential expansion. It was served by a branch railway and had a good range of shopping and recreational facilities which needed more customers. It was decided that North Berwick's future lay primarily in expanding it as a high class residential town rather than as a tourist resort. Any development not conducive to this objective should be refused planning consent. For instance an old proposal to build a promenade along the west bay was not included in the Town Plan and all applications for amusement arcades were consistently refused planning consent. It was also policy that Quality Street leading to the harbour should remain residential and so it was saved from tawdry shops selling beach trash and fast food which characterise other seaside towns. This policy was not so tightly drawn as to prevent the building of a conference/ballroom suite onto the Marine Hotel which is well used by local organisations and we even tried to persuade Joe Lyons, who at one stage owned it, to install an open-air artificial ice curling pond. However the main development thrust was turned to subdivision of the larger houses rather than their conversion to small hotels and bed and breakfast establishments. In fact the decline in residential holidays led to the closure and conversion of many hotels to flats. The timing of major residential development was made contingent on the provision of a sewage treatment works, the resolving of the traffic difficulties in the High Street and the provision of further local employment—all of which we proposed but did not realise.

Plate XI   North Berwick

A fine view of the parliamentary burgh showing the High Street in the centre, Forth Street to the left, and Kirk Street to the right. It shows the Harbour promontory with its four storey buildings dividing the West Bay from the East Bay. In the distance are the Bass Rock and Tantallon Castle.

Whitekirk

Whitekirk had been rather spoilt by a row of Orlit prefabricated houses built after the war at its southern entrance. I am glad to say that no further building has taken place in Whitekirk. The village and its surroundings were made a Conservation Area, thereby trying to maintain its sacred character, with the main road leading direct to the fifteenth century church porch.

Dunbar

Dunbar is served by the main-line railway and by the A1. It also serves as the urban centre for the Hillfoot parishes in the east of the County. It has a fine wide High Street with plenty of shops and interesting old riggs running off it. It has a good flat hinterland, limited by the railway

Plate XII   Whitekirk Church

The fifteenth century church got a better deal from the County Council, who installed floodlighting, than it had from the suffragettes who burnt it down in 1914, after which it was carefully restored by Robert Lorimer. I spent some time with Dr Jimmie Richardson, retired head of the Ministry of Works in Scotland, trying to locate the Holy Well which is recorded as having attracted 15,000 pilgrims in 1413. To have found it might have given a boost to the tourist trade but agricultural drainage had obliterated all signs of its whereabouts.

line, which if it was to be crossed had to be done in a big way to avoid having a ghetto like development across the tracks. It also has fine beaches and space for development within the town. It has all the features suitable for expansion both for residential purposes and tourist facilities. Its expansion would strengthen the case for improving the A1 and result in the diversion of traffic away from the overcrowded A198 to North Berwick. It would improve the fortunes of its shopkeepers and encourage them to invest in their fine buildings. It was only slowly that this idea caught on and I elaborate about it later in Chapter Twelve.

COASTAL CONSERVATION

The other problem examined in the Survey Report was the alarming devastation of the coastline and the misuse of coastal lands by the public. This was to become a major interest of the Planning Department and we became a "world authority in Scotland", as they would say in Denmark. In 1970 we published "*Dune Conservation, A Twenty Year*

Record of Work in East Lothian". The major works at Gullane Dunes will be dealt with in Chapter Ten but our work extended along the whole 42 miles of the coastline.

Seton Camp

The dunes start at Bruce's Holiday Camp just east of Port Seton. This was a hutted camp dating from the 1930s when a whole assortment of old railway carriages, bus bodies and later wooden huts had been placed on barren land. Our 1951 survey recorded that there were 386 individually-owned structures of which 129 were in poor or bad condition. I shared the general opinion that they should all be removed until one evening, when I was returning to Edinburgh, I gave a lift to a family who owned a hut in the camp. I insisted on taking them right home. Home was the fourth floor of a tenement block in Gorgie and it made me appreciate the wonderful outlet that a weekend by bus to Seton Camp provided for them and their children. After that I did my best to protect and improve the camp. This was of course long before the commercialisation of holiday camps that has occurred since.

The camp owned the foreshore and had built a small concrete retaining wall and paved area where teas were served in the 1930s. The concrete wall resulted in the tides scouring the sand away and undermining the wall and paving. The sea was then threatening the road which had been excessively widened on the seaward side. The County Road Surveyor had protected his footpath by a wall of old railway sleepers but it was not until the mid 60s that this stretch of coast was made secure by the sea-lyme grass which I had planted either end of the sleeper wall. It grew slowly across the front of the sleepers, gathered sand at the foot of the wall and generally built up the beach—a case of the soft protecting the hard. This demonstrated the value of cheap vegetative protection in preference to costly civil engineering works which guided all our dune conservation work.

Longniddry Foreshore

Further east the narrow dunes were being heavily eroded. Studies by Napier College proved that this was not sea erosion, as many people thought, but wind erosion arising from public use, and the winning of sand and the burying of the coastal defence blocks. This is generally true of the coastline as a whole. The erosion of the dunes was so severe that the trees on the golf course south of the road were being destroyed by salt-laden wind. We advanced the dune edge 20 feet by brushwood fences, trapping sand blown along the beach which was subsequently planted with sea-lyme grass which then held the sand. Car parking was prohibited and this first stretch of the shoreline was dedicated to cyclists, and to pedestrians coming from the bus terminal at the Camp.

Plate XIII Play Boat, Longniddry

When the County Council acquired the Cockenzie Harbour I asked Mr Macnamara, the boat builder, if he could find us an old boat. This is what he provided, duly installed by Councillors Tommy Gunn, Prestonpans, and Bob Cunningham, Longniddry, and others. I confess that it only lasted three summers, as we did not take it in during the winter. It now appears strange that no children were invited to this occasion.

A range of seats was placed to make a useful resting and return point for walkers, and a play-boat was provided.

At the foot of Longniddry Dene the dunes widen to 250 feet and rise to 35 feet. Two car parks were laid out where before the war there had been golf holes north of the road. Sand winning was refused planning consent, the area leased by the County Council and the public controlled by Bye-laws (1952). The foredune was badly eroded by the winter storms of 1953 and 1961 but it was rebuilt by the use of sea buckthorn as groins every eight metres along the shore. These buckthorn fences had the bonus of acting as wind-brakes and clothes-lines for summer visitors. We later carved out "family nests" every seven metres or so within the sea lyme grass.

Much of the wind erosion of the dunes had started by the action of the County Road Surveyor in digging large holes in the dunes with a

Plate XIV Longniddry Dune Rebuilding

Photograph (a) shows the brushwood fences erected after the spring high tides in order to catch the sand blowing along the beach. It shows our standard coast protection board.

Photograph (b) shows the sand accumulated and planted up with sea-lyme grass. Within these mounds we created 'nests' for family parties.

Ruston Bycrus steam shovel to bury the 4 by 4 by 5 feet high five ton concrete defence blocks. These buried blocks disrupted the capillary action of water in the dunes and so prevented the growth of the dune grasses. A few years later they were once again exposed by the wind and another blow-out created in the dune. Every winter blown sand blocked the coast road and the Highways Department religiously carted it away until I instituted my annual planting programme which fixed the sand on the dunes. The protection of these heavily-used public dunes requires an annual programme of maintenance just as any other work in a public park. I always used to contrast enviously the large budget and manpower devoted to the little-used burgh parks with the neglect and vastly greater numbers using these coastal open spaces. We were fortunate that Lord Wemyss, who had leased these foreshores to the County Council, was also willing to allow his versatile forestry gang, led by Mr Gordon, to carry out thatching, fencing and planting work on repayment by the Council.

The large 'free-range' car park No 3 was established using wartime tracks at Ferny Ness. Here the rocky foreshore presented no erosion problems and grannies could sit in their cars on the shoreline watching their grandchildren disporting themselves on the beach or the sail-boarders on the waves. This they could not do at the other two organised car parks which were behind the dunes. A small group of the defence blocks erected in 1940/41 were left at Ferny Ness on a rocky outcrop as a memorial to the waste and futility of war. These miles of blocks would only have impeded a German invasion by a few minutes. They took me years of cunning to remove.

Two distinct species of dune grass were used on our coastal work. Marram grass (*Amnophila arenaria*), the traditional grass, and sea lyme grass (*Elymus arenarius*), which had been brought into the County by a Longniddry greenkeeper to protect his two holes on the north side of the road. From these few clumps at Longniddry sea lyme grass was planted along any threatened sections of the shore-line and my children call it "Daddy's grass". Now it is self-establishing, being washed about by the storms and drifting from beach to beach, gets smothered by blown sand and shoots away in the spring.

Gosford

Beyond Gosford the coastal footpath continues along the edge of Harestanes Wood to Shell Bay. This wood is quite remarkable in showing the effect of wind on tree growth. The prevailing wind from the south-west prunes the stunted canopy of the growing trees. At the shoreline they are scarcely two feet high, rising at an angle of 15 degrees to full-height trees as seen from the lee-side, the east, sheltering the agricultural land. Inside the wood the twisted vertical stems of the sycamores provide macabre evidence of their age-long struggle to grow against the force of the salt-laden wind. Beyond the wood is Harestanes House, now the Green Craig Hotel, the last of the isolated houses to be built along the shoreline.

My principle was that the shore should be enjoyed by all and not be the private preserve of any owner as I had seen developing along the Mediterranean coastline. It was not enough for the Scots to have their traditional liberty to walk the foreshore. It should be a fine experience into which man's artifacts did not intrude.

Aberlady Bay

Beyond Harestanes House at Shell Bay is Aberlady Bay. The problem here was the indiscriminate shooting of wild fowl, which was becoming a menace, not only to the birds but to the participants. The answer was to create a Local Nature Reserve, the first in the United Kingdom,

Plate XV Gosford Bay—Coast Protection

The North Berwick road, A198, runs along the top of the marram grass bank in front of Gosford West Lodge. As erosion of this bank was threatening the road, the County Road Surveyor proposed to build a sea-wall. My planting of sea-lyme grass and the sand and beach debris it collected provided a living, growing protection at a fraction of the cost.

under the National Parks and Countryside Act, 1948. It is not owned by the County Council, merely controlled by Bye-Laws and managed by a Committee and a warden. It was established in 1952 after considerable local opposition on the grounds that it infringed the ancient right of Regina Major which enabled Scots to use the foreshore. However it was decided by the High Court that an Act of Parliament could vary this right. I fixed its boundary along the edge of the north pavement along the A198 east of Aberlady to thwart a scheme by the County Sanitary Inspector to reclaim the roadside saltings by the deposit of domestic refuse. What a fantastic area with access across the attractive wooden footbridge over the Peffer Burn—which Nigel Tranter, the author, calls the "Footbridge to Enchantment". We were not so lucky with the eastern boundary. So concerned were we with the plight of the birds and the need for a defined boundary that the line of defence blocks was taken as the boundary. As we later found this excluded the best wild-flower areas and included a green of the Gullane Golf Club who own the northern half of the reserve. The Club had to be stopped gassing rabbit burrows on the Reserve which often as not held breeding shelduck—an interference they resented.

It was a great thrill when the during the mid 1960s all four species of tern nested in the Reserve on the sand spit, thanks to the constant watch provided by old Willie Watt. To celebrate this and the degree of care involved, the roseate tern was chosen as the emblem of the County Ranger Service in 1970.

It was also decided that in the interest of science no action should be taken to check the natural movement of the sand. The dunes on the Reserve should be allowed to blow and a very fine wild sight they make in the winter. In the spring the snipe drum overhead in the great East Lothian sky. In the summer the dune slacks behind the dunes are rimmed with orchids—another glorious sight. But perhaps the best sight of all is in the winter when the geese come in to roost off the sand-bar. Flocks come flying in from feeding in fields throughout East and Midlothian and as each skein arrives those already settled rise from the sandbar and there is a ballet in the sky as they mingle and then all settle down again until the next skein comes in and the ballet starts once more accompanied by loud honking. The Rangers regularly count 30,000 geese in the roost. What magic and enchantment, made all the greater for me by the contrast with Cockenzie Power Station some 5 miles across the Bay as a tern might fly. I was able to make Gladhouse Reservoir in Midlothian, the inland goose roost, a Local Nature Reserve when I got to the Lothian Regional Council.

The Reserve finishes in the north at the Hummell Rocks—tall volcanic crags which guard the approach along the shore from Gullane. In all it includes 1,439 acres above and below the High Water Mark, which is receding, and 4.5 miles of coastline—a haven for large flocks of wading birds throughout the year.

Gullane Bay

Gullane Bay presented a massive erosion problem with sand menacing the Open Golf Championship Course at Muirfield and a whole packet of visitor troubles. Chapter Ten tells of these troubles and the steps we took to cope with them and the long task of recreating the foredune. I was determined that the County Council should not open-up new beaches without first attending to the Gullane Dunes.

Beyond Gullane and the Black Rocks to the sea-ward of the Muirfield Golf Course is a 3 mile stretch of wild dunes built up into a series of dune and valley formation by the wind and the valleys stripped down to the raised beach of gravel. I persuaded the Hon. Evans Lombe, then Secretary of The Honourable Company of Edinburgh Golfers and Jimmie Dallmeyer, the Captain, that they should acquire this land at £2 an acre to safeguard themselves, and to have the possibility of an extended or additional course in case urban pressure got too great on their inland course. I also persuaded the Forestry Commission to lease and plant up 40 acres at the west end—Jamie's Neuk—to stop the wind funnelling up the valleys. I had an ulterior motive as I wanted a handy source of brushwood from forestry thinnings for use in the future maintenance of the dunes. In the event the forestry trees did not grow sufficiently well to be productive but well enough to block the wind. Last year I found fine thick turf on the gravelly valley floors between the dunes which now would make it easy to create a golf course there. There is a fine public walk from Gullane to Dirleton, enjoyed by many people, partly along the rocky shore and partly within the shelter of the dunes.

The Eldbotle Woods, at Archerfield, had been breached by a moving sand dune which was being lorried away by George Baxter, a Tranent quarrymaster. His planning consent was not renewed, as removing this plug of blown sand would merely result in higher wind speed stripping more sand from adjoining dunes and blowing it further into the Wood. The correct treatment was to plant the sand where it lay and this was done.

Yellowcraig

Yellowcraig, beautiful Yellowcraig, had been given to the County Council in 1944 for the enjoyment of the public by the generous Colonel Grant of Biel and Dirleton Estate. Here I found cars parked on the dunes. The most frequent activity seemed to be people brushing out their cars onto the dunes and the wheel tracks were breaking up the fragile but floriferous turf. The solution involved the widening and surfacing the old Ware Road, which had allowed from time immemorial the parishioners to gather seaweed for fertilising their fields; and bringing the cars back from the dunes to a car park provided west of Yellowcraig Wood. A caravan site for 120 touring vans was created in a back corner. This had the advantage of the site warden being there and exercising discipline through the hours of darkness. A mown ball-game area was provided for the many who wished to spend part of their outing playing football or cricket with their children. The wood was selectively felled and replanted, opening up a nice woodland walk to the Yellow Craig, a small gorse covered volcanic plug. East of the Craig a fine woodland adventure playground and tree house were provided, although this was tame compared with those currently being developed. A nature trail was laid out in the dune meadow and a booklet prepared which regularly sold 2,000 copies annually. There were permanent numbered metal discs and movable numbered wooden posts which were re-sited each year by Mr Gibb of Gullane, a member of the Scottish Wildlife Trust, as the elusive annual plants came up in different places. In this way we won the respect of the public and their appreciation of the beauties of the place.

We instituted a nursery germination programme to replace viper's buglass. This is a plant with a two foot spike of blue and red flowers which was too tempting for the public to leave alone. To me it seemed a shame to protect it by heavy-handed enforcement of the bye-laws thus spoiling people's day out, when it could so easily be replaced. Our County Ranger also had success one year in keeping a green woodpecker, a rare bird so far north, in the wood all winter by feeding it nuts in suet.

The beach faced Fidra Island and was a nice mixture of rocky outcrops, grass and sand. I established a rim of sea lyme grass along the low dune foot so that public wear could never cause erosion. To the east are the high foredunes of the Broad Sands protecting North Berwick's West Golf Course, which we also maintained for the Town Council.

Tantallon Castle

East of North Berwick are small inlets below the grassy cliffs and the magnificent Tantallon Castle consisting of a 50 feet high masonry wall curtaining off the top of a 100 foot high cliff. Across the inlet to the west was the former Admiralty Radar Research Establishment— Ginhead, as it was appropriately called. This was considered an eyesore but I rather liked the contrast it illustrated between the two methods of defence, the solid masonry of the fifteenth century, protection against armies on foot, and the revolving steel and wire of twentieth century

Plate XVI Yellowcraig, beautiful Yellowcraig.

Yellowcraig has it all—an old wood, a small rocky hill, a wide dune meadow, leading to a low dune edge. It has that magical combination of dune grass, sand, sea and rocks with Fidra island in the background. Here we laid out our first Nature Trail and published our first booklet, which ran into many editions and must be treasured in many thousands of homes in the Lothian Region.

radar protection against aeroplanes in the sky. The buildings proved a great enticement to the American company Ranco Ltd who wanted to establish a research base in Scotland. It was eventually agreed that the Admiralty retained the ownership of the buildings and the ultimate obligation to demolish, but leased them to Ranco with the requirement under the general development order that the colour of the building had to have planning permission. I was asked to both devise a colour scheme and a planting plan, using buckthorn and sycamore that had done so well at Harestane Wood.

Beyond Tantallon lies the private beach of Seacliff where we advised on dune protection and obtained for the owners a Countryside Commission grant for a lavatory. Further on, where the coastline turns south facing the North Sea and behind the dunes the Dales had established a novel agricultural rotation of caravans and carrots. It was agreed that in place of the caravans the Dales would get consent for modest sand-winning from the back of the dunes and for temporary tented camps. Amendment No 21 to the County Development Plan zoned this stretch from Seacliff to Tynemouth and its agricultural hinterland up to the A198 as an Area of Great Landscape Value in which there would be no further commercialisation of the coast.

Tyninghame

The Peffer Burn separates Seacliff from Ravensheugh to which access is provided from Tyninghame Links. This beach is approached by a mile long walk through the woods. It is a real 'Man Friday beach' (and only 25 miles from Edinburgh), a place where your footprint could be the only one in the sand. We kept it that way by restricting the size of the car park. It was eventually included in the John Muir Country Park. This was not without its struggle as the County Road Surveyor, ever keen to reduce the mileage of roads to be maintained, fell for the proposition put forward by the Tyninghame Estate to take the road off the list of public highways. Little did he know of the affection in which this beach was held, of the old public way across a ford in the River Tyne, or anticipate the political storm that arose in the Roads Committee. It was this and my offer to provide a road-end car park and some supervision through the newly-established Ranger Service that won the day and kept the road on the list of public highways. Ever since, the Tyninghame Estate has been most co-operative.

This description of the coast is becoming rather lengthy but it is one of the glories of East Lothian and its conservation and opening up to the public of Central Scotland was one of my proudest achievements. Never was I more pleased with myself than when I reached an agreement that gave the public rights over Belhaven Sands, Tynemouth and Ravensheugh Sands, all now embodied in the John Muir Country Park.

Beyond Belhaven Sands lay the rock-girt town of Dunbar. It had only a small town beach which attracted vast accumulations of seaweed in the winter and many complaints from visitors in the summer. It had a working harbour and a rock-cut swimming pool, since demolished. Visitors had to look outside the town for their beaches and we gave them motor access to Belhaven Bay and White Sands.

Barns Ness Coastal Lands

South of Dunbar are the attractive Dunbar Golf Club links strung along a low rocky shore and, beyond them, the White Sands and Barns Ness. It became a strategic objective to draw day visitors down the A1 to relieve the pressure on the coastline to North Berwick and provide overnight camping sites to draw travellers up the A1 and into the County.

White Sands, an attractive sandy bay, is separated from Barns Ness by the limekilns at Catcraig which were restored together with the calciner's house, thus maintaining a bit of industrial history. One of the limekilns, a three draw kiln, was restored with money from the Associated Portland Cement Manufacturers. The research for the authentic restoration of the lime kilns led me to the Library of the British Museum. The kilns were composed of a 20 feet high brick-built bottle kiln supported within a large square masonry structure to enable carts to load it from the top. Coal was brought in by boat with moorings still visible on the beach. The burnt lime fell to the bottom and was loaded into carts from the three arched draw holes which also served to provide the draught for the fire from whichever direction the wind blew. Dramatic accounts exist of lines of farm carts racing to be first at the kiln in the morning.

Information boards showed this whole process from the excavation of limestone taken from the exposures on the beach and in the quarries, to the carting up the ramps to the top of the kiln and tipping in.

There are seven limestone bands exposed on the beach distinguished by their fossils. We laid out a geological trail along the shore with a specimen fossil embodied in a concrete milestone as geological drawings do not give a very real idea of the fossils. One of the limestones is particularly rich in fossils—like a plum pudding. It was nick-named "Dunbar Marble" and several local farmhouses have mantelpieces made of it. It polished very well but had a dull brown unappetising appearance. At Catcraig I also nearly committed a howler by filling in a surface quarry into which had been dumped the rusted barbed wire fencing from the wartime coastal defences. This was both unsightly and dangerous, but it provided a safe resting place for tired migratory birds attracted by the Barns Ness lighthouse. In the end a compromise was arranged with some tidying up and additional sea buckthorn planted round the edge.

A large camping site was provided by the Camping Club of Great Britain and Ireland intended to draw tourists up the A1 and provide them with a stimulating holiday. Needless to say, we produced a fine booklet describing all that can be seen on the land and on the shore.

Skateraw

Further east the owners of the little bay at Skateraw with its limekiln refused all my approaches. But it came into public ownership when the South of Scotland Electricity Board had to acquire it as alternative public open space in substitution for the public open space, dunes and beach, which they needed for building their nuclear generating station. The story about this is told in Chapter Five.

Thorntonloch

The County Council had acquired the beach, some coastal land and

Plate XVII Barns Ness Coastal Lands

The Associated Portland Cement Manufacturers were persuaded to donate the uncultivated coastal lands to the County Council, a strip two and a half miles long. At the bottom of the photograph is Barns Ness Lighthouse and above it the limestone rocks displayed on the shore. To the left is the Camping Ground behind its ramparts. Above that is the calciner's house and stables at Cateraig and beyond them the White Sands with toilet block. Beyond White Sands the Dunbar golf course hugs the shore-line and Dunbar harbour can be seen jutting out in the sea.

buildings of the disused Thorntonloch farm steading abandoned by the Department of Agriculture for Scotland when they built new buildings for their small holders. It was a good beach where in 1947 a school of whales had got stranded. In the 1950s we had to persuade the Department that ramshackle accommodation for pigs was not a suitable use before they would dispose of it for public recreation to the County Council. The Council, being short of money, then leased the land to a caravan operator on various conditions including the provision of a car

Plate XVIII Cateraig Limekiln

What you see is the massive stone walling and arches which supported a brick bottle kiln in a matrix of sand with clay bands. This structure enabled carts carrying coal and limestone to be tipped into the top of the kiln in alternate layers. The burnt lime was drawn out at the bottom and loaded into carts standing in the arches. This kiln had to be largely rebuilt by John Allan, Builder, of Ormiston. There is an older kiln alongside to the right which has not been excavated.

park and lavatory for day visitors. I also considered that it was essential for the County to acquire and stabilise the dunes that stretched to the north-east in advance of its increased use by the public. It was these dunes and land behind that were required for the nuclear station. In retrospect I am rather ashamed of this caravan site that stretches along the coast and reached agreement that it would be removed when the nuclear station came on power, but this was after my time and has not happened. It is very unsightly and the conditions that all vans were overwintered in a little paddock and various buildings removed have not been enforced. It strengthened my view that the coastline belonged to all visitors and should not be monopolised by individuals.

The conclusion of my twenty-five years of active involvement is that the public authorities must take responsibility for the maintenance of coastal open spaces, that it is possible to prevent erosion and even to rebuild and extend the dunes by a programme of annual maintenance, and that where the public is informed they will respect both the natural phenomena and the measures undertaken to safeguard them. I also believe that there should be a limit to the capacity of beaches and open spaces, just as there are for cinemas or halls and that excess numbers should be turned away to go elsewhere.

I am proud that I was able to bring so much coastal land into public ownership and provide a pleasant and rewarding experience for its visitors.

3

THE COUNTY DEVELOPMENT PLAN 1953
AND ITS IMPLEMENTATION

The Planning Act 1947 • Survey Report
Public Consultation • Town Surveys and Plans
The County Development Plan • The Four Principles
Their Implementation

1 THE PREVENTION OF SUBURBANISATION
The Edinburgh Green Belt • Exodus to Work Reversed

2. THE CHECKING OF RURAL DEPOPULATION
The Development of Dunbar • Town Expansion Scheme
Retention of Old Buildings

3. REGIONAL RECREATIONAL PROVISION
Managing the Beaches • Protecting Interesting Old Buildings

4. THE CONSOLIDATION OF EACH COMMUNITY
Stenton an Example • Corporate Planning

The Planning Act 1947

There have been planning acts in force in the United Kingdom since 1909, but the Town & Country Planning Acts of 1947 for the first time required County Councils to produce Development Plans based on Survey and Analysis of all their area for the approval by the Central Government and gave them compulsory powers to secure the use of land in conformity with the Plan. It took away the right of owners to change the use of land or develop it without the consent of the local planning authority in order that it complied with the approved Development Plan and Policies subject to the developer's right of appeal to the Central Government.

It also took away the right to financial compensation for refusal of consent and provided for the acquisition of the Betterment Value arising from approval. The development rights on all land were to be acquired for a global sum of £300,000,000, allocated proportionally to those landowners who could establish that their land had development potential. It did not interfere with the ownership of the land which was expected to change hands at existing use value. For example if an agricultural field was approved for housing, the developer would pay the agricultural value to the owner. A Development Charge, representing the added development value, would be paid to the Government who would share it with the Planning Authority. This Section of the Act was never fulfilled—landlords were not prepared to sell land at existing value and the Labour Government did not force them by Compulsory Acquisition under the terms of the Act. On its election in 1951 the Conservative Government soon repealed this section of the Act and so all the increase in land values, the betterment, went straight into the landowners' and developers' pockets, less an element of capital gains tax. No money came to the Local Authorities.

Oh, Oh, how wealthy the Government and the local planning authorities would have been if this Betterment system had been made to work. There would have been sufficient capital for all the reinvestment required in roads, railways, parks, economic and social infrastructure, physical amenities, etc. As it was it was all frittered away into landowners' and developer's pockets, despite the fact that they had done nothing to make their land developable. All had been done by community growth and public provision of services.

The other parts of the 1947 Planning Acts remained in being and have had more or less enthusiastic support from both political parties.

Survey Report

It was the first time that the County Councils had been charged with the duty to survey the areas they administered. Previously their knowledge was limited to the functions they carried out. For instance, they knew the number and age of the school pupils as they had to educate them. They knew their roads, and the public health and other services. After the Planning Survey they knew in a systematic way the industrial and employment structure and travel-to-work patterns of their people, the distribution and age of their citizens, the age and condition of the housing, the agricultural value of each field and much else. I would be deluding myself if I thought Councillors really appreciated all this information at the time, but the knowledge gave the Planning Department a great sense of confidence. The Development Plan process made the County Councillors take a long view and make some decisions that would influence the County for the next twenty years.

Public Consultation

The process also required the County Council to consult widely the Government departments, bodies such as the Agricultural Executive and other advisory services, the Nature Conservancy Council, the Royal

Commission for Ancient and Historic Monuments in Scotland, and with other bodies including the bus and rail and port authorities, the trade organisations, private house builders and chambers of commerce, the Burgh Councils and citizen groups and the public at large. In the late 1960s more organised citizen participation became a feature of the planning system. But in the early days consultation was sufficiently novel for the Council to raise some difficulties and accusations of going behind the Councillors' backs. Nonetheless it gave the County Council a higher profile and won a better understanding of the Development Plan as eventually finalised.

Town Surveys and Plans

The Town and Country Planning (Scotland) Act 1947 took away their planning powers from the seven small burghs in the County. This did not seem to upset their Town Councils who had not made much use of the provisions of the Town Planning Act of 1932. They had a great sense of their own dignities and were responsible for most other local government functions except education and the police service. They had part-time Town Clerks who were usually solicitors in private practice in the towns, and full-time Burgh Surveyors who carried out all the other functions and built and managed the housing stock.

It was a slightly difficult relationship for me coming in and telling them how their towns should develop and approving, or worse, recommending refusal of their building plans. However I always cast myself in the role of a planning consultant working with them and not as a County official laying down the law. In time this difficulty vanished as I outstayed all seven original Burgh Surveyors, and I had the information base to help their successors.

The Regulations required that the County prepare a separate Survey Report and Town Plan for each of the Burghs. Three were Royal Burghs: Haddington, Dunbar and North Berwick, with charters dating from the middle ages and 1951 populations ranging from 4,000 to 5,000. The other four were Police Burghs established in the nineteenth century. Tranent was the most populous at 5,690, the other two mining burghs, Prestonpans and Cockenzie, were around 3,000 and East Linton, the smallest, had a population of 990. Each Survey Report had a description of the Burgh's site and its history, which in the cases of Haddington and Dunbar were illustrated by a chart showing its and its parish's development since 1801, plotted against significant general events (mainly wars), and its social, industrial and transport developments. The reports contained an analysis of the Town Form illustrated by the first Ordnance Survey Plans of the 1850s and a table of the Buildings Listed as of Historic or Architectural Interest. Each report had an analysis of its population, its past growth, its changes by natural increase and migration since 1921, and a diagram of its age and sex structure in 1931 (the last year then available) comparing it to the county's profile and showing the changes since 1831.

Each report went on to describe the employment by sex and industry, and the travel to work destinations. All industrial premises were noted with the name of the firm, the number of employees, the condition and adequacy of the premises. The Communications Section described the road network, its traffic use, its weaknesses and the traffic accidents which showed up the black spots where the road layout or inappropriate land uses were giving rise to an accumulation of accidents. The Survey Report also described the minor road pattern and parking problems, for which we carried out surveys. Each town report also considered the bus services and the rural areas from which they brought people into the town which effectively defined their sphere of influence in the surrounding countryside.

Utility services, particularly drainage and surface water disposal needed a good deal of unravelling, for many burghs had no plans of these, merely accumulated unrecorded knowledge.

On community facilities the Survey compared the shopping facilities of the larger burghs in relation to their spheres of influence and to each other. We recorded the type of shop, the class of trade and their apparent prosperity. It was not a very refined study and while it showed up the remarkable differences in the character of the towns, we were not able to make much use of this information. I remember however trying hard to persuade Woolworths, who had a shop in North Berwick, that they should build another in Haddington which had a much more populous catchment area, as the presence of a Woolworth store in a shopping centre was then a great attraction.

Education was thoroughly dealt with, showing the catchment area of all schools and their spare capacity. Similarly public open space was measured and compared with the minimum standards laid down by the National Playing Fields Association. It showed that while the total open space was adequate, thanks to the large acreage of golf courses, pitches for team games were generally deficient. Later on, when we had the detailed tables from the 1951 census, I produced estimates for the Education Committee which combined both the age and structure of the present population and the likely increase from

Plate XIX   Haddington   Population Growth and History

This diagram on the right was one of three included in the Survey Report and shows the relation of population growth to the facts of history, both general and local. It also shows the declining family size that accounted for the physical growth of Haddington although the Burgh's population was remarkably static. It shows as well the normal expectation of growth to 1971 and the accelerated rate of growth on which the Development Plan was based.

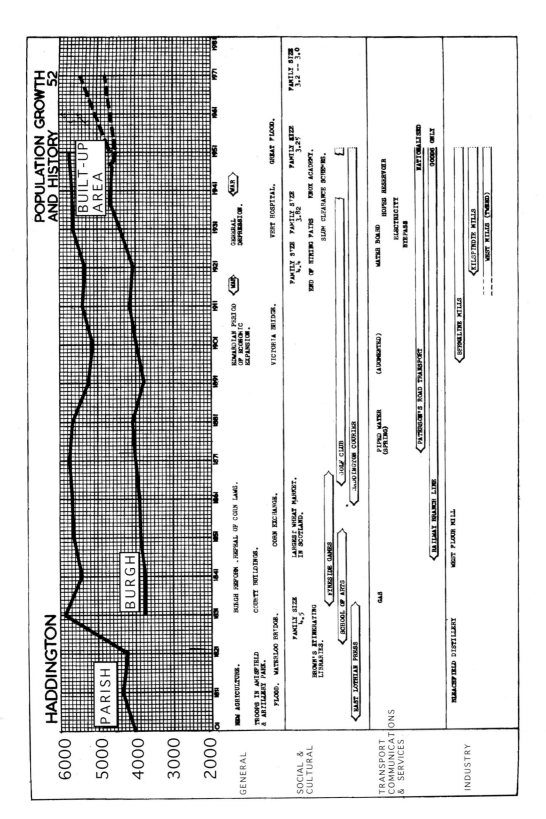

HADDINGTON

POPULATION GROWTH AND HISTORY 52

6000
5000
4000
3000
2000

PARISH

BURGH

BUILT-UP AREA

GENERAL

NEW AGRICULTURE.

TROOPS IN AMISFIELD & ARTILLERY PARK.

FLOOD. WATERLOO BRIDGE.

BURGH REFORM. REPEAL OF CORN LAWS.

COUNTY BUILDINGS.

CORN EXCHANGE.

EDWARDIAN PERIOD OF ECONOMIC EXPANSION. WAR

VICTORIA BRIDGE.

GENERAL DEPRESSION.

VERY HOSPITAL.

WAR

GREAT FLOOD.

SOCIAL & CULTURAL

FAMILY SIZE 4.5

BROWN'S ITINERATING LIBRARIES.

EAST LOTHIAN PRESS

SCHOOL OF ARTS

FIRESIDE GAMES

LARGEST WHEAT MARKET. IN SCOTLAND.

GOLF CLUB

HADDINGTON COURIER.

FAMILY SIZE 4.4

FAMILY SIZE 3.82

END OF HIRING FAIRS

SLUM CLEARANCE SCHEMES.

KNOX ACADEMY.

FAMILY SIZE 3.25

FAMILY SIZE 3.2 — 3.0

TRANSPORT COMMUNICATIONS & SERVICES

GAS

PIPED WATER (SPRING)

RAILWAY BRANCH LINE

PATERSON'S ROAD TRANSPORT

(AUGMENTED)

WATER BOARD

HOPES RESERVOIR

ELECTRICITY

BYE-PASS

NATIONALISED

GOODS ONLY

INDUSTRY

MUNGOSFIELD DISTILLERY

WEST FLOUR MILL

BERMALINE MILLS

KILSPINDIE MILLS

WEST MILLS (TWEED)

55

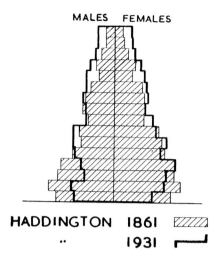

MALES FEMALES

HADDINGTON 1861 ▨▨▨
" 1931 ⌐_⌐

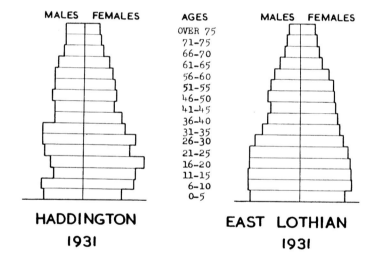

MALES FEMALES	AGES	MALES FEMALES
	OVER 75	
	71–75	
	66–70	
	61–65	
	56–60	
	51–55	
	46–50	
	41–45	
	36–40	
	31–35	
	26–30	
	21–25	
	16–20	
	11–15	
	6–10	
	0–5	

HADDINGTON
1931

EAST LOTHIAN
1931

HADDINGTON : AGE & SEX

Plate XX   Haddington: Age and Sex Profile

Similar diagrams were reproduced for all the burghs showing the changes between 1861 and 1931, with in Haddington's case the ageing of the population although there was an increase in the economically active population aged 26 to 45. We also compared each burgh's profile with that of the County as a whole and Haddington's characteristic was the predominance of women, no doubt attributable to the work available in the mills and service industries.

additional house building. These proved more accurate than the Scottish Education Department rule of thumb, used by the Director of Education, of so many primary and secondary school pupils per house. It was not long before they accepted our estimates.

The Survey Reports dealt with housing which was a function both of the Burgh Councils and the County Council which was also building houses adjoining the Burghs. The two had never been co-ordinated nor had the public housing programme ever been co-ordinated with the speculative builders' production. We produced plans showing the use, age and condition of all the buildings which enabled us to describe areas of obsolete development and bad layout. This justified plans for the Comprehensive Development of small areas in Haddington and Tranent. These designations gave the County Council, as planning authority, a direct real estate involvement in the Burghs.

We also extinguished the old road widening proposals which had laid down widening lines equidistant from the centre of the road. This blighted property values, made the purchase and demolitiion of properties on both sides of the road so expensive, and involved so much human disturbaance, that they were seldom carried out. It was more sensible to decide which side of the road should be widened, acquire the whole property and so have land on which a new frontage could be built within a definite time scale—as happened in the Hardgate in Haddddington.

"Comprehensive Development" later got a very bad name particularly in Glasgow where 29 large areas were defined in order to build the Ring Road and get some real estate value from it. Because of their scale these areas resulted in massive blight and outstripped the capacity of the City to carry out the redevelopment or rehouse the people.

The Burgh Survey Reports drew conclusions which were then addressed in the Town Plans and provided the justification for the policies, the zoning and the proposals adopted. Sites for housing, both public and private, for the next twenty years were zoned. They provided valuable guidance for the Utility Boards who previously had made provision for general expansion in all directions in their forward planning. This selectivity alone justified the expense of the planning process. Similarly sites were set aside for industry and individual sites chosen for schools and other institutions where these were needed.

The planning process is seldom given the credit for the smooth way that the post-war housing boom was co-ordinated with the supply of utility services, schools and other institutions which was vital for the people's satisfaction. This was the basic technical job of the town planner and good design was an added bonus.

The County of East Lothian Development Plan was approved by the County Council on 9 February 1953 and submitted for the approval of the Secretary of State for Scotland together with the Survey Report and Written Statement. They were both bound in post-office red covers backed with holly green tape and accompanied by a roll of plans.

In those days the plans had to be hand coloured with special coloured inks produced by Winsor and Newton. For instance "Residential Zone" had to be coloured Red-brown 3.1, industry purple 1.2. These colours had been worked out by the Ministry of Town & Country Planning and were adopted elsewhere in Europe, as Mary and I found when we visited a Planning Exhibition in Dubrovnik in 1958 and could understand the maps but not the words. This hand colouring was tremendously time consuming and finicky work on A2 sized paper which I remember we backed with shroud-cloth, a supply of which we obtained from the Haddington coffin maker, James Stark. When this proved to be too flexible, we bought cheap checked cotton material from the Co-operative haberdashers, rather than go to the cost of having them professionally mounted. Self-help was always our way.

The Plan consisted of a County Map to the scale of one inch to the mile and six Town Maps at six inches to the mile as Prestonpans and Cockenzie were on the same sheet. There was also a Comprehensive Development Area Map with accompanying Designation Maps at a scale of 25 inches to the mile. These included the Hardgate/Newton Port area of Haddington to enable us to carry through the road widening proposals, and an area of Tranent to make the civic square, and a Designation Map for the compulsory acquisition of a site for a new telephone exchange in East Linton where the Post Office was having difficulty acquiring one. It also had a Written Statement of 54 pages describing the proposals in the Plans and a Memorandum on the Policy and Assumptions behind the Plans. We received a number of objections including some from the National Trust for Scotland who objected to the proposed destruction of certain buildings in Haddington, Tranent and Prestonpans. A public inquiry was held where the National Trust was represented by Jock Cameron, then Dean of the Faculty of Advocates, and the County by George Emslie, Q.C. The Plan was finally it was approved by the Secretary of State, with minor amendments, on 20 May 1955. It was not the first plan to be submitted but the first County Development Plan to be approved by him. This was not bad after our late start.

It was a requirement of the regulations that after approval Development Plans should be made available at reasonable cost to the public. In no way could we spend time hand-colouring the maps and so we pioneered the use of the County's Multilith printing machine, which was used to churn out the Council papers in black and white. It was however capable of doing colour work and we drew the colour separation sheets direct onto the multilith plates, although we later had them photographed. Jacky Saunders, the County printer, keenly co-operated with us despite the nuisance of having to clean his machine between colours. Later we offered this plan reproduction system to other authorities and we printed both the Midlothian and the Arran and Bute plans on repayment. We were beginning to be commercial.

The Four Principles

The Plan laid down four interlocking principles which, slightly paraphrased, were:

First—The prevention of suburbanisation of the County—by a strong green belt policy, by building up local industries and expanding the facilities of Haddington, so unifying the four disparate parts of the County.

Second—The checking of rural depopulation and maintaining a large and contented agricultural population by developing the social and recreational facilities in the market towns, especially Haddington.

Third—Provision for the legitimate recreational needs of the Edinburgh Region, the protection of coastal amenity, the enhancement of the beauties of the countryside and the protection of interesting old buildings.

Fourth—The consolidation of each community including adequate provision for the increase of the population, and a full range of social, commercial and recreational facilities.

The population basis was an overall increase by 1971 in the County's population of 7,500 on the 1951 population of 52,240, resulting both from natural increase of the resident population and from immigration mainly from Edinburgh. The zoning plans in fact provided for an increased capacity of 10,000 leaving a margin for choice.

I suppose that as a Londoner I was over conscious of the suburban threat to the County. Before the war the Edinburgh tramways had run out to Port Seton. There was as yet no great demand from Edinburgh people for houses in the three western burghs which still had reputations as rough places due to the influx of miners in the 1900s. However the Regional Plan of Central and South East Scotland, prepared by Sir Frank Mears, and the City of Edinburgh Plan, prepared by Sir Patrick Abercrombie, both recommended the limitation of the growth of Edinburgh. My strategy therefore was to have any immigrant population leap-frog the three western burghs and to expand Haddington as the County Town, thus building up its commercial and social facilities and so drawing people from the Coastal Fringe and the Mining Area to

Haddington, rather than allowing Edinburgh to drain away all their social and economic life.

For me suburbanisation was not just the spread of bungalows out from Edinburgh but the suburbanising of life whereby people left for work during the day and their towns became bereft of the rich social and professional life which they had enjoyed in the nineteenth century. If they became mere dormitories they could not function as urban centres, retaining their surrounding population.

Their Implementation

Twenty one years after the approval of the County Development Plan by the Council I was still in post and in May 1974 submitted a similar red-bound volume with holly-green backing to the Planning Committee entitled *"County Planning Policy, a Record of the policies and achievements of the Planning Committee under the 1947 Town and Country Planning (Scotland) Act and other Acts."* This report consisted of 83 pages of text and maps and 12 Appendices listing the 47 Amendments to the Plans and 16 Article 4 Directions which required planning consent for developments which normally did not require it. It also listed some 160 significant reports approved by the Committee, an analysis of the changes in employment, a list of the industrial sites owned by the County Council and their 45 industrial tenants, a record of the changes in parish populations, and a list of 27 tourist and countryside publications prepared and published by the Department. Appendix 7 listed the 14 projects carried out and the 8 underway in the Countryside Programme. It listed 14 projects for the Rehabilitation of Derelict Land amounting to 298.8 acres and the 15 programmed Environmental Recovery Projects costing £47,300. It listed the 20 Sites of Special Scientific Interest in the County and the 13 Tree Preservation Orders approved or in preparation and finally it recorded the 22 Civic Trust Awards and Commendations won in the County. My wife, Mary, won two of the Civic Trust Awards for the conversion of the smithy and carpenter's workshop at Dirleton into a house for Lord and Lady Guest and for the restoration of Harbour Terrace, the flagship project in North Berwick for Dennis & Co, and two Commendations for her work at Stevenson House, Haddington. The County Council themselves won 7 Awards or Commendations and I must say that the Planning Department had a hand in many of the others.

The purpose of this document was not just to be a record of achievement under the four principles of the Development Plan but to inform the incoming authorities, both Region and District, of the policies, decisions and proposals that the County Council had made for the future. It was written in narrative form but was fully indexed for easy reference. It was a hand over document, but I must confess that once my staff had moved to other jobs I seldom heard of it being referred to by the 'new boys'. It just shows that it is people and not paper that is important in planning as in other matters. After I got the Director's job in the Region I was able to influence developments in East Lothian up to my retirement in 1983.

The Report stated that the Development Plan had proved an adequate framework for development over the 20 year period. The statutory requirement that it should be reviewed every 5 years had not been fulfilled as we got deeply involved in implementing the Plan. I strongly held the Geddesian view that Plans were useless unless they led to Action. However a series of subject reports had been prepared on the main aspects of the life of the County in the 1960s. 'Main Consideration Reports' had been written for the 7 burghs and 3 large villages and approved by the Planning Committee both for consultation purposes and to guide the control of development. Thus the Committee and Town Councils were kept abreast of events. I do not think that a formal Review and revised Development Plan would have achieved more than we were able to do by our practical work in influencing the development of the County. The following chapters deal with aspects of this work, which was running at about £1,000,000 annual capital investment in land and buildings at pre-1979 inflationary prices. The 1996 equivalent would be of £6,000,000.

The 1953 Development Plan had assumed a population growth from 52,258 in 1951 to 59,750 in 1971. The actual 1971 total was 56,639, and rising fast. Only a modest growth of 420 occurred in the first ten years, before the planning policies were being actively implemented.

My 'end of term' Report recorded the progress in realising the four principles of the Plan.

1. THE PREVENTION OF SUBURBANISATION
The Edinburgh Green Belt

The Edinburgh Green Belt, first designated in the County's Development Plan 1953, had subsequently been approved in 1957 by the Edinburgh Corporation, the other Lothian Authorities and the Scottish Development Department. It was at its narrowest, one mile wide, and least lovely between Musselburgh and Prestonpans, the foreshore defiled by colliery waste from coastal bings. However by 1974 this foreshore was being reclaimed by fly-ash from the Cockenzie Electricity Generating Station and the bing had been reshaped into playing fields and simulated links. The site of the colliery itself was also being developed as the Scottish Mining Museum of which more is written in Chapter Twelve. Various other eyesores had been removed including the moving of the medium-sized haulage business from Bankhead, west of Tranent on the A1 and in the Green Belt to Muirpark on the east side of the town and outside the Green Belt. All the advertisement hoardings had been challenged and removed, Tree Preservation Orders were in place on all significant clumps of trees, and the rights of way had been opened up.

Development control was also strict and in the case of Burns' Yard worked to everyone's advantage. When I first met Mr Burns he ran a small firewood business behind the high walls of Prestongrange on the coast road from Musselburgh to Prestonpans. One day he began buying old furniture in bulk, initially for the kindling it could provide, but later for its resale value. It became a happy hunting ground for couples wanting to set up home. He applied for permission to erect a shed to hold this furniture but of course this was against Green Belt policy and was refused, and continued to be refused until after I left. The result of this was that Mr Burns had to sell the furniture stacked under trees and other make-shift shelters quickly and therefore cheaply. Hence his popularity and his business throve. A motor car scrap dealer got much shorter shrift and was the subject of a Waste-land Removal Order.

In 1966 I thought that the County should make some temporary camping provision for the Commonwealth Games which were being held in Edinburgh. With the help of Mr James Watt, the Burgh Surveyor of Prestonpans, a temporary camp was set up in the wooded policies of Drummohr in the Green Belt. This was a great success all round. However some years later, against my advice but founded on this precedent, the Planning Committee approved the current caravan site at Drummohr. It just shows how careful one must be.

Exodus to Work Reversed

The other positive side of the anti-suburbanisation policy was to provide jobs in the County to reduce commuting. In 1974 I was able to report that the net exodus of 146 from the Haddington Employment Exchange area in 1951 had changed to a net inflow of 485. There had been some 'massaging of the figures', as it was later to be called, with the extension of the Haddington area to include the Macmerry Industrial Estate. We had also absorbed a loss of 3,415 jobs, 14% of the work force employed in the primary industries of mining and agriculture, by a gain in service industry jobs. We had developed a golf club making industry, building factories for leasing to Ben Sayers in North Berwick in 1963 and to Lee Traveno in Dunbar, and establishing a third in the old School in Gifford and a fourth at Winterfield, Dunbar. It was an ideal craft for the County and led to several boys becoming golf professionals and so gaining social advancement. Tourism was at last being viewed as an industry.

2. THE CHECKING OF RURAL DEPOPULATION

The development of Haddington as the County Town unifying the four parts of the County is written in the next Chapter, The Haddington Story, illustrating the Geddesian philosophy of Development through Conservation. The Burgh's population had declined between 1931-51 but rose from 4,518 to 6,591 in 1961 and 7,787 in 1971. In 1975 it was the fastest growing town in Scotland after Thurso, which housed the Atomic Reactor workers.

The Development of Dunbar

Dunbar also was important as it provided the services which would retain population in the eastern hillfoot parishes. It was 30 miles from Edinburgh and although the construction of the Musselburgh and Tranent bypasses had shortened the travel time, the volume house builders, as the speculative builders liked to be called, said it was still too far away, despite its main line train service, to be part of the Edinburgh Housing Market. A modest expansion took place as we built for the housing needs of its two large new local industries—cement and electricity. The town grew from 4,115 in 1951 to 5,700 in 1971. This expansion was first stimulated by a Glasgow Overspill Agreement for 150 houses, mainly built at Riggonfloors in a scheme designed by Wheeler & Sprossan. This with its three storey flatted towers at the corners was nick-named 'Barlinnie' after the prison! This expansion justified the building of new primary and secondary schools and we adapted the old grammar school for industrial use until its useful life expired. It has now been demolished and the site used by the Scottish Special Housing Association for housing the electricity workers. It had housed several uses: a textile darning unit where the sharp eyed Dunbar girls picked up the stitches and faults that the workers in the Borders mills had left in the cloth; kitchen joinery in the former gym; Cooper-Walker precision engineering; a craft pottery for the Hassalls from whom we commissioned several large works, and a biological laboratory, together with storage and other minor uses.

The redevelopment of Dunbar's older parts by the harbour had been given a great start immediately after the war by Basil Spence's inspiring design for a group of fishermen's houses. These in their fresh interpretation of the local pantile and harl traditions set a fine example of developing the sense of place. Unfortunately more recent attempts have deteriorated either into pastiche or bland mediocrity. These houses were built as part of an effort to attract fishermen and their boats from the smaller harbours down the Berwickshire coast, but none came as the fishermen had such strong local and community ties. Eventually they slowly moved but to Eyemouth, not to Dunbar, and the Dunbar harbour lay underused, as its rock-girt entrance deterred

Plate XXI Dunbar

In the centre foreground is the 1530s fort flanked by the Cromwellian harbour to the left and the Victorian harbour to the right. Between the harbours is the earliest warehouse in Scotland and the site of the demolished Custom House. The photograph shows the start of the housing along Colvin Street and in the background the railway line and the site of the Town Development Scheme at Lochend.

all but the most powerful boats. For a short time we were able to re-establish a boat-builder in the old Cromwellian Harbour.

Town Expansion Scheme

The expansion of Dunbar was limited by the mainline railway that ran in a long curve to the south of the town with only one road underpass at Spott Road and another at Belhaven. I considered that it would be socially disastrous to build small housing schemes across the tracks and that development must be of sufficient scale to have its own schools and amenities. The County Council therefore commissioned Peter

Daniel, who had just left his job as Chief Architect Planner of Livingston New Town, to produce a Town Expansion Scheme. This proposed to double the size of Dunbar to 10,500 and enlarge it right up to the A1, which bypassed the town three quarters of a mile south of the railway. Previously this area had held the Mansion House of Loch End of which only the walled garden, a gateway and some hedges remained. Its grounds had been planted up with conifers. It also had a very fine disused farm steading, known as The Halls. Having seen many Scandinavian towns on our holidays with the children, I thought how splendidly we could develop this area around its woodland, opened up and criss-crossed by drives and rides holding the community buildings, and houses ringing it all about and leading pedestrians and cyclists to the station and the old town centre through a number of existing cattle creeps below the railway.

The Town Council was reluctantly persuaded to accept this vision, much preferring the cosy fading town they knew so well with its rather inbred society. But persuaded they were, and Development Plan Amendment No 37 was submitted to the Secretary of State in February 1973. It was never formally approved but a small start was made. A drainage scheme was put in that could cater for the Town Expansion Scheme and a start made with the industrial site between the Spott Road and the railway. The dog-leg kink was taken out of the approach to the Spott Road railway bridge. A number of houses were built off the Spott Road, including three storey blocks which would remind those living in the old town north of the railway of their new neighbours south of the railway.

However after I left East Lothian the drive to achieve this scheme faded away and the easy alternative of expanding housing and industry in the west of the County was taken up, justified by the philosophy of 'Market Forces'. It needs strong conviction and the exercise of firm control over development to influence the market. It had happened at Haddington, it could have happened and indeed may well yet happen in Dunbar as the A1 is dualled from Edinburgh. How much better to build on the traditions and institutions of Dunbar than to house people in peripheral housing estates. How much better to build where the increased population can attract industries and facilities which will serve the people in the rural area dependent on it. How much better to live by the sea, around a splendid wood with a splendid hinterland of villages, valleys and hills than in a treeless estate built on market garden land on the edge of Edinburgh. But the need for a boost to Dunbar has been recognised with the setting up of the Dunbar Initiative in the 1990s. This has started the same process of development through conservation which had revitalised Haddington in the 1960s and 70s and may yet lead to a town expansion scheme.

I cannot say that the 1971 Census showed that we had reversed the population decline in the foothill parishes but the figures certainly showed that their decline had been checked. In itself this is remarkable in view of the cut-back of employment on the farms. The 1991 Census figures show that the population is now largely stable. Planning is a long term business.

Retention of Old Buildings

Believing that development and conservation could work hand-in-hand, I struggled to keep as many of the old buildings built of the soft heavily-weathered red Dunbar sandstone as possible. Quite early on the last kipperer, situated above the Volunteer Arms, was demolished. It was a very characteristic east coast building, in the form of a wide tall flue with wooden ventilators at the top. The herrings were split and impaled in pairs on wooden dowels—hence the hole in the kippers' heads—which were suspended on racks across the flue. The fire of wood chips smouldered away below and the whole interior was black and reeked of kippers. It was built of red sandstone with a roof of orangery red pantiles. It was an empty, disused, picturesque, dilapidated, olfactory property and as a neighbour to the new houses it had no chance. Similar buildings can still be seen in Arbroath and other fish towns in north-east Scotland.

The other great loss was the Customs House lying between the old and new harbours, a finely wrought classical building in its last stages of decay, being used as fishermen's stores. But there still remains the oldest warehouse in Scotland, used at that time by the Easingwood family who ran an undersea salvage business from the old harbour.

A notable tussle occurred over the retention of the warehouses and maltings in Lammer Street. In particular a three storey warehouse which I nicknamed "The Dreadnought" as it survived demolition attempts time after time. It had had many uses; the last, as the first cinema in Dunbar where early silent films were shown in the 1920s. This use had resulted in a most picturesque outside stair being added up its west gable which divided Colvin and Lammer Streets. At one time when we were building up the tourist attraction of Dunbar, the building was acquired by David Hayes of Landmark for conversion as a marine equivalent to his pioneering Visitor Centre at Carrbridge. That was in the early 1970s and it would have been the first of the popular marine centres if it had proceeded. I now learn that it is likely to become a hostel and store for scuba and recreation divers. Well done the Dreadnought! As other of these harbour buildings became ruinous they were replaced by interesting groups of houses which each in their turn won Saltire Housing Awards. Difficult sites always bring out the best in architects and prevent the stock solution being built.

Plate XXII   Dunbar   Basil Spence Houses

Jim Catherwood took endless trouble to get this photograph which shows the fishermen's houses designed by Basil Spence after the war in their setting by the Harbour. It well exemplifies the placing of new houses amongst the old. These houses set the fashion for East coast Vernacular but few, even those that came later from his Edinburgh office, have the same quality.

An interesting episode occurred when I persuaded Mr Dean who wanted to establish an Amusement Centre at the East Beach to commission Basil Spence to design him an amusement arcade within a high walled enclosure, but although they both got along fine the results were very very disappointing.

3. REGIONAL RECREATIONAL PROVISION

The third principle of the Development Plan was the provision for the legitimate recreational needs of the Edinburgh Region, the protection of coastal amenities and the enhancement of the beauties of the countryside and the protection of interesting old buildings.

This third principle gave us much scope to take an active part in many activities outwith the normal remit of a planning authority. It was part of the job that the staff greatly enjoyed. It brought us a kind of kudos, although many people accused me of stretching the planning system—which indeed I was. Its implementation resulted in East Lothian becoming a county it was a joy to live in.

Managing the Beaches

By 1975 action on this third principle ended up with the County and the Burghs owning or managing 30.03 miles or 71% of the total County coastline and making it available to the public. It resulted in the County Council establishing the first County Ranger Service in Scotland in 1970. These achievements have already been foreshadowed in the description of the Coastal Area in Chapter Two and are dealt with in Chapter Twelve on the Development of Tourism.

The maintenance of the beauties of the East Lothian countryside is mainly in the hands of the farmers and a very good job they make of it. The County Council concentrated on removing the eyesores left by the coal mining industry and the 1939-45 War and on protecting the woodlands. Much of this is dealt with in subsequent chapters.

Protecting Interesting Old Buildings

The East Lothian countryside is greatly enriched by its buildings and villages and I was delighted when Lord Wemyss suggested that we add the protection of the interesting old buildings to the Development Plan's principles. This gave us a more positive role than merely advising on Listed Building Applications. The first buildings that aroused my interest were the free-standing masonry doocots which are so typical of the corn growing counties in Britain, but which I had never seen before arriving in East Lothian. In many ways they seemed to typify the County and, being small and useless, it was possible to acquire and repair them. The story is told in Chapter Seven of how the County became the owner of some twelve doocots. That chapter also tells of the first farm buildings survey that was carried out in Scotland, the water mills survey, and the care we exercised over historic buildings.

Our activities were accompanied by the production of booklets and leaflets to gain support and to add to the recreational enjoyment of the people in the Region. We also put up main road boards drawing attention to the interesting features of the countryside and similar boards in the twelve conservation villages. We justified all these activities by reference to this third principle of the Development Plan.

I look back on all this activity with the greatest of pleasure and just wonder how we found all the time and energy to carry it out. But then 25 years is a long time and as the years went by and I gained the confidence of the Councillors and the Government Departments, everything became easier, and we found the public sharing our enthusiasms.

4. THE CONSOLIDATION OF EACH COMMUNITY

The fourth principle of the Development Plan really goes without saying—the proper development of all communities. Each was analysed by the Geddesian trilogy: Folk—Work—Place. Every attempt was made to ensure that the individuality of each community, both physical and social, was maintained and its deficiencies made up. Both Prestonpans and Tranent got modest new town centres, where before there had been dereliction. Provision was made for old peoples' housing, new schools and recreation grounds. The consolidation of each and every community was our aim.

I was very conscious of what had happened to the West Durham mining villages when their collieries closed and was determined that there should be no talk of dying villages as it was just not necessary, placed as East Lothian was so near to Edinburgh.

The implementation of this principle of consolidation runs through much of these memoirs. So I will enlarge here only on Stenton, a Conservation Village, which is a good example of our approach. It was a key village with an expanding sphere of influence which we wanted to build up to check the depopulation of the hillfoot parishes.

Stenton an Example

Stenton is a most attractive village lying 4 miles south-west of Dunbar on the B3670 road running through the hillfoot villages.

It is arranged informally along a winding road with the school and its clock at the west end and a large nineteenth century 'gothic' church closing the vista at the east, although the village straggled on further to end with a 1930s garage, since demolished. In the village centre rubble and pantiled cottages are arranged round a large square green with an ancient well. On our survey we found that its sphere of influence was the next largest to Gifford's, that it had a healthy age-profile and good social facilities. These included a carpet bowls hall, where those glazed pottery balls which are now such collector's items were still in use, and in 1953 a pub was opened for the first time. There were also a number of houses in need of restoration and over the years we directed people to them and many were restored, bringing in new people from all walks of life. Development control was strict and little spoilt the visual harmony, for no picture windows or box dormers were permitted. The pub was gradually transformed into an art gallery and restaurant. Pride in the village grew and when the local Girl Guides company wanted to mark their anniversary, we designed a replica Tron. This was erected on the original masonry base which remained on the Tron Green, although for many years it had been used as the base for one of the few street lights. Mr Halliday, who ran a farm joinery business, provided an oak post and attached a steel yard-arm. It all turned out

Plate XXIII   Stenton Village

A view from the north showing from the left the William Burn 'gothic' church of 1829, the old sixteenth century church surrounded by its gravestones, the small triangular Tron green framed by its deep pink stone cottages with their orange pantiles, the square green backed by the steading and the school in the fork of the road looking down the curving village street.

handsomely. The roadworks through the village were carefully upgraded and the County Sanitary Inspector gave it appropriate lamp standards. A children's playground and a post bus service were provided.

    South of Stenton lay Pressmennan Loch, a long narrow artificial stretch of water in a deep wooded valley which people said resembled the Rhine! The wood on the southern shore had been felled in the early 1950s, then acquired by the Forestry Commission and replanted, unusually for the time, with a fine mixture of broad-leaf and conifer trees. As part of our policy to encourage more tourists to leave the coastline for the hill villages we persuaded the Forestry Commission to open the wood to the public by creating a little car park and making paths through the wood. We in our turn sign posted it and provided a printed leaflet. It became a quite popular walk—although at one time it gave concern during the brief cross-bows craze when dead and injured roe deer were found in the wood. When the Forestry Commission sold the wood in the 1980s it was so loved that the local people raised money to acquire it for the Woodland Trust.

Plate XXIVa   Stenton Tron

A replica of a steelyard for weighing the wool bales was researched in my office and executed by Mr Halliday, Joiner of Stenton, with an oak post set into the original masonry base. Drawing by Graham Duncan who was very good at this. The photograph overleaf (XXIVb) shows the Tron before the post was installed.

The village thus became alive with a nice tourist attraction on its doorstep. But suddenly the Director of Education proposed to close the village school. The clock had stopped at ten to two, and he considered that time was up for this Village School too. He proposed that the children should be bussed to East Linton where they would get a better education in a five class school. The parents were not of the same opinion and I argued that Stenton's designation as a Conservation Village under the Planning Acts did not just mean to the conservation of its buildings but of its institutions and its way of life. The closing of a school is usually followed by the departure of young families and so I opposed the Director of Education. In local government at that time Education was a very independent self-contained service and the Director resented any interference. He was not statutorily bound to consult anybody but he had to get the consent of the Secretary of State. The Planning Committee accepted my view and that of the parents and finally the Secretary of State refused consent for the closure.

The County Architect started the clock going again. Now the declining school roll has been reversed and it is a three teacher school. The parish population rose from 424 in 1951 to 720 in 1971.

Corporate Planning

This was a typical internal 'battle' between two departmental chief officers and two committees and showed that the County Council as a whole was still a long way from understanding its corporate duties and the need for co-ordinated action following from the principles that they had approved in their Development Plan.

To overcome this problem I sent a reasoned report to the County Clerk recommending that the County Planning Committee should be composed of the Chairmen and Vice-Chairmen of all the other committees of the Council instead of a cross-section of the members. This caused great umbrage. I was hauled up before the Convenor and Vice-Convenor and very nearly got my books—saved, I think, by the Vice-Convenor, Lord Tweeddale, a very fair minded aristocrat who understood my point although he did not press for it. However from that time on I noticed that the more powerful elected members wanted to be on the Planning Committee. Its status rose as its development programmes were implemented and its influence on the life of the County became visible.

Stenton is an example of our securing the proper development of each community, but the next chapter recalls the planning endeavour to build up Haddington as the County Town. This was the linch-pin of all four principles of the County Development Plan.

4

THE HADDINGTON STORY

*1 Bridge Street • The 'Caste' System • The Nungate
The Early Fifties • Haddington's Assets • The Town House
The High Street • Glasgow Overspill
The High Street Face-lift Scheme • Golden Shop Signs
The Butts Scheme • Mitchell's Close • The Great Day
The Lamp of Lothian Trust • St Mary's Church
Housing at Clerkington Avenue • Housing at Gourlay Bank
Haddington Festival • Architectural Heritage Centre*

The main proposal of the Development Plan was the expansion of Haddington to unify the County and so provide some weight against the over-riding influence of Edinburgh. This was depriving the surrounding communities of their social and commercial functions and leaving them in a suburban relationship. Its expansion was also needed to help check the depopulation of its rural parishes, to conserve its fine architecture and secure its proper development.

This is a story of how a triumvirate of young local government officers: the part-time Town Clerk, John McVie; the full-time Burgh Chamberlain, Matt Carlaw; and myself managed in 20 years to transform Haddington from a decaying burgh into a prosperous County Town.

1 Bridge Street

But to start at the beginning. When Mary and I were engaged and started to look for a home, we realised that there were a large number of old houses in Haddington and in the country round about that needed restoration. Mary, being an architect, was well up to the challenge and I made a list of 20 'desirable properties'. The one we eventually fixed on, after several weekends of visits and weeks of negotiation, was No 1 Bridge Street, Haddington. This was a three storey rubble and slated house whose gable-end faced onto the Nungate Bridge with fabulous

Plate XXV Haddington Town House

A fine photograph by Tom Scott showing the majesty of the Town House and how it commands the entry into Market Street on the left and the High Street on the right. Prominent on the gable is Graham Duncan's drawing describing the architectural qualities of the town.

Plate XXVI   1 Bridge Street

(a) On acquisition
The condemned house we bought in 1950 showing the adaptions which had been made for multiple occupation. To the right was a shop with cellar doors to the basement. Its only occupants were the pigeons seen sunning themselves on the roof.

views of the River Tyne and St Mary's, the largest medieval parish church in Scotland, and a less fabulous horizon of a row of Cruden non-traditional houses at Briery Bank built immediately after the war on the skyline. For most of the 1950s the Department of Health for Scotland were promoting these 'builders' brainwaves' which were rushed up and subsequently caused housing authorities a lot of maintenance problems. In addition these were in quite the wrong place, marring a view that should have been kept open.

One Bridge Street had been inhabited by three families and the ground floor by a rabbit skin merchant when it was closed in the 1930s under the Housing Acts as unfit for human habitation, as indeed it was in its subdivided form and without services. However, the Burgh Surveyor had never followed up the Closing Order with a Demolition Order as usually happened, being uncertain whether the house propped up the Nungate Bridge or the other way round. So a rabbit skinner was still in occupation and as we measured the building in the semi-dark the paws of the rabbit skins hanging from nails in the wooden ceiling eerily brushed our hair. There was at that time, before myxomatosis, a good trade in the skins to Belgium to be made into children's fur coats.

(b) After restoration
Our home showing the careful matching stonework by Alister Whitehead and the raised casement windows to prevent people looking into our living room—not an antiquarian restoration but an attractive and eminently sensible one by Mary Tindall.

We acquired the house for £50 and a further £10 for the garden ground behind where a close of 24 houses had been demolished. Our gardening required not a fork and spade but a crowbar and pickaxe and we had to import soil for our raised vegetable bed.

The owner of this property had been Hugh Whitehead, a plasterer, slater and glazier, whose father had acquired a number of ruinous properties. He also held shares in the King's Theatre, Edinburgh, no doubt in part payment for slating, and this entitled him to tickets which he occasionally made available to us. His brother Stewart was a mason and we engaged them to reconstruct our house, although the only estimate we could get from him was a price on the back of an envelope. He would never submit an account for work done and when we heard the Income Tax inspectors were after him we paid him a cheque for the amount Mary thought justified and it appeared to satisfy him. We always remained friends and often allies against what we saw were the idiosyncrasies of the Town Council and the Burgh Surveyor.

Hugh Whitehead had promised faithfully that the house would be ready for us when we returned from a honeymoon spent in Collioure in the south of France and then in Barcelona over Easter 1951. But on our excited, expectant return only the pigeons inhabiting the roof had been netted and sold and a few downtakings achieved. So we had to take lodgings with Mrs Barr, a farmer's widow, in Victoria Park for six months until after constant badgering the restoration was finished. One difficulty was that building materials were still rationed and the Town Council had pledged their £1500 allocation to the Sheriff Depute who had moved into Tynebank and wanted alterations done. We had to get our allocation from the County Council. When finished it made a charming house with three bedrooms and was described at some length in Moultrie Kelsall's seminal book "*A Future for the Past*" which made Scots appreciate the possibilities of doing up rather than 'dinging doun' their old buildings.

The 'Caste' System

We learnt our first social lesson when Mary presented her restoration plans to the Town's Dean of Guild Court for Building Warrant approval and removal of the Closing Order. Shortly afterwards she received a letter addressed to "Mrs Mary Tindall, Solicitor". She had transgressed the small town demarcation of labour—only solicitors were supposed to present plans, architects merely appeared in support of them— although there was nothing in the regulations which stipulated this.

The social class division was very marked in the town. We were only supposed to socialise with other local government officers, the doctors, vets and solicitors. There were two classes of shopkeepers— the established traders and the incomers. Tradesmen were below them, followed by labourers and, at the very bottom, Irish casual workers. The farmers kept to themselves, the back parlour of the Gardiner's Arms being their ground where, each in turn, bought a bottle of whisky to pour among their select company. McKemmie, the publican, spent his afternoons walking the rights of way and kept me informed when he found them blocked, as it was the County Council's responsibility to see that they were kept open. The landowners were a class above all. The only occasion when all mixed was New Year's Eve when Lord Tweeddale held open house at Yester.

Amongst my particular confidants was a group of four traditional tradesmen, Ramsay the bootmaker, Gracey the upholsterer, Kennedy the coachbuilder and Fergus Main the saddler who outlived the others. They kept themselves to themselves and were a cut above the other shopkeepers, and it was their company I sought in the Commercial Hotel, now the Mercat Hotel, to hear the stories of Haddington in bygone days. There was also old Hodgson the window cleaner who till the age of 70 still climbed wooden ladders up to the fourth floor windows on the High Street. He took me, or rather I transported him, to Belhaven Bay to collect cockles and hook flounders on the incoming tides with hand lines flung from the shore. As this was over five miles from Haddington we were, in the eyes of the Law, bona fide travellers and so could stop off at the Railway Inn in East Linton to wash the salt air down our throats.

Our social life and that of others was greatly enriched when Celia Parker opened up Tyne House Hotel on the Haughs. She had been an antique dealer in Manchester and her husband, an Irishman and former Colonel in a bomb disposal unit, worked in the Department of Agriculture and Fisheries for Scotland as a drainage engineer. She was refused a bar licence and so served drinks from behind a four poster bed. She was a wonderful cook who was never at a loss. All poor Paddy wanted was a quiet life when he came back from the office, and a little rough shooting at the weekends, but he found himself tied to the hotel chores. When Celia fell ill he seized the opportunity to sell the hotel, little realising that hotel sales involve lock, stock and barrel and so she lost all her furniture. Thankfully she recovered and successively acquired six hotels, building them up by the force of her personality and selling on when some crisis occurred in her life—a happy stimulating life.

The Nungate

We had clearly transgressed the social mores as our house was on the wrong side of the Nungate Bridge. Traditionally the police only ventured into the area in pairs, such was its reputation for violence and drunkenness. Originally the Nungate had been an industrial suburb outside the governance of the Town Council and the price-fixing of the medieval guilds. Our house was backed by a former brewery, then in use by a fell-monger, who took the wool off the sheepskins bought from the slaughter house. Part of the process involved washing the skins and this was done by men standing in the river, scouring the skins on a concrete table. It also involved drying them and twice the kiln went on fire. The firm, Burns Coalston, was short of warehouse space and applied for planning consent to erect an industrial shed on the river bank opposite St Mary's Church. There were dire threats of moving from the Burgh if they did not get consent. Sir Frank Mears' solution was to give the shed an apse end with windows, thus breaking up the large plain gable. The firm of Burns Coalston eventually gave up its antiquated production and both sites have since been developed for housing. Tyne Court, to the north, got the main Civic Trust award in 1975. On our other side was a sausage skin scraper and a scrap merchant who paid us rent, usually in kind—our garden seat was one year's rent. Beyond was Robertson, a blacksmith, who is still there.

During the 1930s a large Town Council housing scheme had been built in the Nungate, but it housed primarily Irish agricultural workers and some socially less desirable families. Our immediate neighbour was a coal merchant with a fine pair of highly polished leather gaiters and a steam driven lorry. We used to lie of a night in bed, listening to the profanities of those returning over the bridge from the pubs in the town, and were woken early in the morning by the steel-shod boots of the building trade workers going the other way to catch their buses or vans in the High Street. We lived there happily, rearing two boys and with Mary carrying on her architectural practice from the dining room. By 1956 we realised the house was too small as Jemima, our daughter, was on the way and we wanted a better garden, so we bought and restored Ford House, an "A" listed building in the County of Midlothian—about which more later. I had to get the consent of the County Council to live outwith the County, but they gave it willingly as they thought that it might be the first step to getting shot of me. The County Development Plan had been approved by the Secretary of State and the Council saw little purpose in having a Planning Officer as they now had a Plan and had complied with their statutory duty.

The Early Fifties

In the early 1950s Haddington was in a very depressed state and many people were bemoaning the fact that the stray bomb, jettisoned at the beginning of the war by German planes targeting the Forth Rail Bridge, had not done more damage so that there could be a clean sweep. Many of the four-storey buildings lining the High Street were empty and decaying above the shops at street level. They were all painted a dull buff colour which the local painters mixed up from their residues of brown and cream paint. The Town had suffered badly from the great flood of 1948—£950,000 had been paid out in compensation to individuals. The Town House was suffering from dry rot and the Town Clerk from alcohol. The schools were antiquated and the jail behind County Buildings filled up each weekend. It alone of the seven burghs had suffered a decline in population between 1931 and 1951. If the Town was to fulfill the central role it was given in the Development Plan, in unifying the County against the suburbanising influence of Edinburgh and checking rural depopulation, much positive action was needed. The Development Plan had to be implemented against the odds.

Haddington's Assets

Haddington possessed two great assets—its architectural distinction and its fine riverside setting. Its architectural distinction arises from its long (600m) triangular layout. In later centuries this got divided by a middle-row of buildings headed by its masterly Town House, into three streets: Court Street, a fine tree-lined street with grand eighteenth-century buildings set back behind humbler ones; the High

Plate XXVII Haddington

At the foot of the photograph are the riggs behind Market Street and the Kilspindie factory, since demolished. The Town House heads the middle row which divides the original long triangular market place into two, with the High Street beyond. The Butts housing scheme is shown in the middle of the picture and beyond it St Mary's, and in the top left the Nungate with its stone bridge and the gable of No 1 Bridge Street beside it.

Street, an enclosed space completely lined with four storey buildings— like an outdoor room; and Market Street which leads to a thoroughfare across the River Tyne, lined with lesser buildings. The river, with its attractive haughs, watermills and bridges, embraces the town in a wide S bend with St Mary's, its large medieval parish church, as the fulcrum. These were designated as areas of great architectural and great landscape value in the County Development Plan. These assets were wasting away and it was clear that development would come only through their conservation; and that their conservation would give Haddington the advantage in competing for development with all the other small burghs.

Of these two assets, it was perhaps the riverside setting which was most at risk. The Tyne is a narrow river along most of its course, but in Haddington is widened out by the Bermaline Weir under the Victoria Bridge which dams back the water and directs it onto the mill wheels, and so gives a big-river effect. There was much agitation to get this removed as a flood prevention measure. However we were able to prove that in any flood which threatened the town, once the weir was drowned, it had no further effect on the height of the flood. The other necessity was to restore the buildings and fill the gaps in the Nungate, so recovering the waterfront along the Nungate which has since been achieved.

The first step I took was to offer to rewrite the Town's Guide-book to highlight these two assets. Former guide-books had been the standard mishmash of assorted information from a Dundee publisher. I rewrote it stressing throughout the burgh's great architectural value with full page photographs of its buildings and a nice cover with drawings of the elevations of both sides of the High Street. There was a large local demand for this, to the astonishment of the publishers who normally had to give their guide-books away.

The Town House

The new Town Clerk, John McVie, persuaded the Town Council that, instead of pulling the Town House down to ease the traffic bottle neck it caused, they should restore it to mark the Queen's Coronation in 1953. This fine building had a core built by William Adam, and still had its original cells on the ground floor. A handsome assembly room with Robert Adam fireplace and cornsheaf cornice and a fine Venetian window looking west down Court Street had been added in 1788 above an open arched corn market. A very graceful belfry and spire designed by James Gillespie Graham in 1831 completed this superb building, worthy of a Royal Burgh. The carriage drive through the building was built up and the cells turned into offices. Above, its social functions were retained, but the fireplace and mantelpiece vanished and the integrity of the Georgian design spoilt by new windows being let into the north elevation in place of blind ones and, externally, by a metal fire escape. The Planning Department had a lot to learn about the protection of historic buildings even when in the hands of a responsible architect, in this case Peter Whiston who taught at the Edinburgh College of Art. However, restored it was, and the town curfew once again rung out at 7 am and 10 pm. Later this was mechanised when the old caretaker who had climbed the 120 stairs twice a day retired. The bell also summoned the citizens to church on Sunday, thus expressing the dominating role of the Town Council in both lay and religious matters.

The High Street

The next happening was the dispute in 1955 about tarmacing the High Street and installing electric street lights to replace the gas lights. These were carried on short iron columns cast in the town's iron foundry at Rosehall. The form of the casting sheds remains in two courtyard houses converted in the 1990s. By then the care of listed buildings had indeed reached its apogee.

The Burgh Surveyor had proposed to erect 25 feet concrete lamp standards with low-pressure orange sodium light fittings along the streets. But I was able to come up with a design incorporating vertical fluorescent tubes, which were fastened to the walls and first used in the City of London. These gave a nice pale moonlight effect and spilled their light all over the buildings and, indeed, into the sky. I spaced them more closely round the Town House to give a modest degree of floodlighting to the spire, which could be seen from the A1 bypass. This scheme was greeted with much approbation in Scotland and was inaugurated by the Lord Lieutenant, the Earl of Wemyss, then Chairman of the National Trust for Scotland.

I was not so lucky with the tarmac, this road being the County Council's responsibility and disputes between officials and Committees frowned upon. The ladies were also against me as stiletto heels had just come into fashion and these were being caught in gaps between the fine granite setts. The setts had been worn smooth by traffic over the years and been badly relaid where they had been lifted for installing services. These drawbacks could have been overcome, as in Europe, by heat treatment to renew the surface but it was easier to lay a tarmac carpet and the Roads Committee would hear nothing against it. The setts were not lifted so some day the tar can be removed and the setts relaid, as is currently being done in the Royal Mile in Edinburgh. At the time it was a bitter blow, I had gone over the top and very nearly got the sack—saved perhaps by the Lord Lieutenant's approbation.

Glasgow Overspill

What was needed by Haddingtonians was not an affirmation that their town was one of the finest architecturally in Scotland but good new jobs. Ranco Ltd, an American firm making fractional horse-power motors for domestic appliances, had been attracted to the County by the disused Admiralty Research Station at Gin Head, North Berwick. During our discussions they had revealed how in America the firm had always been happy in small towns and how much they disliked the Government's industrial estate at Newmains, Lanarkshire. They felt they had no control over their employees as they sorted themselves out into Catholic and Protestant work-groups. Haddington was clearly the place for them. The Town Clerk and Chamberlain obtained the

Plate XXVIII   Church Street.

(a) Before
These fine properties were acquired by the Town Council for ten pounds to house Glasgow Overspill families, who then had Haddington neighbours in adjoining houses.
(b) After
The external alterations are minimal as they should be, a new pediment over the central doorway, removal of the brick chimney stack extensions and the white harling of the two storey block as shown on an early postcard. The ground floor of the tall block was let as a doctor's surgery.

lease of James Stark's disused coffin making workshop in the Nungate and installed water-borne sanitation and other minor improvements at a cost of £800, spent from the Common Good Fund—that excellent old Scottish device to get round bureaucratic rules, built up by income from property and the product of a tuppenny rate. And so Ranco set up a small trial and training unit and, within two years, built a 20,000 sq feet factory on Station Road. Eventually they occupied 50,000 sq feet in Haddington and employed over 2,000 people in the town. The other big industry attracted to Haddington in the 1960s was Hilgar Electronics for whom the County Council built a factory at Gateside, but the history of that is told in the "Industrial Development" Chapter Five.

Ranco had drained the labour pool which led on to the Glasgow Overspill Agreement. This was an innovative scheme whereby Glasgow Corporation gave a subsidy for ten years to every house built and occupied by one of their tenants or a family on their waiting list. This enabled them to reduce the high densities of people then living in Glasgow and to redevelop the older tenement areas. Initially it was only towns round Glasgow that had shown any interest in receiving "overspill" as it was called, but when the Royal Burgh of Haddington— 60 miles away right across Scotland—showed an interest, it was not difficult to persuade their officials to put our agreement on the top of the first batch to be signed. In consequence Haddington became the first overspill town with an agreement to house 250 families from Glasgow.

In the 1920s there had been a similar influx of people from the Borders to man the textile and knitting mills in Haddington. The difficulty this time was that Ranco did not wish to employ Glaswegians from whose labour practices they were escaping. However many local businesses who had lost labour to Ranco offered employment and we built a higher proportion of two apartment houses to attract retired people. I knew from my New Town experience the desirability of attracting a wider age-range of families and not, as in the New Towns, of housing only those employed by the industrialists. These, not surprisingly, were men in their twenties and thirties, and so the New Town Development Corporations landed themselves with difficult social and service problems as waves of the same age group crowded schools, clubs and jobs. It was the accepted wisdom that older people would never move from Glasgow away from their relatives, pubs, shops, football teams and children. But we had little difficulty in attracting them to Haddington and they proved to be the best at integrating with the local community as they had time on their hands to meet and help others, and were not burdened with children and hire-purchase debts.

We also made it a rule that every Glaswegian should have a

Haddington neighbour. This meant rehousing some of the Haddington families in the new scheme at Artillery Park built for the overspill, and renovating council houses for incoming Glaswegians. It also meant that the Town Council could restore some of the disused tenement buildings in the town. The old barrack block in Church Street was acquired for £1 and restored into six houses and a general practice surgery. In addition a further block of houses was built across St Ann's Place. Thus the town avoided having a Glasgow ghetto.

The Town Council set up a Welcome Committee of local people to visit the incomers, making them feel wanted, as indeed they were, and to tell them about the organisations and facilities in the burgh. The local amateur operatic society obtained the long sought-for tenor, a partner for Betty Black, a pillar of the society; the George Hotel, a new chef, and so it went on. There was also a remarkable improvement in the appearance and dress of the local girls as they competed with the Glaswegians in mini-skirts. We did a settling-in survey five years after the first overspill family arrived, and another five years later when few remembered who was an overspill family. There had been problems such as children who arrived barefoot at school but people rallied round and the over-stretched, desperate mother was helped and so another family was saved. Such were the benefits of the overspill scheme.

Plate XXIX   St Ann's Place.
A little piece of infill linking two derelict sites and so creating a court off Sidegate where before there had been a roadway. We followed our own rules by having the floor level one foot above the 1956 flood level, hence the rather high cills on the new building. Architect: J A W Grant.

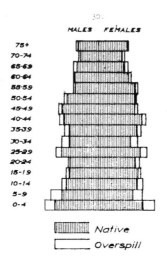

MALES   FEMALES

75+
70-74
65-69
60-64
55-59
50-54
45-49
40-44
35-39
30-34
25-29
20-24
15-19
10-14
5-9
0-4

|||||| Native

Overspill

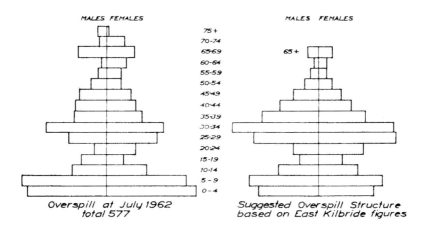

MALES FEMALES

MALES FEMALES

75 +
70-74
65-69
60-64
55-59
50-54
45-49
40-44
35-39
30-34
25-29
20-24
15-19
10-14
5-9
0-4

65 +

Overspill at July 1962
total 577

Suggested Overspill Structure
based on East Kilbride figures

HADDINGTON : Population Graphs

Percentage of population in AGE & SEX groups

Native population from 1951 census
Overspill population from Overspill Survey Aug. 1962

SCALE : 2/10" to 1%

1094
31·10·62

EAST LOTHIAN COUNTY COUNCIL
COUNTY PLANNING DEPARTMENT

Plate XXX   Glasgow Overspill Age-Structure

These graphs were contained in the Planning Department's Annual Report for 1961.
The bottom left shows the young age-groups which came with the Glasgow Overspill.
The bottom right shows a typical New Town population with fewer of the older people
whom we specifically attracted to Haddington. The top graph shows the combined
population with its recruitment to the lower age-groups thus building up a more
"healthy" population profile.

The High Street Face-lift Scheme

The increased population also led directly to the restoration of the classical frontage building "Carlyle House" as accommodation for Lee Hogg, the Burgh Surveyor, who previously had worked from three small rooms above the Fire Station on the Sands. It also led to the shopkeepers' tills ringing more merrily and so they were in a more expansive frame of mind when we started to persuade them to join in a great face-lift scheme for the High Street. This was organised, as much else was, by the indefatigable Town Chamberlain, Matt Carlaw. Eric Hall & Partners, Architects, were engaged to draw up a colour scheme using the elevational drawing bequeathed to us by Sir Frank Mears. The basis was earth colours for the walls, where painted, and bright colours for the doors. Windows were to be white and all architectural detail picked out in colour. There was not a lot of this but the beading on the panelled doors was picked out in white and made the whole scene sing. Obviously, it made no sense to paint rotten window cills, etc, and so the scheme also involved the architects giving each owner a consultation, not only in choice of colour but also on the maintenance or improvement required; thus leaving him or her with a specification of works which could be given to their builders. The merchants had previously been conditioned to brighter colours as my department had been providing colour schemes for shops in strategic positions.

Golden Shop Signs

I also tried to persuade the shopkeepers to continue the tradition of the golden signs. The golden Wellington Boot outside Ramsay the bootmaker, which had mysteriously vanished after his shop was closed, had been traced and returned to Haddington by John McVie and graced the adjoining footwear shop—although once again it seems to have vanished. Ramsay's shop had been bought by Crawfords the Bakers and I persuaded them both to strip the paint off the stone front and to hang out a golden kettle to advertise the little cafe they conducted with the bread and cake counter. Main, the saddler, had a golden horse, both chemists a pestle and mortar, and Godek, one of the Polish soldiers who stayed on after the war, was persuaded to gild the front end of a bicycle. But that was the extent of my persuasion. I could not get Purvis, the licenced grocer, to gild and hang a small sherry barrel, nor Craig, the upholsterer, to hang a chair, although later George Low in Dunbar took up the notion. We had also been into most buildings and drawn up 1/8 scale plans to match the Sir Frank Mears' elevations, so that we could see the potential for each property and make suggestions to the owner. Matt Carlaw offered them generous housing improvement grants on the reasoning that an improved house paid higher rates and so contributed more to the town's finances. The painting scheme was thus more than skin deep.

Plate XXXI   The Golden Signs

(a)   The Wellington Boot, in its original form before the rubber manufacturers transformed it, graced Ramsay the Bootmaker's shop with its splendid lettering, now a cafe. It was taken by an antique dealer, but recovered by the Town Clerk. Where is it now?

(b)   The Golden Bicycle, designed in the Planning Department and erected by Mr Godek, one of the enterprising Polish soldiers who married local girls and made Haddington their home.

The Butts Scheme

Behind the buildings on the south side of the High Street were long closes of old decaying buildings, sheds and stables, and beyond again, strips of unkempt gardens. These were terminated by the Burgh wall, an eight feet rubble wall, not for defence, but to keep out vagrants and others in earlier centuries when the Town Council had to provide poor relief for anyone within its walls. Wicket gates gave out onto a path, the Butts. As late as 1911 the Town Council hired a herdsman who took the cattle put out through the gates to the common grazing at Neilson Park, now the recreation ground.

The problem as I saw it was to get a service road built round the back from which supply lorries could deliver into backshops, thus avoiding both the lorries being double parked in the High Street and the goods being squeezed past customers in the front shop. Such a road would also give the opportunity to convert the buildings in the closes, without everything having to be barrowed through from the High Street, and open up sites for new houses which could pay for the service road. These new houses carried on the line of the riggs and were built traditionally with pantiled roofs. They had footpath access

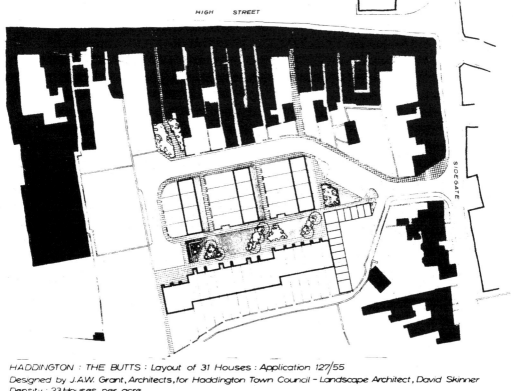

SIDEGATE

HADDINGTON : THE BUTTS : Layout of 31 Houses : Application 127/55
Designed by J.A.W. Grant, Architects, for Haddington Town Council – Landscape Architect, David Skinner
Density : 23 Houses per acre

SCALE OF FEET
50   25   100   200   300

1206
26·8·63

EAST LOTHIAN COUNTY COUNCIL
COUNTY PLANNING DEPARTMENT

Plate XXXII   The Butts

The layout shows the service road provided for the backs of the shops on the south
side of the High Street and the tight little housing scheme which paid for it. At the
bottom is the Butts footpath to which the houses had direct access and which led to all
the schools; to the south of the footpath is the public park.

leading to a paved space along which there was built a two-storey terrace
of nineteen terrace houses 12 feet wide facing south along the park
frontage with small gardens giving access onto the Butts. This was the
longest terrace built in Scotland since the First World War, until it was
exceeded by terraces built in the New Town of Cumbernauld. It was of
a revolutionary type which we had examined at Peterlee. They were
economically built between party walls and had metal roofs. This block
mirrored the continuous elevations of the High Street and, being only
two storey, maintained the views to the hills enjoyed from the upper
flats on the High Street. Garages and car parks were situated at either
end of the paved area which had rose-beds and a small play area. The
actual line of the service road was determined by the thirty feet lengths
of Hugh Whitehead's wooden ladders which had to be kept under cover
to comply with the new Health and Safety Regulations. This enabled

modest expansion of the High Street properties. Most of these have undergone restoration but Mary's plans to convert a warehouse block to single apartment flats behind No 48 High Street for Mr Di Rollo were turned down on the recommendation of the Burgh Surveyor who considered that they would be used by prostitutes. I had argued that, even if they were, it was an essential trade in a County Town! The Town Council acquired Ross's Close, restored the frontage building and erected a row of new houses along the Close, which led directly to the Butts.

Mitchell's Close

The County Council, under their Comprehensive Development Area powers, widened Newton Port and restored Mitchell's Close incorporating a Health Centre at the head of the close and craft workshops along the east side as well as the four-storey frontage building. This restoration was done in a fairly free style, that retained its atmosphere, not pedantic as things are done now. It used the stone from the stairs of the Fisherman's House at Prestonpans for access to the weaving loft which was felicitously let to Mr Mitchell, a designer-weaver, who had been made redundant when the Patterson Cloth Mill closed. Twenty-five years later when he retired he was given a party in the loft to which I was invited. I apologised for the basic structure of the loft, without a ceiling and bare walls, but recalled how he said that the cold and damp was ideal for his wool if not his chest. Below him was Mr Davy, the plumber, and sanitary ware was often left outside. But the main sight was the hanging loo behind Mr Gracie's property which formed the south-east corner of the close. It has since been removed when the property was restored, something I had avoided doing. The restoration of the close was declared open by Lord Muirsheil, Chairman of the Scottish Civic Trust.

While this construction was going on there were some 126 owners to be persuaded of the merits of the co-ordinated painting scheme. Those of little faith and with some mischief held back until we had persuaded Hugh Whitehead to paint his building in the centre of the south side of the High Street. Here on the ground floor was his scarcely used office and above six small flats. It was a shameful property — cobbler's bairns—and Hugh a very thrawn character. But once he brought out his wooden ladders and started painting, all the remaining owners were shamed into painting their properties also. But suddenly a maverick appeared. The Italian ice-cream shop appeared with yellow walls and puce woodwork, of which Mr Forte was inordinately proud. It was garish and spoilt the whole carefully worked-out colour scheme. The day was only saved by the Town Clerk and me offering to pay for it to be painted for the day in conformity with the scheme. The penalty

Plate XXXIII   Mitchell's Close

(a) On acquisition
(b) After restoration

Photographs of this close off Market Street before and after restoration carried out by the County Council. It comprises a shop, three houses, a weaver's loft, a plumber's office and workshop, a health clinic and, on the left out of the picture, a craft workshop. Practical, not pedantic restoration. 1964.
Architect: Campbell & Arnott.

was that we had to repaint it to his colours within a year. I also had to fork out for painting the unoccupied but historic pantiled house at the West Port. Here I used copperas, a lime wash tinted with sulphate of iron to a very striking rich tan colour, which we had used on our house at Ford and which I had been trying unsuccessfully to get used on all the awful grey cement rendered council houses in Haddington. It looked splendid, but it did not persuade Mr Hogg or any other Housing Manager to use it. It was too old fashioned, too cheap and had no guarantee. It was not until the 1980s that the campaign to brighten up council houses throughout Scotland took off, and by then proprietary cement based paints were used.

The Great Day

The great day arrived on 22nd October 1962 when the Secretary of State for Scotland, Michael Noble, led a great column of Provosts and Conveners from throughout Scotland down the High Street. All had been invited to lunch and to attend a ceremony to mark the completion of the Town Centre Refurbishment Scheme by the Civic Trust, a London organisation, led by Sir Duncan Sandys and Michael Middleton, the secretary. This again was the first such face-lift in Scotland and the Civic Trust was promoting these schemes following on their initial projects in Norwich and Windsor. A great luncheon for 500 people was held in the Corn Exchange. The Civic Trust demonstrated a new

Plate XXXIV   The Great Day.

The Marquis of Tweeddale, my Chairman, wearing his trilby hat, Provost Gardiner and
Michael Noble, Secretary of State for Scotland, lead the procession of Conveners and
Provosts and their wives down the High Street to admire our co-ordinated painting
scheme. Ex-Provost Bill Crowe and John McVie, the Town Clerk, in his wig and gown,
are in the second row.

machine for transplanting trees and anchoring them by underground
stays, but the three ash trees that were planted outside the Corn
Exchange had not been adequately prepared by previous root pruning.
They are still there but never recovered from the shock although they
did draw attention to the importance of trees in towns. My department
mounted an exhibition of ten 4 by 4 feet boards in the Town House
which told the Haddington Story and the Secretary of State unveiled a
plaque on that little gem of a classical building, Carlyle House, the
Burgh Surveyor's new office in Lodge Street. This building with its
Corinthian pilasters and denticulated cornice with urns had clearly
been built from an eighteenth century pattern book. However it is
only 23 feet wide and 20 feet high and so was less than half the size of
the mansion house for which it had been intended. Nevertheless it
epitomised the pride of eighteenth century Haddington when the Town
Council was sending resolutions to Parliament at Westminster. It
reflected the pride that Haddington certainly felt that day in 1962 and
its reputation, and mine, were spread throughout Scotland.

Plate XXXV   Carlyle House

The little palace fronted house was restored by the Town Council for the Burgh Surveyor who needed enlarged offices as the result of the overspill population. The Architect was Sir Robert Matthew. The left hand Corinthian capital was carved in situ from a new stone. The chalk blobs on the windows remind the tradesmen that they have been glazed—an old custom.

The Lamp of Lothian Trust

The Haddington Story does not end there. It was taken up by the Duchess of Hamilton. After the war the ducal family had left Hamilton in the Clyde Valley and acquired the mansion house of Lennoxlove two miles south of Haddington, and bought a number of farms in the County. They had not played much part in local life until the 1960s. It all started when the Duchess realised, as we had, that it was ineffectual to build up the social life in her estate village of Bolton, when what was needed was a bridge between the life on the farms and life in the towns.

So she established the Bridge Youth Club in the row of old miller's cottages behind the Poldrate Corn Mill and subsequently the Visual Arts Centre for adults in a house on the Sidegate.

She found that this combination of new socially worth-while uses and the restoration of old buildings was a powerful attraction for charitable funds and, of course, it helped to be a duchess. She then acquired Haddington House in the Sidegate, the finest of the seventeenth century houses left in the town with a 4 acre derelict orchard sweeping back to St Mary's Churchyard and down to Lady Kitty's garden by the river. This had been acquired by the Earl of Wemyss for the East Lothian Antiquarian and Field Naturalist Society in the 1940s and was lived in by a retired fruiterer, Mr Faunt, who was well beyond the age when he could look after it and the Society had not adequate funds to repair it, let alone do anything with it. Mary and I tried to acquire it in the mid 1950s to restore it once old Mr Faunt had died, and provide the Society with rooms for their meetings and their library. We always regret that our offer was not accepted, but the Society fell for the Duchess. The house was restored by the architect Schomberg Scott and it was used in a multiplicity of ways as a Community House. It was the headquarters of the Lamp of Lothian Trust, for organising community events, such as exhibitions and concerts. Rooms were set aside for senior pupils to do their homework for university entrance but this never took off. The upper floor was used as lodgings for various community volunteers and workers. There were meeting rooms and stacking chairs in the fine seventeenth century panelled rooms. But somehow it never really became the cultural heart of the community, as intended, and it was put up for sale in 1994.

The restoration of the garden however was a great success under the joint direction of Sir George Taylor and Sir David Lowe, and with the financial aid of the Stanley Smith Garden Trust and, latterly, of the East Lothian District Council who provided a gardener. The Apple House, which had originally been a doocot, was restored as a memorial to the tenth Duke of Hamilton. A laburnum walk, following the famous one at Bodnant, North Wales, led from the House to the gate into St Mary's Churchyard. A sunken garden planted with seventeenth century plants was laid out in front of the House. The public garden is a great joy, attracting many return visits by locals and always popular with tourists.

St Mary's Church

The greatest project in Haddington was the restoration of St Mary's Church which John McVie, the Town Clerk, had initiated with the Kirk Session. The Duchess assumed the responsibility for fund-raising. St Mary's Church, the largest medieval parish church in Scotland had been damaged in the siege of Haddington in 1548, when the English held the town against a combined force of French and Scots. The tower had originally supported a masonry crown like St Giles in Edinburgh, but it, together with the choir and transepts were ruins in the care of the Ancient Monuments Department. Only the nave was roofed and used by the Church of Scotland congregation.

The first proposal was to put a flat roof over the choir and transepts, and open up the whole church to the growing population of the town, not only as a place of worship, but also for cultural events.

I rather liked this romantic ruined church in the great bend of the River Tyne with the large copper beech tree at its east end. I knew that the pillars of the choir were unstable because of the ebb and flow of the river through the gravel beds which underlay the S bend in the river with at least as much water flowing underground as in the open bed of the river. Anyhow, the crass re-roofing could not be recommended for planning approval, and if it was to be restored, the church must be restored properly with vaults inside and a pitched slated roof outside. I had thought that this would finish the matter but the architects, Ian Lindsay & Partners, came forward with the proposal for a glass fibre vault to replicate the original. My other concern was that the colours and size of the stones used in rebuilding the walls should match the original masonry which was built of large coursed square rubble from the characteristic mixture of stones found in local quarries. Over the centuries the stones stonemasons use have got smaller, and small stones are a sure sign of a modern patch-up. The architects told me that to comply with this condition they had to transport stone from 36 demolition sites in the Lothians, but they honoured the condition nobly, as can be seen in the south-west corner of the north transept. Internally, there were also problems with the floor level as some of the column bases had sunk and it would have been wrong for the pillars to appear without bases. That explains why the floor is cut back round some of the columns in the choir. The choir looks naked without its wooden choir stalls, but with the table placed centrally under the crossing it meets the liturgical needs of the Church of Scotland and makes it more suitable for large musical performances and other lay activities.

The Duchess had established links with Yehudi Menuhin and his Music School performed in the Church most years and has given a great boost to music throughout East Lothian. Her other great venture was the conversion of the old Poldrate Mill in the Sidegate into a Visual Arts Centre with facilities for painting, pottery and sculpture in the granary building, and the Mill itself into a rather odd meeting and exhibition centre. I had opposed the demolition of its tall brick chimney which acted as a visual landmark to the southern edge of the town,

Plate XXXVI   St Mary's Church

(a) Before
The largest medieval parish church in Scotland. 62.8m long, 0.7m longer than St Giles, Edinburgh. But until its restoration only the nave was used and the aisles had been raised with rather English-looking parapets and pinnacles.

apart from its historic significance. The architects were not prepared to be convinced and it is difficult to beat a Duchess—so a metal flue pipe was erected instead, incongruous both inside and out.

Finally, the Duchess honoured one of Haddington's heroines, Jane Welsh Carlyle, by acquiring her father's house and furnishing the drawing room with Victorian memorabilia. It is a condition of the tenancy of the house that the room is open to visitors during the summer. This is certainly better treatment than the bronze plaque that marks the birthplace of Samuel Smiles on 62 High Street. His best known book *"Self Help"* was much mentioned in support of the free play of market forces during the Thatcher years. His politics were in fact much further to the left than she would have liked, if only she had read the book and not just the title.

None of these activities would have been possible without a substantial influx of new people into Haddington. At one time there were over thirty architects restoring property, living in Haddington and enriching its social and cultural life. In particular, I remember Jim Macdonald who spent his evenings painting large semi-abstract pictures with broad brushes and acrylic paints. His wife, Irene, with her

(b) After Restoration
The reroofed choir and rebuilt north transepts. Popular history says that the tower carried a stone crown like St Giles but Colin McWilliam states that there is no positive evidence that one was actually built. The photograph shows the rebuilt stonework on the north transept where it was a planning condition that it should be of similar size and colour, matching the original courses. Architects: Ian Lindsay & Partners.

knowledge of early pottery, established a shop in the Elm House coach house that drew people into Haddington. It was quickly followed by Peter Potter's Gallery which adapted the former Fire Station into a space for the sale of well-known craftsmen's wares with a coffee room above in the loft where the fire hoses had been laid out to dry horizontally, as witnessed by the louvres, which it was a planning condition should be retained. They add to the quaintness of this building which looks south over the oldest bowling green in Scotland—no longer used since the firemen, who maintained it, left for their new station in Court Street. This is next to the Police Station, another listed building, and a former doctor's house, which I had persuaded the Police to acquire and erect a 'Dixon of Dock Green' blue lamp over the door in the old wrought iron fitting.

Housing at Clerkington Avenue
In the 1960s the speculative builders considered Haddington too far from Edinburgh for them to build and sell houses so, to force their

hand, the Town Council acquired the field at the west end—the posh end—of the burgh and offered it not for outright sale but on a grassum, an old Scottish legal term which involved the builder acquiring the right to build and the real money and real title only changing hands between the Town Council and the house owners when the houses were sold. This left the feudal superiority, with its control over use and appearance, in the hands of the Town Council. It was a great attraction to the builders as they did not have to lay out money in advance for land acquisition. Four builders put in schemes and offers. The most interesting was one from Bells, the large Newcastle builders. In the North-east of England there was a tradition of owner-occupation reaching much lower down the social scale than in Scotland. There, the builders priced their houses on what they cost to build plus a profit. In Scotland, with its smaller middle-class market, builders charged what they thought the market would bear. Bells also had staff architects and therefore it was no surprise that they submitted the best layout and their houses were the best value for money and so were chosen. It was their first Scottish venture and they complained about the Scottish Building Regulations which at that time were more stringent than the English regulations, and they considered, added £1,000 to the cost of a house.

It was always my intention that the St Lawrence Burn and the policies of Clerkington should mark the western edge of Haddington. This was reflected in the design with a continuous chain of similar houses linked by their garages facing over a burn to the open farmland beyond with a public footpath along the dell beside the burn. The development attracted a lot of talented people and I was delighted to receive, although I was unable to attend, an invitation to the open-air party that they organised for the 25th anniversary of the Estate. I wonder how many times this has happened on a speculative housing estate.

Housing at Gourlay Bank

The Adam Housing Association built another innovative scheme at Gourlay Bank. This was the first post-war Housing Association scheme in Scotland and was designed by James Gray, Architect. The scheme was a very delightful start for this important initiative. It consisted of

Plate XXXVII   St Mary's Church Interior.

A photograph looking east showing the glass fibre vault and ribbing supported on the old stone columns. The ceiling bosses were also fibreglass but rather crude and without the medieval humour but the Planning Officer's writ did not run as far as designing bosses. Outside the east window is the great copper beech tree.

a series of 32 single and two storey houses in two cul-de-sacs. Between the remnants of the old orchard was a common green, and this, together with the rest of the planting was maintained jointly by the owners who had quite small individual gardens. It too attracted many young professional people to Haddington.

In 1980 the Bield Housing Association also built a charming scheme of sheltered housing as an extension of our Butts scheme, retaining much of the old rigg walling and a doocot and providing pedestrian access back onto the High Street.

Haddington Festival

The mid-1960s saw the need to integrate these incomers, both overspill and owner-occupiers, into the community. Accordingly the Town Council organised a Festival Week in May during which all the organisations in the Town put on events and tried to win new members.

Plate XXXVIII   Trail Leaflets

(a) Architecture (b) Trees

These two booklets were produced by my department as their contribution to the first and second Haddington Festivals and were designed to open the eyes of newcomers and natives alike to the wealth of beauty all around them in Haddington. The Architectural Trail cover and illustrations were drawn by Graham Duncan. The trees frame the monument (1880) to the eighth Marquis of Tweeddale who looks out at the traffic on Court Street. Both were on sale 24 hours a day at the Police Station.

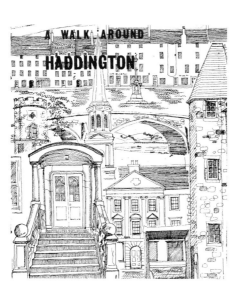

Plate XXXIX   Architectural Heritage Centre

Lady Kitty's Doocot was restored in 1975 and its undercroft used as a modest Architectural Heritage Centre. As the undercroft was only 16x16 feet the display boards were demountable and could be taken out into the garden for telling the story of Haddington and describing its architectural grandeur to school parties. Human access to the Doocot above is by ladder. The pigeons get access through a central glover on the roof.

Again, this was the first of the Town Festivals which have now become commonplace as tourist occasions, but this one was for community building. The Planning Department, I remember, designed and had manufactured the long banner flags emblazoned with the goat, the Haddington crest. It also produced the *"Architectural Trail"*, a booklet available 24 hours a day from the Police Station, and melamine boards which picked out the architectural features of the Town—another first which remains in place to this day. The following year we did a similar booklet *"Trees about Town"* which identified the trees and the part they played in the Townscape. The labels we placed on the trees were soon removed as collectors' items but the trees have earned greater respect which was the purpose of the exercise.

One of the most spectacular events put on, if I remember rightly, by the Rotarians, was racing bedsteads in the High Street, which was closed to other traffic. In those days there were plenty of old iron bedsteads with casters and these were raced from one end of the High Street to the other, with various classes of occupants in suitable sleeping attire. What a laugh, what spills, what a spectacle in the refurbished High Street with its newly-painted walls and the Goats presiding from their flagpoles. The Commercial Hotel served beer on the street and this added to the sense of liberation and the casting off of old inhibitions and caste prejudices.

Another aspect of community consolidation was to control the rate of new house building so that newcomers had time to put down their roots and the community to absorb them. I remember the astonishment on the faces of Bells' directors when I told them that planning permission to continue their successful and much admired Clerkington development south across the Pencaitland Road had been refused planning consent. On my advice they moved to Dalkeith and subsequently to Dalgety Bay where they continued their developments. This policy got me into trouble with the headmaster of Knox Academy who thought the school was too small at 800 pupils, and though I could point to its good academic record and the limited capacity of its new buildings by Alan Reiach and Eric Hall, he never gave up.

Architectural Heritage Centre

In 1975 we pulled together *"The Haddington Story"* in an exhibition in the small undercroft of Lady Kitty's Doocot. It had a vaulted ceiling and a fireplace and so must have been a garden "howff" at sometime. The exhibition was mounted on canvas frames that could be lifted off their hooks and taken outside in the sunshine to lecture school parties. The eight boards told the story of Haddington from its origin in the twelfth century, its growth through the centuries, its form and character, its industries and people, and finally, the efforts of the last 25 years, all shown through its architecture as in the original guide-book. This was, in the parlance of the time, the first Architectural Heritage Centre in Britain, although it only measured 15 feet square. Access was gained by borrowing the keys from Peter Potter's Gallery. This worked well for many years and it was visited on average a dozen times a week in the summer. Access could be obtained to the Doocot by a ladder, but this and its several replacements were stolen. Then unfortunately the exhibition was vandalised in 1983 and the District Council never had the energy to revive it. It recorded that Haddington had grown from 4,518 in 1951 to 7,787 in 1971 and its age profile had widened out in the form of a pyramid with more young people at the bottom than elderly at the top. The travel to work outflow of 146 had been reversed to an inflow of 485. The whole spirit of the place had changed and it had an air of quiet prosperity. Of the 129 buildings on the 1972 List of Buildings of Architectural or Historic Interest, 43 had been restored, the future of 69 was secure and the future of only 11 was in doubt. What a nice story and how nice to have the figures to back it up.

5

INDUSTRIAL PROMOTION

2,979 Jobs Created • Richard Adams • Dunbar Cement Works
Macmerry Industrial Estate • London Promotion
Prestonpans • Morfax • Haddington • Gateside • Tanberg
The Plessey Debacle • Village Factories • Only One Bad Debt
South of Scotland Electricity Board
1960s Cockenzie Coal-Fired Power Station
Cockenzie Pylon Lines • 1970s Torness Nuclear Power Station
Torness Pylon Lines

During the 1950s it became clear that it was the development of local industries and the creation of jobs that were necessary, both to support the conservation effort and to give new life to the County.

It was a time of job losses with collieries closing, agricultural manpower declining rapidly, pre-war and wartime industries failing. The figures were dreadful: a decline in the insured population from 13,503 in 1950 to 11,396 in 1960, and in 1960, 2,509 people travelling out of the County to work compared with 823 travelling in.

There was pressure on the County Councillors to do something about it. The Council was not then empowered by statute to run a job creation programme, but under the planning and associated acts it was empowered to designate and acquire industrial sites and build factories. It was entitled to build houses for incoming industrialists; and, through its general planning powers, could help or hinder the establishment of new industry and sustain the existing industries.

2979 Jobs Created

This chapter describes the part the County Council played in establishing a new industrial base for the County and creating jobs. While currently much is being done by direct investment by Enterprise Boards and other Government agencies, the planning powers and support services of the local authorities are vital as the following episodes show. Later I was able to boast to the sceptical Industrial Officer in the Lothian Regional Council that East Lothian County Council had created, in one way or another, 2,979 industrial jobs by 1974. It was more than Livingston New Town achieved for many years. How it was done and some of the more significant of our ventures and escapades are remembered below.

In 1970 the County Council authorised me to employ an Industrial Officer. We had a lot of unsuccessful businessmen and women responding to our advertisements in the Scottish papers but I had also advertised the job in the *New Statesman and Nation* which I read weekly. This had attracted Richard Adams and his wife, both graduates of Newcastle University. Their life ambition was to help the Indian sub-continent. They wanted to get some training, he with me and his wife at the Edinburgh Royal Infirmary. It was agreed that his appointment would be of limited duration, in fact until his wife obtained her nursing qualification. This did not prevent him restoring and living in the house at West Port, Haddington. He started our tradition of 'avuncular help' to industrialists and of nurturing 'home-grown' industries. We assisted in practical ways 50 of the 60 manufacturing firms which were attracted to the County, either by providing buildings for 45 firms, houses, publicity, intervention with utility companies and government departments, etc. He set the pattern for subsequent Industrial Officers and for what is now called the partnership approach. By 1974 the County had invested £1.5M in industrial sites and buildings. All this endeavour was recorded in Annual Reports submitted to the County Planning Committee. In 1971 the Report had a front cover showing the press coverage we had received, in 1972 the eleven factories we had then built and in 1974 photographs of the seventeen managing directors of the firms who had been recently established in the County.

Richard's life plan was to help the rural people of India by buying their agricultural produce to supply the growing number of ethnic restaurants and the growing taste for out-of-season fruit and vegetables in Britain. The third member of the group was out in India preparing the small farmers while Richard, when he left me, concentrated on the marketing. To learn the tricks of the trade, he acquired a greengrocer's business in Harrow. At the same time he built up a series of contracts with customers in the Midlands and awaited with great excitement the first plane load of vegetables to arrive at Birmingham Airport. To his horror, these had turned to pulp and were quite unsalable so he had to acquire stuff at Covent Garden to honour his contracts and await the next week's plane. But that second load was no better than the first. The Indians had only been used to picking ripe fruits for the local markets and had not been able to change this inbred habit. The business had to be moved to East African suppliers where the British and Italian farmers had been longer at the European trade, but this was not Richard's goal. He therefore switched to importing durable goods— amami wares and other craft goods made in the villages of Bangladesh. He built up a big ethical company supplying the charity shops that were beginning to boom under the name 'Tradcraft'. I hope he remembers us and his early apprenticeship in East Lothian. A very interesting fellow, leading a very worthwhile life.

Dunbar Cement Works

The need for a Scottish cement industry had been highlighted by the hold-up in cement supplies during the hard winter of 1957, when cement trains from Kent could not get round London, and work on Highland hydro-electric dams was held up for months. About that time a cement company was exploring the possibility of establishing production at East Saltoun. This was to be fired in a vertical kiln which is not so efficient, nor produces such a pure product, as the larger horizontal rotating kiln used by the Associated Portland Cement Manufacturers—The Blue Circle Group. Late one Friday afternoon one of their directors, John Taylor, came into my office—a big man, in a very long heavy overcoat, who clearly considered that County Planning Officers were great to eat for breakfast. He was of that unique breed—a Fife Coal Company lawyer, but a lawyer who, with a group of others in the 1930s had led the campaign for an independent socialist Scotland. He had emigrated south and was now the legal and tax director of the APCM and as such in charge of their development programme. This had brought him into fierce confrontation with planners throughout England, although I did not know it at the time of his first visit.

I got off on quite the wrong foot with him as I thought he was coming to discuss the East Saltoun project where I knew a drilling team had been exploring the extent of the limestone deposit. This team had also been involved in drilling at Oxwellmains, Dunbar, for the Coltness Iron Company and it was canteen tittle-tattle that had alerted the APCM to these larger deposits. So much for their statement at the subsequent Public Inquiry that the Company had explored all possible sources and that Oxwellmains was the only one that could sustain a production unit of their size. He was also in some embarrassment, as his surveyors had got consent for an exploration programme at Oxwellmains without first having agreed a price and obtained an option. That apart, he had done his homework and knew everyone in the County who held shares in APCM. Luckily I had recently sold my mother's shares.

I, of course, welcomed the proposal for this new industry exploiting the County's natural resources and fulfilling a national need. It was in the right place with access to the main line railway and near the coast where the smoke and stour would be blown out to sea by the prevailing wind. It was also in an area of rapid depopulation which it was the County Planning Policy to halt.

Regrettably, the plans he unfurled were quite unworkable, with an open-cast quarry stretching from the coast across the A1 road to the main line railway. It would not allow the cyclical restoration of this best grade agricultural land which I told him would be a non-negotiable planning condition. His reason for proposing this was that he knew the owner, Sir James Hope, was near bankruptcy and the adjoining owner was the Duke of Roxburgh. As he said, he was not prepared to take on the House of Lords. His ploy was that, once he established a works, he could extend the quarry by means of a piece of Victorian legislation which enabled railway magnates to compulsorily acquire land to complete their lines.

All this and his plans were quite unacceptable to me and as we had to promote our first 'Amendment to the County Development Plan' I said that we would designate for compulsory acquisition the land on the south side of the railway for both works and a quarry. This would enable the Company to work the limestone by open-cast methods from north to south, restoring the agricultural land as it went. He was clearly nonplussed by this but, as I knew he was staying the weekend at the Caledonian Hotel in Edinburgh, I invited him out to my house at Ford on Sunday evening, thinking it essential to try to make a friend of him. The friendship was sealed over a bottle of Drambuie which we finished that evening—with a pact that Dunbar was to be the finest cement works in Britain.

However the Company was not convinced by my proposals and invited the Planning Committee down to inspect the works at Shoreham, West Sussex, where the Scots Saltire was flying from the mast as we approached. The hospitality was magnificent, the dust not so noticeable and we adjourned for a meeting and dinner in the Hotel Metropole in Brighton, before being put on the train back to Dunbar. John Taylor put us under great pressure to agree with his proposals and I remember getting up and shaking the County Clerk, by now a little worse for drink, and saying nothing must be decided until we got back to the Council Chambers in Haddington. And nor it was.

In the end, Associated Portland Cement accepted our proposal and the Development Plan Amendment but demanded a price—that the Council rebuild the humpback bridge over the railway. It was commonly thought that the works would increase the County's rateable value and this would more than compensate for the expenditure. As it turned out, the Company argued that much of their plant was moveable, and with the operation of the rate equalisation scheme, the County got no financial benefit from the cement works. Nevertheless there was substantial economic gain as we persuaded them to train local people, rather than bring in workers from their other plants or take on the contractors' men, who would have needed housing. Some housing was necessary and the Company paid the same subsidy to the Dunbar Town Council for the right to nominate tenants as applied under the Glasgow Overspill Agreement.

Plate XL Dunbar Cement Works

An early view showing in the foreground the human scale buildings, offices, laboratories and canteen on the left and the workshop and yard on the right. The conical coal store is extreme right with the kiln building above it, the mill buildings are in the centre and the silos to the left. The top of the picture shows the opening up of the quarry. Barneyhill House and park is shown on the left.

There were great arguments over the design of the big asbestos sheds specified by Oscar Faber. John Taylor challenged me to suggest better industrial sheds and I showed him those that Basil Spence had designed for the Scottish Agricultural Industries fertiliser plant at Leith, where the eaves were made of curved sheets linking the roof and walls, so avoiding gutters and greatly improving the appearance. Although floored he would not depart from his normal buildings. He accepted my argument that all the buildings in which personnel worked, the offices, canteen, laboratories, workshops, etc, should be grouped at the site entrance and not scattered through the plant; that 20 feet should be lopped off the height of the buildings; and that the chimneys should be

Plate XLI   Oxwellmains South Quarry

A dramatic view of the cyclical restoration showing on the right the upper glacial material being moved across the cut to the left by the transporter sitting on the upper limestone. On the extreme left is the restored agricultural land. At the top of the picture a dumper truck can be seen moving the upper limestone to get at the lower limestone and shale seams. A far cry from the 'hill and dale' landscape left by Stewart & Lloyds when working ironstone near Corby, which I saw as a school boy.

raised 100 feet to carry any deposit across the agricultural land into the sea. He put great faith in his landscape architect, Sheila Haywood, who produced charm but very sparse planting. His final sticking point was his refusal to accept that, in addition to stripping the 18 inches of top-soil, the Company must also strip and replace separately 18 inches of the soil parent material of broken stone and minerals which lay directly under the top-soil. This was to be put back on top of the sandstone overburden that had to be excavated to get at the two 20 feet seams of limestone and their associated shales. It was on this small difference of 18 inches that he forced a public inquiry at which of course he was in his element. The Reportor found against him, and I must say that standing up against him did me no harm with the agricultural community and introduced me to a whole new world of soil science.

The first quarry manager, Mr Hamilton, was a qualified town planner and, while he was there, the quarry was a magnificent precision job with vertical benches, although it got less so as it met more difficult geological conditions. The restored land was growing barley within three years of its excavation. Recently I have learnt with horror that, after all our efforts, planning consent has been given to turn this restored land into a refuse mountain for Edinburgh. Changed days.

John Taylor did not in the end ask the County Council to compulsorily acquire the Duke of Roxburgh's land as he did not want the District Valuer, who would have negotiated for the Council, to be privy to the Company's financial calculations. The Duke also preferred to deal direct with APCM as he wanted to offload not just the designated land but all the land he owned in the area, the Mansion House and policies at Broxmouth (the former dower house of the estate), his tenanted farms and the coastal lands comprising Dunbar golf course, and the White Sands and Barns Ness. At my suggestion the Company gave these latter areas to the County Council and it paid for the restoration of the limekilns at Catcraig in exchange for permission to demolish similar kilns at Oxwellmains. The Company also paid for printing a booklet on 'Lothian Limekilns', produced at my suggestion by Basil Skinner with his Edinburgh University Extra Mural local history students.

The action by the County Council in designating land for the profit of a private company astonished the Edinburgh legal fraternity. They were used to County Councils compulsorily acquiring land for their direct functions—roads, housing, schools—but compulsory purchase to secure development in conformity to the development plan showed the power of a local planning authority in a new and, they thought, dangerous light.

These negotiations lost me one of my first friends in the County,

Mrs Robert Hope, to whom I had had a letter of introduction from my Greek godmother. I had sought a meeting with Robert Hope, who farmed land at Oxwellmains and lived in the fine house at Barney Hill, to explain the national and local interest in having the cement industry at Dunbar and to try to win his support for my quarry proposal. But it was all too much for them and he 'threw' me out of his drawing room. It was the only occasion this happened to me during my professional life and I could well understand his feelings. However, out of the deal he acquired Broxmouth Park and ended his days comfortably in a new house there. He became very deaf, but at the end he must have forgiven me, for he made a generous donation of Broxmouth South Lodge and £5,000 to the Lothian Building Preservation Trust of which I was the Director. It was a surprise when I was included in the list of 100 guests which Mr McGregor, a tenant farmer affected by the cement works, had composed to be invited to a dinner at the North British Hotel in Edinburgh one year after his death. A little circle of friends was built up by John Taylor as he made his annual visits to Dunbar. He was very proud of the works, which we had struggled to improve together, and thought it was the best looking works in the Company and a notable contribution to the economy of his native Scotland.

By 1970 the Company had worked out the limestone on the south side of the railway up to the Dry Burn and turned their attention to the land they owned to the north of the railway. It was then of course they appreciated the impossibility of working these deposits without moving the A1 trunk road, as I had foretold. It would have meant sterilising, for safety reasons, 100 metres either side of the road. The Company could live with the railway as it operated to a timetable with signal controls which could be co-ordinated with the timing of the blasting. Traffic on the A1 could not be expected to tolerate the delays involved. There was only one thing to do—move the road. The Company curiously preferred to realign the road along the coast, but I preferred the inland route as constructed right off the limestone deposits, which would not give rise to undue pressure for development of the coastal lands. It was our policy to approach the coastline from branch or dead-end roads where access could be controlled, not a corniche road, which I think rather appealed to John. Not surprisingly he insisted that, as the Company was paying for it, the road should be constructed of concrete! As this northern quarry would operate at least thirty years, I insisted that the Company used the overburden from the first cut to create a cultivatable downland area to the sea-ward of Broxmouth Park which would be there for all time. This was good thinking as, after my time, the Company refused, and got away with it, to move the unsightly heap of overburden from the first opening up the quarry, south of the railway, to fill up the excavation left along the Dry Burn.

The north quarry was then logically worked at right angles between the railway and the coastal strip, restoring the land as it went, much in the same way as double digging a garden plot. The principle difference being that it needed a 15,000,000 Deutschmark transporter to carry the excavated material over the 300 feet deep trench. For the record, there is a planning condition that when cement production ceases, the works buildings and structures must be demolished and the whole site restored to agriculture and other appropriate countryside uses. Let us hope the Planning Authority of the day enforces this.

Macmerry Industrial Estate
The County Development Plan had zoned the former Royal Air Force technical site to the south of the A1 road at MacMerry airfield as the main industrial site to serve those thrown out of employment in the mining and agricultural industries, and to provide increased employment opportunities for women from the mining areas. In November 1960 I recommended that the County Council acquire it, remove the coal bing and service it so that they could quickly build

Plate XLII Macmerry Industrial Site

My Chairman, Provost George McNeil of Tranent, cutting the first sod at Macmerry Industrial Estate in 1964. A very happy day for me as the Planning Committee, from merely being a regulatory body, also took on a development function.

factories for incoming firms. It was acquired in December 1963 and the County Council built speculatively a row of Butler prefabricated buildings along the northern frontage. These were not great buildings but were quick to erect and very serviceable as we knew from the first of these American buildings to be erected in Scotland at Goatfield, Haddington. Trees and daffodils were planted along the A1 frontage but I very much regret that we did not persevere with the virginia creeper planted on the sides of the factories. By December 1974, 15 firms were established within the estate, employing some 900 people. Eight firms had moved out from Edinburgh, two originated on the site and five had been 'won' from England. Elliott's Prefabricated Building was won on the back of the Education Committee's visit to Peterborough to buy some of their prefabricated classrooms. Webber Marking Systems which produced stick-on labels for supermarkets was won as the result of our industrial exhibition in the Bank of Scotland in the Haymarket, London.

London Promotion

This exhibition, mounted round high cardboard drums to make the most of the limited space, was planned to last three days with receptions for industrialists with whom we were in touch, and their professional advisers: bankers, surveyors and estate agents. I managed to persuade Arthur Neil of the Open Arms, Dirleton, to drive his outside catering van to London. It had never before been further than the Borders for hunt balls. They brought good fresh East Lothian food—shell fish and game and malt whisky—doing what cooking was necessary in one of Arthur Neil's friend's hotels and serving it up from the bank's first aid room. The guest list had thinned for the last day but the rota of Councillors who came down to preside were astonished that the numbers grew at each of the receptions. The Londoners clearly appreciated our smoked turkey, lobsters, pheasants, quails' eggs and were coming back for more. The total cost for food was no more than the estimates we had received from London caterers for their tired old canapes. The direct benefits of this promotion were 150 jobs but the indirect benefits were incalculable. East Lothian, from being a late starter, was now known to be in the hunt for jobs and offering the best fare in the business. A similar exhibition and industrial drive was held in an hotel in Reading later that year. As well as the Macmerry central industrial estate other small industrial estates were established at North Berwick, Dunbar and Prestonpans which all slowly filled up.

Prestonpans—Morfax

Fowler's Brewery in Prestonpans was closed down in the late 1950s, having been absorbed into the Tennent Caledonian Brewery Group, and its substantial stone buildings on the shore at the east end of the Burgh attracted the attention of Tom Morse. He was one of the early post-war Cockney entrepreneurs. When he was discharged from the RAF he acquired a motor bike and sidecar, mounted welding equipment on the sidecar, and went round south London fixing up the cars that owners had laid up during the war. Cheekily he bought his first workshop with a sack full of sixpences as the owners demanded cash. Their solicitor later became his man of business and an old RAF colleague, Reg Baldwin, who lived in Coventry, his building surveyor. When I travelled down to meet him on his own ground at Mitcham I found his company, Morfax Ltd, housed in a four-storey immaculate machine shop, doing precision engineering of the highest quality for the Ministry of Defence and others.

He had already acquired the old school at Newton in Midlothian and set up a sheet metal business under the name "Aviamac". When he needed to expand he found that the school playground and the surroundings were undermined and considered so unstable that they could not be built on. He was so furious with Midlothian County Council, who had not warned him about this, that he turned to us on the advice of their Planning Committee Chairman, Councillor Gaynor, a publican.

Three times we attempted to acquire the old Brewery for him and each time Tennents asked an impossible figure which in no way met the District Valuer's price, to which the County Council was tied. But we did not give up and our efforts were appreciated by Tom Morse. At the fourth time of asking, some three years on, we had narrowed the price down to an acceptable figure on condition that Tennents Caledonian put the building into a wind and watertight condition. They had teams of glaziers working round the clock to achieve this by the deadline. This was fixed for lunch-time after a Housing Committee meeting as Tom Morse had demanded that fifty council houses were made available for the skilled staff he thought he would need to move up from London. That number was way above the two or three that we normally allocated for key workers and represented half that year's council house building programme and so was a major decision for the Committee. However, my enquiries among engineering firms showed up the remarkable all-round abilities of ex-miners and their adaptability to learn new skills. I advised the Committee to accede to Tom's requirements as it was unlikely they would ever be taken up and so it turned out, only eight houses being needed. This was a great tribute to the local work-force and one that featured in all our subsequent industrial promotions. There were two other problems. Firstly Tom's insistence that the County Council made over the foreshore to him as he thought it would be useful if he got a Ministry of Defence order to adapt amphibious fighting vehicles. This went against my principle of 'the foreshore for the people', but a form of words was hammered out whereby the County Council bound itself to giving him a lease of the foreshore if this or other contracts materialised subject to there being a public walkway across it. Again, this was never taken up. The other problem spotted by Reg Baldwin was that the Tennent Caledonian's glaziers had not painted the putty which held the new glass into the frames and so it would shrink and the panes fall out. This nearly held up our back-to-back deal but was successfully resolved by the County Council and Tennents reducing their price to cover the costs. Thus the documents were signed and we all proceeded to have a fine lunch in the Harvesters' Hotel in East Linton.

Tom Morse embarrassed us each Christmas by giving handsome presents, which I understood he normally gave to the Ministry of Defence officials. I had strict rules about presents as it was then a normal practice for builders and developers to send bottles of spirituous liquor to me and other County officials. They were difficult to refuse, but were religiously shared out in my department amongst all the staff, and went to supplement the samples taken from hotel bars and public houses by the County Sanitary Inspector exercising his duties under the Public Health Acts. These samples were divided before the licensee's eyes into three: one was sent for analysis, one retained by the licensee and one by the County Sanitary Inspector. It was the last that fuelled the joint New Year's Eve parties our two departments enjoyed. However Tom's presents were more personal and less easily shared out than bottles. I still have a fine Swiss watch inscribed "MORFAX 25 years TOM 50 years Thank You."

Tom also treated his trips to Scotland as great holidays, but I am glad to say that he made a friend of Willie Merrilees, the Chief Constable of the Lothian and Peebles Police Force, who detailed a police car to keep an eye on his night's activities and see he came to no harm. It was one responsibility that I was not prepared to take on.

His firm had the most sophisticated computer-controlled machine tools in Scotland which were publicised in the County's Industrial Directory. The firm carried out work of an indescribably complicated nature, being involved, amongst other contracts, in the Cern European project for the smashing of atoms in a vast circular steel tube. He was greatly disappointed that he never got enough work in Scotland and had to move contracts up from Mitcham. It was a great pleasure to see these wonderful machines working in the old stone brewery buildings which he and Reg took a delight in adapting. After his death, the flow of work dried up and Morfax first moved to smaller premises in the industrial site at Prestonpans and then left the County altogether. But its experience and its trained work-force was an important factor in attracting other engineering firms to the County. The brewery has now been demolished and the site used for housing. Other industrialists, not having Tom's flair and imagination, prefer the standard factory. But over a third of the manufacturing firms attracted to the County were engaged in engineering activities, thus providing a solid base for the future.

Haddington—Gateside

As we worked out attractive financial packages for industrialists, the County Treasurer was always complaining that I did not bring any 'blue-chip' companies to the County, only small start-up and unquoted concerns—our "home-grown industries". I assured him that I was not turning away any 'blue-chip' companies, and the reason they were not coming was that there was not a large enough pool of skilled labour available. Miraculously, one day in 1967 the managing director of Hilgar and Watts, a quoted company with optical works in London, came into my office. He was proposing to set up a new company with Ferranti to make computer-controlled optical instruments. They wanted a site not far from Dalkeith, where Ferranti had their factory and research laboratories for producing computer-controlled machine tools. As many of their staff lived in the County, Haddington was a natural choice. Hilgar Electronics (Scotland) Ltd was formed and was greatly attracted to Haddington with its colourful and prosperous air. We had just managed to get Baird's Maltings to relinquish the Gateside site at the west end of Haddington, where its massive buildings and silos would have been a visual disaster, and develop a site at Wester Pencaitland. Gateside was zoned for a single prestigious industry in a parkland setting, and Hilgar Electronics clearly fitted the bill. The difference in price between what we had to pay for the site and what we could get from Hilgars was bridged by the legal device of an escalating feu duty. This was an initial fixed sum that went up with the extent of buildings erected on the site. I had never heard of such a device, but George Ritchie, the deputy County Clerk of Midlothian, put me up to it and it satisfied the District Valuer.

Then I made a great mistake which took years to redeem. I went along with the decision of Mr Campbell, Hilgar's managing director, to give the job of designing the factory to his old school chum, Percy Smith, despite the fact that the Council was paying for the factory. The result was a vastly expensive old-fashioned building with a two storey reinforced concrete office block in the front and north light roof trusses behind with only 10 feet headroom—just like the pre-war factories along the Great West Road in London. It was not the image I wanted to create but there was no moving them. The building may have suited Hilgar Watts, but its reletting value was about half the annual charges the Council was paying on it.

Hilgar Watts' main achievement was making an instrument that could count the stars in the Milky Way. A great achievement but not one in great demand. The company was bought out by Ranks who wanted to move their work to their own plant in Fife. The work-force rejected this proposal and found a 'White Knight', Paul Coradi, a Swiss Canadian, to acquire the factory. He had a more promising line in digital mapping machines. Sadly this also was short-lived as the Chicago Rope Company withdrew their finance. The staff, still very reluctant to leave their homes in Haddington and the County, managed to set up a smaller company with local backing, but this too failed. The rump was taken on by Whitwell Data Systems and the County Council managed to let much of the production area to Rancos for storage. The factory was fast becoming a white elephant for which I was responsible.

We had managed to write off some of the capital outlay as the guarantors of the successive leases were made to pay up, but it was still a charge on the County Council, empty to all intents and purposes and skilled people remained unemployed. Subsequently it was leased to and then bought by Tanberg who extinguished the escalating feu duty. A pity, as it turned out, for the vast expansion of the factory by Mitsubishi in the 1980s would have paid the Council handsomely.

Tanberg

Tanberg was a very successful Norwegian television manufacturer, who had eleven factories around Oslo and produced TV sets, which due to their reliability, were the mainstay of the British rental companies. Their sets were not assembled on a production line but individually by a "family group" of workers responsible for all stages of the sets' production and inspection. The firm was wishing to tap into the British research and university circles in order to broaden out to other television applications.

Otto Kaltenborn, the young Norwegian engineer charged with establishing their UK plant, came to us with an introduction from the Norwegian Consul, Maxwell Harper-Gow, who lived at Longniddry. After careful consideration, Otto narrowed down his choice to Livingston New Town, Morpeth in Northumberland and Haddington. We wrapped up our white elephant in an attractive package and introduced him to the pool of skilled labour who had been trained in electronic assembly by Hilgar Electronics and their successor Paul Coradi. Years later, I asked Otto what made him choose Haddington, and he admitted, rather shame-facedly, that in the last analysis it was because I was wearing a rose in my button-hole when we first met in my office. It was not the good business package, the nice meals, the fine environment, or the splendid people of Haddington, but the Charles Mallerin rose in the County Planning Officer's button-hole!

Plate XLIII Otto Kaltenborn

The young Norwegian engineer sent over by Tanberg to find a site for their first overseas plant. He chose Haddington and took over my 'white elephant', set up a very successful plant making television sets and employed some 400 people. He became a great friend and we still exchange visits.

Although Haddington was Otto's choice it still had to be approved by the Tanberg Board in Oslo, and we foresaw two obstacles. The founder of the firm, then retired and living in the company's hospitality building, and the company trade union who had two seats on the board, needed to be won over to the idea of a foreign plant. With big Jim Carnegie, who really was big, our industrial officer at the time, we worked out the following tactics. The company had invited us to send a deputation to Oslo and we decided to fly direct, not adopting the usual route by British Airways to London and SAS to Oslo, but to charter three small planes and fly direct from East Fortune airfield some 5 miles east of Haddington. In the outcome this was not possible, as the planes had to return to Edinburgh for customs clearance, but there was enough truth and bravado in the plan to impress old Mr Tanberg, especially as it was in the depth of winter, 9th December. It was a beautiful sunny day as we flew low over the North Sea and then saw the Norwegian children enjoying their winter sports.

We had little to persuade the trade unionists except goodwill and we showed this by taking six crates of Belhaven beer brewed in Dunbar and kindly donated to us by Sandy Hunter, the proprietor. These crates caused us customs delay when we landed at Oslo and so we arrived late for the board meeting. Through an oversight the crates were brought into the boardroom behind us. They must have thought that the Scots went everywhere with their own booze. However, it did the trick and we got their goodwill, and they, the beer. At dinner we met

Plate XLIV Tanberg Haddington

The 'white elephant' on the left and the charming new wing to the right commissioned by Otto Kaltenborn, which not only transformed the appearance but also the work practices. After the demise of Tanberg in Norway the building and the trained workers were taken over by Mitsubishi. Architect: Michael Calthrop.

the five staff members and their wives who would be coming to Haddington, and the following day toured their factories in Oslo which appeared to have just about as much floor space devoted to recreational and social facilities as to production. Outside each factory was a bronze sculpture presented by old Mr Tanberg and it was then decided that he would present us with two contesting goats—the armorial beast of Haddington—which now fight it out on the corner of the High Street and Sidegate. On the third day we had lunch at the Oslo Folk Museum, and once again there was a goat, a table decoration made of straw and dressed in red ribbons, which was presented to me, and I still bring it out each Christmas.

Full of schnapps, food and good cheer, we left at 4 pm for the airport and the journey home—and what a journey. Not the smiling sunny sea but a wild night with St Joseph's fire flashing round the propellers. My colleagues, some 14 in all, with bursting bladders, were frozen as the small planes had no heaters. At the pilot's suggestion we jettisoned the hot coffee to take the urine. We flew very low to minimise the cold and appeared to be skimming the huge waves—what a flight! The Provost of Tranent, George McNeil, our Chairman, never flew again and the young girl reporter from the Haddingtonshire Courier was hysterical. We landed three hours later, safe but shaken and delighted that the "White Elephant" was in someone else's charge and a fine new industry had been secured for Haddington.

The Tanberg operation was a great success and the firm soon built up a work-force of 400 people. After two years, they exercised their option to acquire the site and built a most attractive new entry hall, assembly room and hospitality wing, designed by Michael Calthrop, which brought the complex forward to the road and put Percy Smith's dull building in the background. But it was not to last. The Japanese outsold Tanberg in Europe, and the firm went bankrupt. Their Haddington plant was always profitable, but clearly it could not be kept going on its own, and once again the Gateside factory was empty when I left for the Lothian Region. Mitsubishi, their Japanese rivals, were persuaded to acquire the factory by the Scottish Development Agency and greatly benefited from the legacy of the skilled and well-motivated labour force trained by the Norwegians.

The County Council had managed to keep this factory and the electronic industry going through seven changes of company, and succeeded in establishing skilled employment in the town. It had even managed to move the last remnants of Whitwell Data Systems, the last of our Gateside tenants, to the Macmerry Industrial Estate, before it too collapsed. What an uncle! What nephews, who were determined not to leave the home town of their choice.

The Plessey Debacle

It was in 1967, when the Labour Party was in power and Tony Wedgwood Benn was Minister of Trade, that the County, and Scotland, were robbed of their greatest industrial prize. There were at that time three companies in Britain developing the computer control of machine tools: Ferranti at Dalkeith, Plessey at Plymouth and a Midlands firm that later, under the name of Matrix Churchill, got involved in the arms to Iraq affair. It was Tony Benn's ambition to bring these three firms together to make a world leader. Plessey was the only profitable one at the time, but the innovative work was all being done by Ferranti which then had more the reputation of an inventors' club than a commercial firm. The Ferranti people had chosen the industrial site at Mid Road, Prestonpans, between the A198 road and the railway, as the location for the combined factory. This had been zoned for industry in the County Development Plan though in view of its high agricultural value it was County policy not to sub-divide it, but to retain it for just such a major user.

Negotiations proceeded with Plessey and with Mr Walkinshaw for some additional land which had to be acquired as it would be a big plant. The County Council delayed the demolition of the disused

Preston Lodge Secondary School, opposite the railway station, so that it could be adapted as a training centre. Securicor and guard dogs were hired as the buildings were being vandalised. An outline deal was fixed up but Plessey, who were always a greedy company, wanted to secure traffic light contracts in Scotland. At this stage it appeared that, now Prestonpans was their preferred Scottish site, it was a Scotland versus England contest. I thought we should bring in the Scottish Development Department on our side and Plessey was sent to try and fix up their side-deals with the Scottish Roads Department. I confess that this was a great mistake but I was pretty confident of the outcome as it so happened that I knew personally Plessey's Company Secretary, Maurice Haddon-Grant. He had married a Cambridge girlfriend of mine and our boys had been educated together. However, after an awful six weeks of waiting, Maurice telephoned me to say that Sir John Clerk, the Plessey Chairman, had acquired the historic Argyle motor-car factory in Alexandria, which had been converted to a torpedo factory, for £100 with all its machine tools. The new plant was to be set up there. He was very sorry but Sir John, he said, could never resist a bargain.

The only way we could find out what had happened was through John Mackintosh, our Member of Parliament. For years he had been kept at arm's length by the County Council as he frequently raised what were considered hostile questions on behalf of his constituents concerning education, housing and other matters. This was the first occasion on which the County Council allied themselves with their MP, and I am glad to say that, as the result of this case, a permanent liaison was built up on the planning side, in which I involved him a great deal until his premature death—such a fine intelligent fellow.

What appeared to have happened in the Scottish Development Department was that the Under Secretary, one MacGuiness, who was later described to me as having ice-cold water flowing in his veins, considered that the west of Scotland was in greater need of this development than the east, and so the treachery started. It all ended in disaster as MacGuiness had not appreciated the human side, so well known to us from our experiences at Gateside. The Ferranti people, the key to the whole amalgamation, were established in the east and would not move to the west. The Glasgow image at that time was so bad that it proved impossible to attract the staff from Plymouth or the Midlands and so the whole thing fell apart. Sir John Clerk sold off the machine tools, and the fine building fell derelict and Tony Benn's initiative to create a great British computerised machine-tool industry never got off the ground. I am quite sure that if the Scottish Development Department had been wiser, less devious and had realised the human as well as the political dimension, that a great industry could have been built up at Prestonpans. The living conditions in the County met entirely the expectations of the incoming personnel, there were trained operatives in the area and strong links with Edinburgh University departments. It was a grand site and we had offered the firm a good deal.

Some years later, after a service in Nunraw Abbey, I met and challenged MacGuiness who lived in Glasgow but travelled daily by train to St Andrew's House in Edinburgh. He admitted that he had not been so clever and that Scotland had lost a great new industry. The County Council was left to pick up Securicor's large bill and the Mid Road site was subsequently split up for McMillans, a firm of copper fabricators, whose noisy processes had driven them out of Edinburgh, and Morfax when they left the former Fowler's Brewery on the shore at Prestonpans.

Village Factories

One of the reasons leading to rural depopulation is the lack of employment for other members of agricultural workers' families. We had found this out in our village surveys and it is substantiated in the literature. So I seized the opportunity which arose with the closing of some of the village schools to take these over from the Education Department onto the Planning Account and let them to small firms. For this they proved ideal. Most comprised a school house and garden, playground, outside storage, usually two classrooms and a little office. They were solidly built, had good daylight and some heating and were in reasonable repair.

The first school we let was at Garvald, the children having moved into the new school built at Gifford in October, 1971. It was let to Mr and Mrs Leighton from Edinburgh whose brother ran a souvenir shop in Dunbar and they set up a firm, Joyleigh Ltd, to manufacture souvenirs—Mrs Joy Leighton being a very competent potter. This was an ideal little industry as not only did they employ eight young people in the school but also put out work for wives to do in their own homes. The Industrial Report of 1972 noted that "although they had not been able to get as many employees as they had hoped from the village, they were extremely happy with their move from Edinburgh and their business was expanding rapidly". The school house was later sold to them and, after I had left the County Council, the school as well. It has now been converted into houses and so the village has lost this communal activity.

Another former school at Crossroads, near Ormiston, has had a succession of occupants. It had been built in 1871 on an isolated site in the middle of the parish so that all children had an equal distance to walk to school—a typical Scottish arrangement to spread the misery,

Plate XLV Crossroads School, Ormiston.

One of the nine schools transferred to the Planning Account and leased as industrial units to keep some life in the countryside. The combination of house, schoolrooms and playground proved very attractive to incoming crafts people and there have been a succession of these. It is currently occupied by Kenny Munro.

rather than building a school in the village. The first firm was Callan Electronics, who manufactured electronic cow-feeding doors for dairy farms, and it is currently let to Kenny Munro, an artist craftsman, who tells me he finds it quite ideal. The same arrangement happened with other village schools at East and West Barns, Dunbar, at Gifford, at Pencaitland, at Kingston, at Oldhamstocks and at Whittinghame. The larger schools at Cockenzie and the old Dunbar High School were also pressed into industrial service, so providing employment and maintaining some communal activities in all these places.

Two other schools were used to develop the tourist industry. At Gullane the old primary school was used for golf training and other recreational sports, and the school at Innerwick was developed as a countryside centre for the use of school parties as described in Chapter Eleven. Bolton school was turned into a village hall rather incongruously as it had been agreed by then that social provision was better provided in Haddington.

Such was the prominence of these schools and their new uses that Councillor Brian Foulkes, then Chairman of the Lothian Region Education Committee, on his inaugural tour of East Lothian thought he was on a Planning Tour! Brian was one of the cadre of very bright young politicians elected to the Lothian Regional Council in 1974 who subsequently became Labour Members of Parliament. These included Alistair Darling and my first Planning and Development Committee Chairman, Eric Clarke.

As well as old schools, other village buildings such as disused churches and wartime huts, were pressed into industrial use. These all provided distinctive and extensive accommodation at cheap rents and, for many industrialists, were preferable to the nest factories which we were also building at the time at Macmerry. They also fulfilled the vital role of maintaining a communal element in the villages and, by providing employment for secondary earners, helped check rural depopulation.

Only One Bad Debt

In all those years we had only one bad debt and a development that had no lasting effect. Several small firms went bankrupt, but they left behind a trained workforce, which attracted other firms. The bad debt was Fox Biology for whom we had adapted part of the old Dunbar High School. The small rooms, which no one else wanted, were converted at a cost of £950. The firm's business was in preparing specimens for school and college biology classes. The local fishermen brought the firm catfish and other specimens, and they employed school leavers to make slides and other demonstration and dissecting material. It seemed an ideal little firm, but it started to supply laboratory equipment as well and found itself in financial difficulties before vanishing into the moonlight. We found no one to take over the business or the trained girls. All we got out of it were a number of nice old earthenware crocks in which the firm had kept their specimens.

Contact with all these people struggling to establish or maintain a livelihood gave great stimulus to life in the Planning Department in Haddington. Their progress was noted in the annual Industrial Reports submitted to the Planning Committee by the succession of industrial officers—Richard Adams, already mentioned, Michael Cox who came to us from Northern Ireland, and Big Jim Carnegie from the Irvine New Town Development Corporation. However the really big industrial developments were the two large electricity generating stations, which caused us much concern—coal-fired at Cockenzie, and nuclear-powered at Torness.

South of Scotland Electricity Board

I know I am going to have difficulty writing this section as the location and design of the two stations span the twenty-five years of my life as County Planning Officer. I found the South of Scotland Electricity Board, now privatised as Scottish Power, a narrow-minded overbearing body, very smug and boastful about how they brought light and modern living conditions to everyone. They totally rejected the idea of a National Energy Policy and of Combined Heat and Power. They defiled the countryside by using multiple pylon lines when one line would carry the electricity generated by the largest station. They badly misled the consumer when, as we were to find out later, they first promoted cheap off-peak electricity in the 1960s and then upped the tariff, leaving much human misery behind as people could not afford their electrical space heating, especially underfloor heating. Although they were a nationalised industry they certainly took little account of the wider national or local interests.

I was handicapped in dealing with the Board, as I lacked both the technical help of a consultant and the support of my Committee most of the time. There was no one in the Scottish Development Department overseeing the Board's activities except a junior administrator, who seemed only concerned that the Board had gone through the correct statutory procedures, whatever the outcome. It was only when I got to the Lothian Regional Council that I had the political backing and the financial resources to employ consultants and challenge the Board; but, by then, it only remained to decide the route of the supergrid pylons out from Torness. The Regional Council also took up the question of whole city heating by utilising the hot water which the Board wasted in the generation of electricity to the extent of 65% to 68% of the calorific value of the fuel they used. This hot water could have been pumped round the City, heating the buildings, as is done on the continent, instead of being wasted into the sea, but the Board would have nothing to do with it. Anyhow, to start at the beginning: in 1952, the Board was searching for a new site to replace the Portobello Power Station, which had been built by Edinburgh Corporation and which had heated the open air swimming pool built alongside it with its waste heat. The power station was on a cramped site, the SSEB wanted a new modern station and so it was demolished and, as a consequence the pool closed.

The Board sought a site on the East Lothian coast for their new 1,200 megawatt coal-fired station. I thought this a grand opportunity for a combined development with the new undersea colliery, still proposed at that time, feeding coal direct into the power station—a model that the Board later adopted at Longannet. There were great difficulties: a narrow whinstone dyke on which the building must be founded to avoid subsidence damage, a massive reclamation of land from the sea and a difficult route out for the pylons over Prestongrange policies and through the proposed Edinburgh Green Belt. However it seemed preferable to me than siting this massive building at Prestonlinks where it stands today, sandwiched between the two burghs of Prestonpans and Cockenzie, and wasting 240 acres of top class agricultural land. Such a loss would not have occurred at Prestongrange where the despoiled foreshore could have been reclaimed for the coal store.

I remember having a happy time getting hold of power station and colliery plans and trying to fit it all onto the Prestongrange site. The Board was most unwilling to be involved in any joint ventures with the National Coal Board, and, although the wartime Ministry of Fuel and Power still existed, they were not prepared to play any real part in pushing my grand design. The County Clerk made it quite clear that if I persisted too far and lost the power station to the County I could expect my books. In the end I had to accept that a combined venture by these two nationalised bodies in the national interest was not on, and that the Prestongrange site was not suitable for a power station by itself, with its difficult access for the coal trains from the mainline railway. And so my great innovative dream ended, my sketches were discarded and I had to take up the planning officer's normal job of modifying the horrific plans that the SSEB's chief engineer had produced for Prestonlinks.

1960s Cockenzie Coal-Fired Power Station

Prestonlinks was a short stretch of public open space between the old coal harbour at Cockenzie to the east, which Robert Stevenson had built in 1822 for the Cadells, and the disused Prestonlinks colliery with its coal bing to the west. The links had been traditionally used by fishermen for drying their nets and for casual public recreation.

I put the County Council in the driving seat by proposing an Amendment to the County Development Plan as I had done for the cement works and the Board were pleased to accept this, in view of the many owners involved and the local opposition they anticipated. The Board's chief engineer had proposed building this vast station, 800 feet long and 200 feet high, only 40 feet from the centre of the main road and at road level. On the south side, and equally close to the centre of the road, he proposed a vast open-air switching and transmitting station, both to be surrounded by high security fences. This would have been visually devastating and was quite unacceptable. I pushed the buildings back and down onto the rocky foreshore some 220 feet from the centre of the road, and insisted that as they had to excavate to the rock outcrop anyhow for the foundations of the building, it should be built at rock level. At a stroke this eliminated the need for the oppressive security palings as a 15 feet drop was as good as a 12 feet high fence and all the works clutter, associated with running the station, would be hidden from below the eye-level of people passing along the road. The station would appear to rise from a grassy lawn like a mansion house behind its ha-ha. I did not foresee that later on the station management would cut up this lawn with oval flower beds!

Plate XLVI   Cockenzie Power Station

A most handsome Station designed by Robert Matthew, Johnson Marshall, job architect
Chris Carter. In the foreground is the former Prestonlinks Colliery bing transformed
into coastal links and, in the background, Cockenzie and Port Seton Burgh. On the
extreme right is part of the 40 acre coal store contained by grass banks and the cranked
covered conveyors to the Stations's four boilers. In the centre is the rectangular indoor
transmission station and the circular Scottish Gas Board holder. All as neat as could
be! It won a Civic Trust Award in 1972.

There was more difficulty arguing against the open-air transmission
station. But my luck was in, as a complete black-out occurred in the
English Midlands lasting several days, caused by industrial dirt on the
outdoor insulators and switches. I argued how much worse salt
accumulation would be beside the sea at Cockenzie and so won the
argument for an indoor switching station. Eight years later, when I
was going round the station with a party, I was amused to hear the
manager say that, because of salt contamination, the Board always built
indoor sub-stations. Little did he know of the fight I had to get this
accepted. Indoor switching stations are much more expensive and the
Board was most reluctant to build one. They were also greatly offended
when I lined up their new transmission station with the existing gas-

holder on the site. How these rival nationalised fuel boards hated each other! It was also a requirement of the Development Plan Amendment that Crown Square, the coal company's housing scheme, was demolished before the station was commissioned as I considered that no-one should be asked to live so close under its shadow. The site of old Prestonlinks colliery was to be cleared and the Board proudly offered us a public playing field there. They were flabbergasted when I turned down the offer of these cold exposed football pitches in favour of the existing dune shapes, which would at least reduce the apparent height of the buildings as seen from Prestonpans and would provide the opportunity for a small pitch and putt golf links for summer use. A further condition required the Board to provide a promenade for pleasure on the seaward side of the station and alternative boat launching facilities to replace one which had been occasionally used on the links. The 'pleasure' bit has never been implemented, and I confess never thought out, and they drew the line at providing a yacht club and compound. It was before the days of "planning gain" when it would have been accepted practice for them to offer, and the County to accept, such a provision, and so nothing was done for the local people. For their part the County Council provided a concrete slipway over the unstable foreshore made of colliery refuse from the Prestonlinks Colliery and provided a compound for dinghies and a car park. Later Mr James Watt, the Burgh Surveyor, provided a disused prefab house and adapted it as a club house, so the people of Prestonpans once again can enjoy sailing and have a modest tourist attraction, no thanks to the Board.

I also tried to persuade the Board's officials that the station would look better with a single taller chimney rather than the two they proposed, but their engineers produced a wealth of arguments that this was quite impossible. A few years later these same engineers built a single chimney for their Longannet Power Station which has the great advantage that it could be maintained from the inside and men did not have to climb ladders fastened up the outside, as at Cockenzie. I had to accept their arguments but, nevertheless, raised their chimney from 400 to 500 feet to ensure that the stour blew well away from our coast and the surrounding towns. I often wonder whether it is the dilute carbon dioxide from these chimneys which causes the acid rain in Scandinavia. At least it did not ruin our market garden crops.

I tried as well to get two other things out of the Board. First, that they should pipe some of the waste heat to Port Seton swimming pool as had been done at Portobello, but they would not change their sloppy method of clearing the cooling water intake channels of crustaceans by dumping occasional sacks of chlorine into the water rather than by regular measured dilute doses. We could not risk poisoning the bathers and again they would not take any measures to help the local community. The other proposal was that, as they were taking so much top-grade agricultural land, they should provide piped hot water to Lowe's french garden at Prestonpans which could then produce four crops of vegetables a year instead of two. This also failed as they would not guarantee a continuous supply or insure against its breakdown, which could blight a whole crop. (After my time this fine productive garden has been built over by private housing.) No wonder a keen young socialist planning officer showed such deep disdain for this narrow crabbed outlook of a nationalised industry. How much worse will they be as a privatised industry?

Finally there were two matters which remained to be settled. Firstly where was the Board to dispose of vast quantities of fly-ash, as fine as face powder, which they wanted to lorry to a dry valley at Airfield by Ormiston, previously acquired for the disposal of hard ash from the Portobello Station. Secondly, when this was full, to tip in other dry valleys in the Lammermuirs. What a fleet of lorries coming and going along our country roads! However they were persuaded to adopted my suggestion for the reclamation of the 240 acres of degraded foreshore between Prestongrange and Musselburgh, thus neatly making up for the quantity, but not the quality, of the land they were using at Seton Park.

Cockenzie Pylon Lines

The other outstanding matter was the route of the pylons which the Board was not prepared to discuss at the Development Plan Amendment stage. Their stated requirement was for three pylon lines for this 1,200 megawatt station. One 400Kv line from Blyth, Northumberland, bringing in power to construct the station and two 275Kv lines to export power to Edinburgh and the west of Scotland. The engineers had left room for only these two lines between the coal store and the old mineral railway along the east side of Prestonpans—so the 400Kv line had to be strung out to the east and then come back round the Meadowmill bing. It was a very difficult decision to make—whether or not this line would be better to the east of Tranent with the consequence that the burgh be encircled with pylons. I decided it would be best to group all three pylon lines together and march them three by three, like soldiers, to the west of Tranent and on to the Smeaton sub-station. I had seen such an arrangement in an alpine valley in Italy and the discipline of the 'marching' lines was most impressive. This was agreed with the engineers but ignored by the Board's wayleave officers who, as was their wont, adjusted the pylon positions to suit the farmers and so the pylons stepped out of line like ill-disciplined troops. When the proposals came to the Committee for planning approval I recommended refusal for the lines but my Committee would not support me. Few of them had ever travelled abroad and seen how much better things are managed there. Now the pylons appear to be randomly scattered and the countryside seems full of them. It was only later when I was at the Lothian Region that I learnt that only one 275Kv pylon line is necessary to carry the production of a 1,200Mw station and the other two merely constitute belt and braces twice over.

The design of the station building was entrusted to Sir Robert Matthew and his firm Robert Matthew Johnson Marshall. I remember the utter astonishment with which the engineers and general manager met his stipulation that he needed the weekend to decide which way round the station should face. He decided, quite rightly, that the offices and human-scale parts should face Cockenzie harbour and the coal conveyor be at the west end. The Board's engineers would have had it the other way round, with a shorter coal conveyor and one less change of direction.

Sir Robert produced a most elegant building and Chris Carter, the job architect, never lost control and even dictated where the engineer's pipes came through the roof—a fine job. It was therefore with great dismay that I learnt that the firm RMJM was not to be employed on the Torness Power Station. It was given to Howard Lobb, an old chum of the Board's chief engineer. My heart fell, as I could see that in no way would he or his job architects be able to win the inevitable arguments with the engineers and so we got a greatly inferior design. He did not even support me when I wanted the station sited on dry land, although his perspective sketch deceptively showed it in this position and not projecting out on reclaimed land.

1970s Torness Nuclear Power Station

It was in the late 1960s that the South of Scotland Electricity Board came back at us saying that they wanted to build a nuclear power station on the East Lothian coast and offering us a choice of four sites which met their requirements. This decision to build was predicated on their assumption that the demand for electricity would double every ten years and, more curiously, that they should build alternately in the west and in the east of Scotland. Having just completed a useless oil-fired generating station at Inverkip on the Clyde, which has never generated any electricity, they said it was East Lothian's turn again. This time they were looking for a site to accommodate four 1,200Mw plants—four times the size of Cockenzie, such was their difficulty in getting planning consents and the expense of the site preparation works. No Government body ever appeared to question these silly assumptions. The market for electricity was falling and growth on a geometric progression of this order is logically impossible. It was absurd to switch from west to east as the vast amount of process water, 50,000,000 gallons an hour, was then available only in the east if it was withdrawn from Loch Lomond in the west. It became even more absurd when it came out that they would need a pylon line to take power generated on the east coast to run a pumped water storage scheme at Ben Cruachan. This involved using off-peak power to pump water from Loch Lomond to an upland reservoir for discharge through turbines, at times of peak load, to supply electricity which could be sold to the English National Grid. Logic or economy was never the Board's strong point.

It was also their ambition to build another nuclear station although they had not yet decided on the type. This was based on their long-standing feud with of the National Coal Board. The mining communities realised, only slowly, the implications of this decision which spelt the end of their industry in Scotland, but at that date they were not very vocal. This time the Board decided to proceed under their own Electricity Act and not under the Planning Acts as at Cockenzie.

The four alternative sites they offered the County Council were: Yellowcraig by Dirleton, Ravensheugh by Tyninghame, Barns Ness, and Torness. They said they were prepared to leave the initial choice to the County Council. The sites were all dreadful and infringed County Planning Policy, sites of special scientific interest and all other amenity considerations, which they never considered. It was sufficient that they were all five miles from a major settlement, which is a necessary locational criterion for a nuclear station, and had the appropriate geological condition of a low flat rocky foreshore to provide good foundations and low pumping costs. The least damaging was clearly Torness, where there was some chance of getting power lines away— hidden in the foothills and not striding across our beautiful County on their way to the west of Scotland. It was also nearest to the railway for bringing in construction materials and removing the spent nuclear fuel, although the Board was not prepared to specify that their suppliers used rail in place of road as we asked. They did build a slipway to bring in the heavy loads by sea-barge to avoid having to rebuild several road bridges on the A1 to carry the weight. The actual site at Torness was not of great recreational value and was called "the stinking hole" by the locals as seaweed gathered and rotted on the rocky shore. It also had the great advantage for the Board of being owned by the Department of Agriculture and Fisheries for Scotland, although they were aghast when they learnt that the County Council owned the dune strip and rocky foreshore that I had bought in the 1950s. This proved a trump card, but the County Council was not prepared to play it. In no way would they doubt the wisdom of the Board or engage in the nuclear controversy that was just gathering momentum. The whole power station issue was to be dealt with as a local planning matter, and I just

Plate XLVII   Torness Power Station

The photograph shows the agricultural land that was mounded up to hide the lower buildings and the human clutter round the Station. This has been most successful in integrating the vast building into the fertile corn lands. I always thought that the white sheeting on the Station was too reflective. Architect: Howard Lobb.

had to fit the building into the scenery as best I could. Our trump card, played astutely by Archie Elliott, Q.C., at the public inquiry, proved to be worth £2 million as it forced the Board to offer to underground the first 2 km of their proposed twin overhead pylon lines to a take-off point in the foothills of the Lammermuirs. The Board was prepared to pay this to avoid the delay and questions in Parliament which they thought might have arisen from the compulsory purchase of public open space. It was no doubt small change in their billion pound project, but extremely valuable in protecting the natural landscape of the coastal plain where it widens out at the southern entry to the County. In exchange for the coastal lands at Torness, the County secured that other half mile of coastline at Skateraw, which the Board succeeded in buying from Mrs Bowe where I had failed. The campaign against nuclear energy produced good witnesses who spoke well at the inquiry but their case was brushed aside.

I had four other main goals to score. First, that the station should not encroach on the natural shoreline. Second, that from the landward side the station should rise and be screened by cultivated arable ridges in place of the grassy bunds that the Board was proposing. Third, that the caravan site which I had established, was closed and the Department of Agriculture's small holdings were relocated, so that no one lived under the shadow of the station and highlighted its enormous size. Fourth, that the large work camp, which the Board proposed to site on the A1 alongside the construction site, should be sited inland at Thurston Mains which had been designated as a holiday village in the County's tourist proposals. In addition it should be limited in size so that the maximum number of local people were employed. I confess that I scored only two goals, the second and fourth. What dignity the station has arises from it being seen across the reshaped agricultural land which hides the inevitable human clutter from the A1. The fourth point was not fully achieved as the Board was not prepared to depart from their normal arrangements with their contractors importing their own men onto the site. However, by limiting the accommodation we forced them to employ and train more local people. The camp at Thurston Mains was built and is now in use as a holiday camp, thus fulfilling its designation in the Development Plan.

The worst feature of the station is perhaps the reclamation of a large area of the rocky shore by dolos blocks—big cuff-link shaped concrete castings interlocking on the seabed and below the seawall in Germanic proportions. This stems from the Board's decision to build the station at a higher level, as the result of a flooding incident at its other nuclear station at Hunterston and the reclamation was scarcely necessary. I had always admired the photographs of the fast reactor at Thurso rising from a natural shoreline, but I could not persuade the Reporter at the Inquiry to go and see it. The Board argued that, without the land reclamation, the site would be too small for eight reactors with a total capacity of 4,800Mw, although they were only applying for two reactors or 1,200Mw.

If I had had the opportunity to proceed by way of a development plan amendment the story would have been very different. The A1 road would have been moved to the west of the railway, a rail siding taken into the site, tree plantations established off the site to screen the long distance views of the station, and the agricultural holdings would have been relocated.

Torness Pylon Lines

Once again the Board refused to discuss the routeing of the pylon lines until they had consent for the station, although they produced an indicative plan showing the two lines running in tandem along the foothills of the Lammermuirs to Edinburgh. I argued that the pylons were an essential element in siting the station and had to be settled before the site was approved. In addition their proposal for lines in tandem was quite unacceptable. The Reporter decided that as there were alternatives he need not delay the inquiry until the route of the overhead lines had been agreed, so greatly weakening our hand.

I proposed to the Board that, just as they had brought the power lines to the Dunbar cement works from Eccles in the Borders, they should route one 400Kv pylon line south from Torness along the same route. This proved very beneficial to the Board as much of the power generated at Torness supplies England, although they would not admit this at the inquiry. I recommended that the second pylon line should be tailored to fit along the foothills with the other human artifacts rather than cross the Lammermuirs and run over virgin moorland which had little other evidence of man's occupation. I never thought I would persuade the County Planning Committee or, later, the Regional Planning and Development Committee with this philosophical argument. Indeed, when it came to the crunch, the East Lothian District Council, responding to local opposition, supported a half and half proposal where the line crossed to behind the Lammermuirs at Elmscleugh and back again at Prior's Nose.

The public inquiry into the pylon routes took place when I was with the Regional Council who took the view that there should be no more pylons in Lothian, and that the lines should be undergrounded on both amenity and public health grounds. As this meant a sixteen times increase in the cost of the lines, I knew I could never sustain such an argument. The undergrounding of lower voltage, wood-pole lines was financially possible, as the Dutch and other Europeans had proved, but for 400Kv lines with their special needs for coolants it was not possible. After discussions with lecturers at Heriot-Watt University, I adopted the argument that one 400Kv line was quite sufficient to take all the power generated at Torness even when they had eight reactors there, not merely the two for which they were seeking consent. As it was necessary only to extend the agreed 2km kilometre underground cable by a further 4km to the County boundary on the Eccles route, and anyhow they were saving the entire cost of the second line I had an arguable case. I was authorised by the Regional Council to engage consultants, Mertz McClellan of Newcastle, who had been responsible, amongst other projects, for installing a single pylon line over the Andes at 14,000 feet to supply the city of Buenos Aires without having any significant interruptions of supply. They were quite adamant that the production of 4,800Mw was capable of being transmitted on a single pylon line. Each pylon line carries two separate circuits, one on either side of the tower, and the Board argued that they needed four circuits on two pylons to ensure continuity of supply with security against vandalism, earthquakes and other causes, and this was especially necessary because of the difficulty of closing down a nuclear reactor in case of an emergency! God help us. Archie Elliott, now Lord Elliott of the Land Court, who was appearing for the Lothian Regional Council, secured an adjournment of the inquiry so that the Board could produce figures of the number of occasions and the duration in seconds when both circuits on their pylon lines had been out of commission at the same time—'double outage' in their jargon. The figures proved this to be quite infinitesimal.

I noticed at the resumed inquiry that there were two new faces in the room, those of engineers from the Central Electricity Generating Board who run the national grid. They were greatly concerned, for if we had won the argument, they could see half the pylon lines throughout Britain being challenged. Blessed vision. However, it was not to be. The Reporter was a retired town planner who, like me, had always accepted that every power station required two pylon lines reaching out over the countryside, and our job was to fit them into the landscape as well as possible. It was also a fact that the Regional Council had not enough time to prepare its case and get nationwide support for it from amenity societies and other bodies. The Board was also able to rubbish our public health arguments by saying that none of their workers suffered any ill effects from working on the lines, ignoring completely the case that it was not fit working men who were at risk, but the old, the young and the infirm with deficient immune systems. But there it was, the Reporter found against us. I confess that I am ashamed that I never wrote up the case in the technical journals because it was about that time that I retired. The SSEB and other electricity boards still continue with their old working practices erecting unnecessary double lines at great capital cost, although perhaps the new private owners will stop the damnable habit. So ended my twenty five year tussle with the South of Scotland Electricity Board without the crescendo of pylons being felled throughout the land!

6

HOUSING LAYOUTS
Kadugli, south-west Sudan

LOCAL AUTHORITY HOUSING
Mid Road, Prestonpans • Radburn Layout, Tranent
'Pondorosa',Prestonpans • Gourlay Bank, Haddington

SPECULATIVE BUILDERS
Broadgait Green, Gullane • Brodie's Avenue, North Berwick
Somnerfield Park, Haddington Harts' Developments, Tranent

PRIVATE FEUING
Glassel Park, Longniddry • Muirfield Park, Gullane
The Glebe, Pencaitland • Pencaitland Village Expansion

The design of housing estates has been one of the specialities of the town planner since the 1909 Housing and Town Planning Act which gave Local Authorities power to prepare schemes for new peripheral areas round towns. The Town Planning Institute stipulated a fee per acre for preparing housing layouts. However the English innovation of the Garden City had never really taken root in Scotland except at Rosyth where the Admiralty employed A.H.Mottram to lay out the housing for their dockyard workers, and where in some streets you might think you were in Welwyn Garden City. What did take root were low density housing estates with drab grey cement-rendered council houses, as there were no facing bricks made in Scotland, either semi-detached or four in a block, divided either horizontally or vertically, lined up along streets with poorly kept gardens, front and back, and ramshackle fences. East Lothian had its share of these. Some were of course more comely than others. I remember challenging J.A.W.Grant to build a curved block of eight at Caponflat Crescent in Haddington. What a pleasure the old architect got from this deviation from the norm and what dignity it gives this entry off the Edinburgh Road!

Kadugli, SW Sudan
My first housing layout was built in Kadugli, in south-west Sudan in 1944. I had been asked to take a near mutinous company of the Sudan Defence Force back home to Kadugli from Tripoli by lorry, rail, Nile

steamer, Sudan railways and, finally, truck. Kadugli is 140 miles south-west of El Obeid in the Nuba mountains which are a series of extinct volcanic hills rising steeply from a rich flood plain. After arrival I discharged the soldiers, and got a great shock in seeing my tall, dark, handsome soldiers, well turned out with khaki shorts, shirts and turbans, with First World War puttees and sandals walking out of the little 'Beau Geste' fort stark naked. Each had a long stick over his shoulder carrying in a bandanna, Dick Whittington style, the loot he had managed to accumulate following the Eighth Army doing guard and prisoner-of-war duties all the way from El Alamein to Tripoli, where they had got rather restive. They walked back to their hill with its individual clan structure, a chief and a witch doctor/priest who kept them thirled by the rumbles which rose occasionally from their volcanic hill.

I was left with the core of Sudanese non-commissioned officers, only one of whom could read and write, and this in Arabic. He appropriately was the quarter-master sergeant and had to buy all the rations in the market. These fine soldiers had a genuine grievance in that their married quarters were in a terrible state and in part it was their wives' unheeded complaints that had reached them in Tripoli that turned them mutinous. In part of course it was the attention of the British Military Police who failed to appreciate that after their long campaign they thought their due reward was loot, rape and rapine!

I got authorisation to rebuild the married quarters and instead of rebuilding them on the old lines, sunk a new well, surrounded it with stone paving and four thorn trees and arranged the houses in diamond formation around the well which served as a social centre. The houses were circular mud huts with conical straw roofs—'tuckels' as they were called in the Sudan. The contractor was a Greek, as were most of the merchants there. I was very hard on him, checking the amount of straw mixed in with the mud for the walls, the amount of dung mixed in with the clay for plastering the insides and the straightness of the poles for the roof structure. Many a camel load of these brought in over twenty miles from the bush I rejected. When finished, with their white-washed walls and golden new thatch, the new quarters looked very smart. I left at the end of December 1944 to rejoin my Rifle Brigade Battalion with the Eighth Army in Italy. On Christmas Day I caught the train from El Obeid to Khartoum with my civilian cook, Osman, who had been with me during the whole two years of my posting with the Sudan Defence Force. I was feeling rather miserable, wondering what sort of Christmas my mother and two sisters were enjoying at home in war rationed Britain and recalling Christmases past. Then Osman announced that he had laid out my meal in the next compartment and there, wonderful to behold, was a complete Christmas dinner with paper chains, bells and crackers decorating the carriage and the food to match—turkey, sweet potatoes, tinned peas, plum pudding and a bottle of Cyprus sherry. I inquired from Osman how this fairy feast had arrived and he told me that the Greek contractor had provided it. What a nice gesture, but also what a good lesson that one earns respect from building contractors by being firm and strict, one that I have never forgotten.

LOCAL AUTHORITY HOUSING

Mid Road, Prestonpans

The East Lothian housing problems could not be resolved so easily. My first tentative steps were to rearrange the proposed council houses at Mid Road, Prestonpans, which had been aligned traditionally with large back greens, always ill-kempt, so as to make a large green playing area between the houses and the Mid Road, A198. This was a great success and much liked. Thereafter, I always made it my practice to produce what I irreverently called a 'Burgh Surveyor's layout' following the usual rules and conventions. I then tried to eliminate its faults and evolve a better layout. This could then be compared with the 'Burgh Surveyor's layout' for number of houses, length of road per house and its plus points demonstrated to the committees.

Radburn Layout, Tranent

A more ambitious venture a little later was to introduce a Radburn type layout at Tranent, where the Burgh Council had given a housing contract to a local firm, Harts, and asked me to prepare a layout. This was based on an American model, where vehicular access served the backs of the houses and the fronts were aligned along footpaths that led to the school and community buildings. As well as this novel layout I agreed with the builders that the interiors were painted to four different colour schemes and, although the Burgh Council letting procedures were not done sufficiently far in advance to allow the tenants to choose between the four, it at least gave some variety to the houses. However it proved possible to allow the tenants to choose the colour of their front doors from a range of eight paints. I am sorry to say that this Radburn layout was not a great success, as there was not enough money to build garages in the back courts, which became rather a mess as people erected their own. Everyone used the back courts and the front doors onto the footpaths were seldom used. I do not think the layout was ever copied elsewhere in Scotland, despite Mary's wartime advocacy in the Department's Advisory Plan for Dunfermline. A larger Radburn scheme was built by Professor Gordon Stevenson at Wrexham. Tommy Hart, a bricklayer who had built up his contracting firm from scratch after the war, insisted that I should have some recognition for my efforts

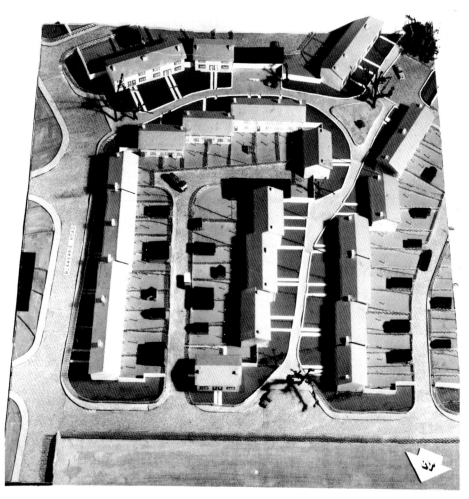

TRANENT: ORMISTON ROAD HOUSING SCHEME - SECOND STAGE

DETAIL OF LAYOUT FOR
NON-TRADITIONAL HOUSES   SHOWING THE PRINCIPLE OF BACK SERVICE COURTS AND FOOTWAY ACCESS TO FRONT DOORS

SCALE   ONE INCH EQUALS SIXTEEN FEET

MARCH 1958   EAST LOTHIAN COUNTY COUNCIL
                    COUNTY PLANNING DEPARTMENT

Plate XLVIII   Radburn Layout, Tranent

Radburn was an innovative layout named after a small American town, in which the front doors of the houses gave access not onto a road but onto a footpath which led safely to the playgrounds, schools and shops. Vehicles came into a back court with garages. I tried it out in Tranent but confess that it was not very successful as children played in the back courts and visitors came in that way as well. However the model 'sold' it to the Town Council.

and my initials are picked out in projecting bricks in a screen wall on a corner of the scheme.

"Ponderosa", Prestonpans

The most notable innovation in housing design took place at Cuthill in the west of Prestonpans. Here a scheme was designed for the County Council by the Housing Research Unit, set up by Sir Robert Matthew in Edinburgh University's Department of Architecture and headed by Eric Stevenson. Eric and Margrethe, his Danish wife, had been amongst our first friends in the County. He then worked in the Planning Division of the Department of Health for Scotland, but he could never shake off the spy-role that he played at the end of the war in Denmark and all his professional life seemed to be based on getting round established practices. No bad thing, but Eric took it too far with this scheme.

It was built on land where the Summerlee Coal Company had built houses, including Bath Street, named proudly after the bathrooms which, quite exceptionally for the 1890s, had been incorporated into these two storey flatted houses. But they had been neglected and had fallen below tolerable standards and were demolished as part of the scheme to widen and straighten Prestonpans High Street.

The Cuthill housing scheme was for 45 single-storey interlocking L-shaped courtyard houses with small enclosed gardens, covered pedestrian access ways with small open-air gathering places, which gave a high degree of individual privacy. A very radical change from the draughty exposure of the normal housing estate. It appeared to be the logical response to the desire for single-storey houses, small gardens and safe areas for the children to play. As well as this new form of layout the houses themselves incorporated many new features such as flat roofs, electrical underfloor heating and an open plan, whereby the kitchen and dining area were an extension of the living room. As the kitchen was also the place where clothes were washed and dried and the underfloor heating was too expensive for some families to run, the houses were plagued with condensation and dampness. As the houses conjoined, the flat roofs with their skylit bathrooms became a playground for peeping-toms. The horizontal board fencing to the walkways gave the scheme its nickname 'Ponderosa' after a wild west TV programme of the time.

The low-rise scheme was vastly preferable to the high multi-storey blocks that other authorities were building at the time, but, like them, it really needed, and never had, a resident caretaker to clean the walkways, check the children, etc, and get a higher standard of maintenance. It resulted in a similar housing density to the tower blocks. The scheme had so many innovative features of layout and design that none could be individually assessed and this reduced its

Plate XLIX 'Ponderosa', Prestonpans

Another innovative layout showing a world of difference between the wasteful, boring two storey houses seen at top right and the compact private courtyard houses with access through covered walkways. The thicket planting, just showing, was an idea brought from Denmark for low-maintenance landscaping. Architect: Edinburgh University Housing Research Unit.

value as a research project. It was well liked by the tenants and it was not demolished in the 1980s as were so many tower blocks, but was revamped with pitched roofs which slightly compromised its new world white and black original colouring. As far as I know it was only repeated once in a scheme in Newcastle-upon-Tyne.

Gourlay Bank, Haddington
A somewhat similar scheme of 32 single and two-storey houses was designed by James Gray for the Adam Housing Trust at Gourlay Bank in Haddington the following year. This was the first of the many housing association schemes that were built throughout Scotland, particularly

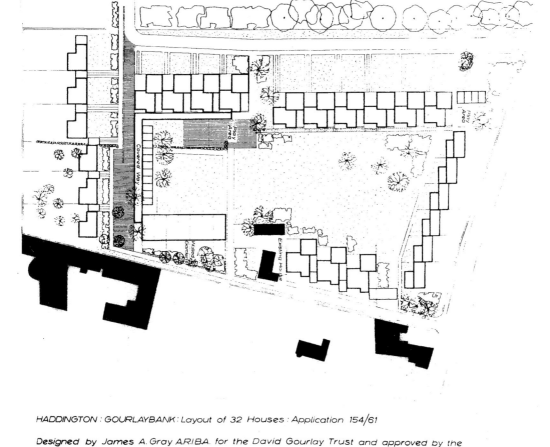

HADDINGTON : GOURLAYBANK : Layout of 32 Houses : Application 154/61

Designed by James A. Gray A.R.I.B.A. for the David Gourlay Trust and approved by the
County Planning Committee -September 1961

Density: 6 Houses per acre
Roadway: 26 feet per House

Private Land   2·73 acres
Common Open Space 1·53 acres
Other Access Areas   0·59 acres

SCALE OF FEET

9·21   EAST LOTHIAN COUNTY COUNCI
23·2·61   COUNTY PLANNING DEPARTME

Plate L   Gourlay Bank, Haddington

This drawing was used to illustrate our Annual Report for 1962/3. It is not quite what
was eventually built but it shows a radically different solution to the normal speculative
builder's scheme with houses well related to their small gardens and to a larger
communal space. The planting retains the best of the old orchard trees and the layout
was a revelation at the time. The key lists the various components such as density of
housing, length of roadway, etc., which were used to compare it with a 'burgh surveyor's'
solution. Architect: James Gray.

during the Thatcher years as the Conservative Government viciously cut back the budgets of the local housing authorities. It was a low density scheme, 6.4 houses to the acre, built round a largish open space with old fruit trees. It has already been described in the Haddington Story, Chapter Four, and is well worth a visit.

We did not have much trouble with adjusting local authority housing where the burghs employed consultant architects and even less when much of the housing to rent was built by housing associations with their own architectural consultants. That system had its drawbacks as the consultants rarely monitored their schemes in use and so did not learn from their inadequacies. This was something we could contribute when we examined their subsequent schemes.

SPECULATIVE BUILDERS

Our main housing design problems arose from the speculative builders, who, in the 1960s, turned their attention to the growing prestige and attractions of East Lothian. On the whole, the speculative builders were building for first time buyers the same sort of houses their mothers lived in or dreamed about: two-storey detached or semi-detached houses aligned along roads with small front and back gardens. It was just such a scheme at Douglas Road, Longniddry, built by Wimpeys which is dealt with in Chapter Fourteen.

Their styling, which to start with was very plain, became more esoteric and foreign to Scotland with half-timbering tack-ons, gothic windows and baronial features all built on to the same pre-war plan. They were selling the houses, but not appreciating how family structure and habits were changing, and completely ignoring the latent demand from older people for more convenient houses. This was the message that I tried, meeting after meeting, as Regional Director of Physical Planning to drum into their representatives' heads just as they tried to drum into mine their need for more greenfield sites. There was no need to build every house with a pram space, etc, when only one in three households had any children under twenty. They completely ignored the needs of retired people, single parents and unmarried people of both sexes, living singly or together who required radically different houses. Houses or flats within the City or town centres, near employment, cultural and social facilities were needed, not houses on greenfield sites stuck away on the periphery and built to the old pre-war plans.

Broadgait Green, Gullane
We were able to introduce some small innovations. Crudens, in developing a small back-land site between Broadgait East and Broadgait

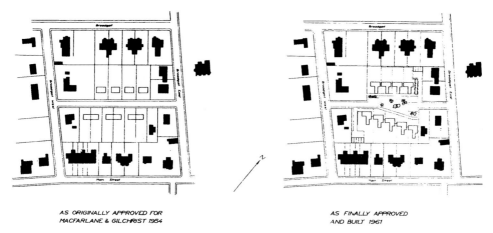

AS ORIGINALLY APPROVED FOR
MACFARLANE & GILCHRIST 1954

AS FINALLY APPROVED
AND BUILT 1961

GULLANE : BROADGAIT GREEN : Speculative Housing Development
Crudens Ltd. Application 176/60

1·83acres 10Houses

1·83acres 9 Houses
Private Land   1·15 acres
Common Open Space 0·68acres

SCALE OF FEET   200   400   600   800

930
21·11·61

East Lothian County Council
County Planning Department

Plate LI   Broadgait Green, Gullane

A drawing from our Annual Report 1961 showing the layout we prepared for Crudens, a speculative builder, who challenged us to demonstrate the principles we were harking on about. The L shaped single storey houses had flat roofs, courtyard gardens facing south and were grouped round a green instead of strung along a road as had previously been approved in 1954. These houses sold very well, but were not repeated.

West in Gullane, were persuaded not to follow the plan the Committee had approved for a previous builder in 1954 which showed a straight road linking through the site lined with detached and semi-detached houses, but to have two cul-de-sacs and a central green surrounded with attractive L-shaped houses well integrated with their gardens. It is called Broadgait Green and is still attractive, but the owners have done little to enrich the green which still depends on the trees and shrubs planted in 1960.

Brodie's Avenue, North Berwick

At North Berwick I persuaded Jack Loudon, who at that time had Peter Daniel working for him, to build a long continuous terrace harled with Barra cockle shells at Brodie's Avenue. No semis here, as the maximum number of houses were given the sea view from their bedrooms and access onto a strip of communal open space at the rear and garages out front, screening one house from the next.

Somnerfield Park, Haddington

Another scheme which cut new ground was Thain's scheme at Somnerfield, Haddington lying behind the Victorian stone built villas on the West Road. Innovative features here were a large common green separating Thain's houses from the villas and the two blocks of flats up near the old station for childless couples, an unheard of departure for a country speculative estate but they sold well. Many of the houses here were also L-shaped with a completely private terrace between adjoining buildings onto which the living rooms gave access. Some years later I was invited to the firm's anniversary dinner. I found myself the only local government officer there and took it as a mark of respect.

Harts' Developments, Tranent

Harts built two nice schemes at Tranent when they were employing two young architects, Malcolm Macdonald, later to be Planning Officer at Berwick-on-Tweed, and Andrew Taylor, later to be the Bank of Scotland's architect. One was Poulsen Park, a small group of white flat-roofed single-storey houses which has been beautifully maintained ever since and the second a larger scheme at Bankpark on steeply sloping land, again with linked housing looking out to the Firth of Forth across a large communal park, where the land was unsafe for building, and garages at the roadside.

PRIVATE FEUING

Glassel Park, Longniddry

As well as the activities of speculative builders, there was a growing demand from people to acquire land and have houses built to their own design— individual feuing, as it was termed. Before the 1939-45 War, Longniddry had been the place for this, but the serviced half acre of larger plots facing the golf course had all been taken up by the mid-50s and there was much discussion with the Wemyss Landed Estate as to how the 56 acres between King's Road and the railway should be developed. I considered it important that there was an exclusive housing area to attract entrepreneurs into the County and I thought Longniddry was the place. I recommended that the Estate commission a layout from a group of architects led by Robert Steedman, a landscape architect. This layout had quite short cul-de-sacs serving the houses with quite small gardens backing onto four common parks and linked through to a central one. The feuars were to be bound to use one of seven architects to design their house and these architects undertook to work to a mutually agreed design code. I had nominated a range of architects, male and female, young and old, red headed and raven locked, to suit all tastes! The common code was that the houses would have red clay pantiled roofs in some areas and flat roofs in others; the houses were to have white painted concrete block garden walls or these could be incorporated into the house; the excavations from the house should form a bank along the back of the garden adjoining the common

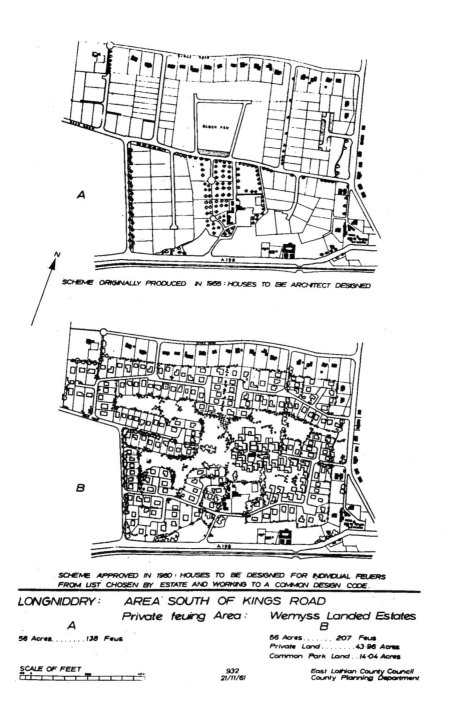

SCHEME ORIGINALLY PRODUCED IN 1955 : HOUSES TO BE ARCHITECT DESIGNED

SCHEME APPROVED IN 1960 : HOUSES TO BE DESIGNED FOR INDIVIDUAL FEUERS
FROM LIST CHOSEN BY ESTATE AND WORKING TO A COMMON DESIGN CODE.

LONGNIDDRY: AREA SOUTH OF KINGS ROAD
               Private feuing Area: Wemyss Landed Estates
     A   B

56 Acres........138 Feus   56 Acres....... 207 Feus
                                  Private Land.........43·96 Acres
                                  Common Park Land...14·04 Acres

SCALE OF FEET   932   East Lothian County Council
                                  21/11/61   County Planning Department

Plate LII   Glassel Park, Longniddry

Only the north-east quarter of this layout was built as planned. Again it consisted of
small individual plots grouped round the larger common park. The design code gave
plenty of room for individuality in the house designs. The other three quarters were
built in the usual spec builders' manner, although there is no through central east west
road across the site as proposed in the 1955 scheme with its half acre plots.

parks. The provision of these common private parks had a precedent in nineteenth-century Edinburgh's Royal Terrace and Calton Crescent and the quality of many Edinburgh housing areas stems from the high stone walls and trees appearing over them. The 1930s development along King's and Gosford Roads in Longniddry is characterised by white painted walls and hedges and very fine features they are. The outcome can be seen in the first quarter of Glassel Park, off Lyars Road, where some forty houses were built to this common code and the effect is very good. I was dismayed, however, when the first house came in for approval to find that in place of a flat roof it had one with a five degree pitch—so much for artistic licence and for codes of design! Unfortunately, the Wemyss Estate, under a new factor, got impatient at the necessarily slow rate of this individual feuing and sold out to Crudens, so only this quarter of the original layout was built. The rest looks like any other 'executive housing' scheme except that the Planning Committee made it a condition that all the front gardens were enclosed by beech hedging which, where it was honoured, gives some character to the development. I was also able to make it a condition that Crudens built a row of shops off Lyars Road and I produced a plan for the Wemyss Estate to convert cottages along the main road into an inn as there was no pub in the village.

I fought the Crudens' application in the Committee which was particularly awkward as Eric Stevenson was acting as their consultant. The County lost out on talented and ambitious people wanting to build their own houses who could have done a lot to stimulate life in the County. But to my Committee Members a house was just a house.

Muirfield Park, Gullane

There are two other private housing schemes which are worth a mention as they were on land in the ownership of the County Council and we were able to set a new standard. The first was a development at Muirfield Park in Gullane on a 24 acre site, which I persuaded the County Council to acquire from the Hospital Board, and to act as a developing laird. It incorporates several elements. Adjoining the main road there is a very attractive scheme by Frank Clark, a bankrupt builder from England, whom we started in a small way with a single plot on which he built a house with his own hands and who progressed to several very nice architect-designed schemes in the County, this being his first. The next element was a cul-de-sac given over to Dorran prefab houses which were sprouting up all over Scotland. I realised I could not keep them out of East Lothian for ever. By setting aside this cul-de-sac I was able to protect the rest of the County from these mean, little houses. Another part of the site was sold to the Link Housing Association and the parts nearer the Championship Golf Course of Muirfield were reserved for individual feuing. The key site, in fact a double plot, was sold to 'Gorgeous George' Pottinger, who had John Poulson design and build a house for him as they had been in cahoots over the construction of the Aviemore Centre. When the Poulson scandal broke in the 1960s, involving so many local authorities, I was called on by a senior officer of Scotland Yard Criminal Investigation Department and the most stony-faced policewoman I have ever met. She clearly thought I had received a back-hander or two. However, I sent them away satisfied that this was a straight property deal and there was no reason why the house and its internal swimming pool should not have received planning approval in the normal course of events. The main entry to the scheme was Lime Tree Avenue leading directly to the Muirfield championship car parks, thus eliminating the circuitous routes previously used. It was to be lined with individual pantiled bungalows and white wicket fences on the east side and the speculative cul-de-sacs led off it on the west side.

It was the mixture of three very different speculative builders, a housing association and individual feuing that I subsequently made a condition of the development of all large housing sites. I felt that no builder should have the monopoly of building new houses in any of our small towns or villages and in this way the monstrosity of large schemes was avoided.

The Glebe, Pencaitland

The other Council-owned feuing area was the Glebe at Pencaitland where the Planning Department feued off the remainder of the site left over from the new school. Here we simply laid down that all the houses had to be single or one and a half storeys high, with white harling and red clay pantiles and a uniform brick to be used for the low front garden walls. This resulted in a very homogeneous and tidy development but with a welcome variety of different house plans individually commissioned. Muirfield Park and The Glebe pointed up the important role that a land-owner can still exercise over the appearance of development on his land. If individuals appreciated the conditions before they bought the site there was little hassle when the plans were submitted for approval to the Planning Committee.

Pencaitland Village Expansion

Perhaps at this stage I should explain the decision that led to the expansion of Pencaitland that has been so severely criticised after I left for the Lothian Region. In 1958 I had recommended to the Planning Committee that Pencaitland should be earmarked for future expansion to cater for the expected demand from Edinburgh people to live in the country. The choice lay between Pencaitland and Ormiston. Ormiston

Plate LIII   The Glebe, Pencaitland

A private housing area feued by the County Council and controlled by the specification of white harling and clay pantiles, the brick for the front garden walls and a limitation to one or one and a half storeys. This has resulted in a calm development much in keeping with the old village. The white line on the roadway is to prevent parking across the driveways when mothers collect children from the adjoining school.

was severely constrained by land liable to subsidence, flooding and drainage limitations. It was also a fine well-established mining community into which it would, to my mind, have been a shame to introduce commuters from the City who could be very socially divisive. Pencaitland on the other hand was already a divided community: a posh Easter Pencaitland and a miner's Wester Pencaitland which badly needed uniting. It also needed a new school, a new sewage works, and enhanced electricity and telephone services. It had a fine wooded situation on the banks of the River Tyne, a big house, Winton House, in need of support and a good situation on the main road and a bus route from Edinburgh to Gifford and the hills. It was also a very pleasant place to live and so the County Council decided to expand Pencaitland and planning consent in principle was given; subject to many conditions controlling the variety and type of development and tenure, a choice of builders, and a steady rate of building, all of which we had pioneered at Muirfield Park, Gullane. There was also to be a main footpath created along the woods giving access to the recreation ground and shops, passing the school and bridging over the Tyne. This provides a link between Easter and Wester Pencaitland without using the narrow main road and old medieval bridge. The boundary of the Pencaitland Conservation Area was drawn to include the expansion area at Easter Pencaitland as an additional control to ensure that housing development would enhance the area that it could not preserve. This was a slightly devious arrangement, but one I hoped would ensure that the quality that had already been established through development control of houses within Pencaitland would be matched in the expansion area.

It was not developed until after I had left the County Council and I, along with many others, was dismayed by the 'Noddylands' that were built with red-brick houses of stock designs and pretentious add-ons destroying the quiet harmony of the stone-built village. The Vinefields development did not take full account of the conditions laid down in the outline planning consent of 1958 and certainly did not enhance the Conservation Area. But there you are, the planning system is dependent on those who administer it. I do however consider that it was the correct place to expand and only regret the way in which it was done. All over Britain similar housing schemes are being built by the national house builders with approval from planning authorities. We should all have been a great deal stronger in insisting that developments match the character and essence of the place where they are built, that independent architects are appointed to work out fully the detail of the schemes, and ensuring that the houses meet people's aspirations for the future, and meet the needs of the wide variety of families of different ages and composition.

Housing associations have recently set a new standard with their schemes and Mary has played her part on the Board of Hanover (Scotland) Housing Association Ltd in raising standards in their sheltered housing developments in Scotland. There are now enough good exemplars, public, private and housing association, to guide the next house building boom. Let us hope planning officers insist that they are followed.

7

BUILDINGS OF ARCHITECTURAL OR HISTORIC INTEREST

Statutory Provisions • The Two McPhails • Lost Buildings
The Tale of Two Towers • Care of Historic Buildings
Conservation Areas • Farm Steadings • Farm Buildings Survey 1968
Crauchie • Water Mills Survey 1970 • Water Mills Conference 1970
Preston Mill, East Linton • West Saltoun Barley Mill • Sandy's Mill
Doocots • Doocot Conference and Tour 1970
Harbour Terrace, North Berwick • The Lodge, North Berwick
Stevenson House, Haddington • Prestongrange Beam Engine
Lady Victoria Colliery, Newtongrange • Newtongrange Mining Village
Lothian Building Preservation Trust 1984-96
Bankton House, Prestonpans

The spirit of a place largely resides in the buildings inherited from the past. This was recognised between the wars by active preservation campaigns to save historic buildings from demolition. The National Trust for Scotland was established in 1931 and did much to save buildings—not only the mansion houses but small buildings in Culross, Hamilton House in Prestonpans and others. The fourth Earl of Bute commissioned Ian Lindsay to make a list of the buildings at risk. This list, as I remember, contained some 8 buildings in East Lothian.

Statutory Provisions

The Scandinavians had meantime been more thorough, producing extensive, well documented lists, and it was their example which was built into the 1947 Town and Country Planning (Scotland) Act requiring the Secretary of State to prepare lists of buildings of architectural or historic interest and to notify owners, who would then be required to obtain listed building consent for any alterations to them. The County had 482 buildings on the statutory list published in 1961 which had to be registered on the owners' title deeds and 310 on a supplementary list, whose owners were not notified. Local planning authorities were instructed to bear this supplementary list in mind when they were considering development applications affecting them.

The original list for East Lothian was compiled by Alan Reiach, an architect whom Mary had known when he worked for the Clyde

Valley Regional Plan at the closing stages of the war. He had just started up his own architectural practice and this was a nice little 'earner' at 10 shillings an hour plus a mileage allowance. He gave me a type-script copy of his list in 1951 and Mary and I had great delight in using it on our early forays around the County. I spent a good deal of time adding to and revising the list and filling out the descriptions. His list was very long on eighteenth and early nineteenth century farmhouses but very short on later Victorian and industrial buildings.

The Two McPhails

The Department of Health for Scotland was very dilatory in approving and publishing these lists. I remember chiding Mr D.M.McPhail, who was in charge of this section, but all the satisfaction I got was a gift of a guide book to Leningrad which he had visited as a tourist by ship in the 1930s after I had told him I was flying there as a delegate. It was not until another McPhail, J.G.S.McPhail, took over the responsibility for listed buildings in the early 1960s that the Department published slim grey volumes of buildings by burghs and parishes, and not until

Plate LIV Knox Academy, Haddington

A Victorian building added to the list by J G S McPhail. Despite being unused for many years and having a condemnatory report from a civil engineer, the County Council refused to allow it to be demolished and eventually the Lothian Regional Council, who had inherited it, sold it for £100 to the Edinvar Housing Association who converted it into sheltered housing and added two wings. Architect: Johnson-Marshall.

much later that they were confirmed and notified to the owners and authorities and authoritative type-script lists produced.

J.G.S.McPhail lived in a fine stone villa on the West Road in Haddington. I had met him in the Sudan where he was the District Commissioner, Shendi, 'a blue ruling blacks'. I had also known Fiona, his wife, when she was a nursing sister in Khartoum and later in Tripoli, where she came to visit me living in state in the empty Italian tourist hotel at Garian. It was a delight to be welcomed by them in Haddington, especially as they shared these memories and a passion for Scottish architecture. When the British political service was thrown out of Sudan on independence he had returned to his native Scotland and joined the Civil Service. To be a civil servant with a passion for Scottish architecture was of course rather awkward, but he was greatly liked under the soubriquet of 'Jigs'.

Another fine ex-colonial was Sir Robert Russell of the Indian Civil Service, who was an Under Secretary in the Department. He greatly encouraged me in my early days and approved our Development Plan on behalf of the Secretary of State. He continued his Indian habit of having a siesta in the afternoon, locking his office door and lying down on a sofa he had brought into his office. These men with their habit of combining field work with administration brought a breath of fresh air to the Department. It was one of the nice things about working as a local government officer in Scotland, in contrast to England, that we had a close contact with the civil servants and indeed with a whole range of well-informed and interesting people.

Lost Buildings

But even these well-intentioned civil servants could not fully activate the statutory listed building provisions of the 1947 Act to protect listed buildings until well into the 1970s. During the intervening period many fine buildings were lost to the County. Notable among these was Archerfield House, a Robert Adam building where the farmer knocked out the front and installed a grain dryer in the hall. Even the Earl of Haddington demolished Hedderwick Hill House without any consultation. Dunglass House was another loss, a nineteenth century building on a most dramatic site. It was greatly admired by Colin McWilliam, who was Director of the Scottish Building Record, a scholarly and doughty fighter for old buildings, who gave us much support. He with Mrs Eleanor Robertson set up the Scottish Georgian Society, later renamed the Architectural Heritage Society of Scotland. He also initiated, with Nikolaus Pevsner, the 'Buildings of Scotland' series and his volume on Lothian is a masterpiece.

After my retiral from the Lothian Regional Council, I joined Mary as their case worker, examining all applications for listed building

Plate LV Archerfield House, Dirleton

The owner, a farmer, cut the Robert Adam interior out of this fine house and installed a grain dryer and hoppers. The current owner has at least boarded the windows up which improves its prospects. Fine drawings of the rooms survive so it could be reinstated. My son, Benjamin produced excellent plans for its restoration, but this has still to happen.

consent and for development affecting conservation areas within East Lothian until 1996. This kept us in touch with what was happening in East Lothian and with young planning officers, but we never felt that they were willing or able to go as far as the Society was recommending in protecting or enhancing these buildings or villages.

I had always considered that planning officers had the duty to watch over the buildings on the Secretary of State's list, and as they went round the County should encourage the owners to look after them. But it was only when the owners had been formally notified and the entry made on their title deeds that they were required by statute to apply to the County Council for listed building consent for any alteration, both internal and external, or for demolition, that we at last began to get a real grip on them and reduce the losses.

Public attitudes were also changing. Some owners quite liked the idea of owning a historic building apart from the additional bureaucratic control. One thing we found difficult to get over to owners was that they should not purchase a listed building if they needed to extend or radically alter it. Eventually the County Planning Committee accepted our line and was not prepared to approve any but minor additions to listed buildings.

Plate LVI   Elphinstone Tower

A fifteenth century tower which was distinquished by the number of small rooms within the thickness of the walls, the usual three halls one above the other, the ground floor with a barrel vault and first floor with a pointed vault. It was well built with coursed ashlar. The structure was unusually complete but badly wrecked by underground mining.

The Tale of Two Towers

The change in public attitude can be illustrated by the tale of two towers. Elphinstone Tower, a massive fifteenth century tower with extensive intramural rooms within its thick walls, was demolished by its owner in the early 1960s despite it being an Ancient Monument. Ten years later there was a similar threat to demolish Preston Tower, this time by Prestonpans Town Council, who wanted the land for housing. Its

Plate LVII Preston Tower

Also of the fifteenth century but with the oddity of a two storey renaissance house, 1626, built off the parapet wall of the Tower. Inside it has two barrel vaulted halls and a dungeon in its small projecting wing. Entry was originally at the first floor by a wooden stair hung from the corbels which are still visible on the east face. It is now in the custody of the East Lothian Council.

demolition was prevented by the combined action of the National Trust for Scotland and the County Council. The Trust assumed the superiority in exchange for some ground off Hamilton House to provide access from the West Wynd. The Council took the building into guardianship and acquired the remainder of the orchard, which is now laid out as a public garden. The original owner was able to sell a plot of land for a modest housing development. This and subsequent developments have created a very charming corner in the historic village of Preston.

Care of Historic Buildings

The care of historic buildings was part of our development control system. We took special trouble to examine them on any pretext which came our way and to encourage owners to carry out the necessary 'stitch in time' repairs. If the buildings were beyond this, and many were, we encouraged them either to restore them with the enhanced housing improvement grants that the County gave for costly restorations, or to sell them to others who would restore them. As a last resort we threatened but never did use, our statutory powers to carry out repairs or acquire them. Our efforts reached a climax in "European Architectural Heritage Year 1975" when we prepared a booklet illustrating 43 listed buildings and monuments on which the Council and private owners were working at the time. These ranged from access to and interpretative boards for Whitecastle, a fine iron-age fort, in the Lammermuir foothills south of Garvald and, at the other end of the scale, Tyne Court, the major housing redevelopment by the Town Council of the fell monger's works behind our house in Haddington's Nungate which received a Civic Trust Award that year. Its photograph embellished the front cover of their publication of all the UK awards. Other schemes included the floodlighting of landmark churches at Aberlady, Whitekirk, Gifford and Pencaitland; the private housing development round the ruined mansion house at Ormiston Hall; the rehabilitation of Doocot Park, North Berwick; the restoration of 29 High Street, East Linton; and the Steading at Stevenson House, Haddington. We had no major mansion house projects that year. Another important but time consuming task was the fastening of 463 handsome bronze plaques, some four inches high, designed by John Reid, to identify listed buildings throughout the County. Only fifteen owners refused to allow us to erect these plaques which shows the extent to which we had won the support of owners in our campaign to protect listed buildings.

It is pleasant to recall that at the presentation of Civic Trust Awards by the Duke of Edinburgh in Windsor Castle to mark European Architectural Heritage Year 1975 a special award was devised to recognise the consistent conservation achievements over the years by

Plate LVIII   Historic Buildings Plaques

Many people and organisations disliked my idea of putting plaques on Listed Buildings.
This design by John Reid, cast in solid bronze by Charles Henshaw, Edinburgh cost
£2.25 each. It was well received in East Lothian but has not been followed by other
local planning authorities or by Historic Scotland.

East Lothian County Council, which while intended for me, was received
by Peter Wilson, the Convener of the Lothian Regional Council to which
I had moved by the time of the ceremony.

Conservation Areas

The County Council took advantage of the Civic Amenities Act 1967
to designate 15 conservation areas which at the time were unique in
that some included not just the historic cores of the towns and villages,
but also the approaches and the countryside about them which were
important to safeguard views into and out of the villages. Among these
were Athelstaneford, Whitekirk, Dirleton, Gifford, Ormiston,
Pencaitland and Stenton, as well as the central areas of Haddington,
Dunbar, North Berwick and Tranent.

In conservation areas only developments which preserved or
enhanced their character were to be allowed and it was incumbent on
the planning authority to take steps to achieve this. No buildings could
be demolished or trees felled without the authority's consent. Thus a
higher standard of development control was enforced and I for one
took the strict view that developments must enhance the area, not just

Plate LIX   Athelstaneford

A typical Scottish agricultural village with the fertile fields stretching away to the sea.
It was built by Sir David Kinloch of Gilmerton House to encourage the settlement of
tradesmen in the eighteenth century and in my time still had a smithy, a joiner and
slater. It is built on a ridge with the church (1868) and manse on opposite sides of the
road at the west end and the school and village hall set back on opposite sides near the
east end. In between, the street is lined with single storey pantiled cottages. The
hedged area to the east of the village is the minister's glebe with some council houses
and along the road to the north is the former brewery.

Plate LX   Smithy Row, Athelstaneford

This charming row of rubble and pantiled cottages is at the east end of the village where the street widens out into a little triangular green. The smithy building is to the left of the row, to the right the cottage of the tiler, with the beautifully swept pantile eaves.

do them no harm. Thus sheds and other buildings, even if not seen from the roads, had to have pitched roofs of slate or tile. However we were not slavishly antiquarian in our approach and allowed, for example, quite stylish new infill buildings in Forth Street, North Berwick, although I was ashamed that my Committee approved a flat roofed house on the north side of the street. The County Council also gave small grants for embellishments and the first of these went to Braidwood in Gifford for the replacement of finials which later came to be known as the "Planning Officer's Balls". The East Lothian District Council established several town schemes where Historic Scotland and the District Council together gave owners 50% grants for repairs and enhancements.

In 1975, European Architectural Heritage Year, I was able to persuade the County Council to put up boards in twelve of the conservation villages containing sketches of the significant buildings and village form by John Knight, who was later to become Historic Scotland's chief architect for the South of Scotland and with a description by John Gifford who was the researcher and author of *'Buildings of Scotland'*. I asked them to do this as I knew that if it was done in-house by my department it would be subject to much criticism as the boards contained many pithy comments which are part of their charm. They are still there. The County Council had these drawings

Plate LXI   Village Boards, Innerwick

One of the twelve village boards we erected in 1975, this board shows the original meandering village street linking the farm to the left with the church, manse, school and the laird's modest house. To the south lies the straight toll-road with the toll house linking the two roads. Twenty years later these boards remain in place drawing peoples' attention to the qualities of their surroundings.

and commentaries made up into a booklet *"East Lothian Villages"* which has been reprinted twice. It was this care and appreciation of historic buildings and conservation areas that distinguishes East Lothian and enriches the lives of many of its inhabitants.

Farm Steadings

After coal the other source of the County's wealth was the advanced farming practices in the Lothians, which led the way in Scotland. Farm buildings were also poorly represented in Alan Reiach's original list of buildings of architectural or historic interest, so I seized the opportunity in 1968 to institute a survey of farm steadings in the County.

The occasion for this was the County Planning Committee's reluctant approval of an application to demolish the old pantiled steading at Saltoun East Mains with its interesting chimney and its replacement by a large steel barn. Many farms had these tall industrial chimneys to operate steam engines installed to thresh the grain, slice the turnips and do other farm jobs. I never saw one of these steam engines, as the scrap merchants had done too good a job during the war, but with coal so handy it was the logical thing for the farmers to have. The Saltoun East Mains chimney was particularly interesting as it had a pattern in its brickwork which we could never interpret—an hour glass, a full wine glass, and a diamond, one above the other facing south.

Farm Buildings Survey 1968

The survey was carried out in the summer of 1968 by Robert Dunnet, a third year student of Edinburgh University's Department of Architecture. One hundred and thirty farms in the eastern part of the County were visited, photographed and their features listed and a grading system applied covering the degree of alteration, the state of repair, historic interest and architectural character. Sixty-two empty farm cottages suitable for reconstruction as weekend cottages were also noted and used to satisfy the enquiries for such cottages being made to the Planning Department. Of the hundred and thirty farms, seventy-five had the standard arrangement of cart sheds with granary over, twenty-six had chimneys and nine had horse mills, that is the octagonal roof which sheltered the horses who walked round and round powering the threshing mill. The Planning Committee made the restoration of a horse mill at Newhouse, Dunbar a condition for the approval of the Shell petrol filling station, where it can still be seen

Plate LXII   Saltoun East Mains

This photograph was used on the cover of 'East Lothian Farm Buildings', August 1968, which was the outcome of our architectural and historic survey. It shows the boiler room, its enigmatic chimney and the long granary building behind the chimney. It was all swept away and replaced by a big steel barn, but it was the last to suffer this fate in my time.

Plate LXIII   Newhouse Dunbar

(a) Diagram   (b) Horsemill
This is typical of what remains of the many horsemills in the County—merely the sun-shade or umbrella as the pair of horses went round and round providing the drive for the threshing mill in the adjoining barn as shown in the drawing we provided. Mr Harwell remembered in his youth in Stirlingshire riding in the central 'trees' as they turned and turned.

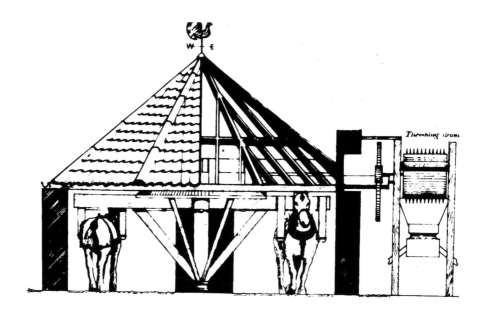

with our explanation of how it worked. Ten steadings had pigeon lofts, two had clock towers and four had relics of water mills. They all had cattle courts where Irish store cattle were kept over winter, fed on turnips, producing large quantities of dung which was spread on to the fields in the spring after the cattle had been sold to graziers in the English Midlands to be fattened up for the London market. These open courts, in groups of four to ten, had roofed feeding troughs, typically held twenty cattle and can still be seen arranged symmetrically round a central store from which turnips and straw were led by barrow to the courts. A nice booklet was produced with plans and photographs of the finest steadings. This was the first such survey and its publication awakened much interest in farm buildings. In particular, it inspired a book by Robert Morton and stimulated the setting up of the Scottish Vernacular Building Society.

The Committee authorised the wide circulation of the survey booklet to the farmers, the agricultural colleges and the advisory services. On the strength of this survey, the Department of Agriculture and Fisheries for Scotland was persuaded, in the case of listed farm buildings and others of scenic value, to give grants for re-roofing with the original materials rather than with the cheapest which were asbestos cement sheets. The Tyninghame Links steading was a beneficiary of this persuasion.

The County Council agreed that the ten best farms identified in the survey should be submitted for statutory listing, which was given, and further agreed to provide a small fund to give grants to farmers to maintain useless, but picturesque, features such as chimneys, horse threshing mills and clock towers. The two empty steadings at Crauchie and Hallhill, Dunbar, were earmarked as possible agricultural museums.

Crauchie

I pursued the idea of turning Crauchie into a museum. It was a led farm, that is the land was cultivated from an adjoining farm and so the steading was redundant. Willie Dale of Lochhouses, who had previously shown his collection of vintage motor cars in the cavalry stables at Dunbar barracks, was also building up a collection of farm machinery. He offered to rent the farmhouse at Crauchie and put in a retired man who would restore the machinery and open the display to the public, much as happened later at his Myreton Motor Museum. Neither he, nor I, could persuade the Trustees of the Gilmerton Estate to enter into this arrangement and so the proposal fell through. Sadly, both this steading and the alternative possibility of Hallhill were converted to houses after my time. The past achievements of the agricultural industry therefore came off worse than the mining industry and can only be seen in a disembodied state in a steel building at Ingliston run by the Royal Museum of Scotland.

Plate LXIV   Monkrigg Farm Steading

Designed by William Burn in the mid-nineteenth century it was the first to be converted into 'residences'. Only one skylight in sight and a few ventilation pipes. The cart-shed to the left is nicely glazed and the cupola restored: a Listed Building saved, not a farm steading cannibalised.

I was always slightly two-minded about the conversion of farm steadings into 'residences', as the estate agents called them. There was a particular incentive for this to happen to the listed steadings as no VAT was charged. I always tried to limit the number of 'desirable residences' to get larger houses and more privacy and to ensure that facilities for the inhabitants to keep small animals were provided, and that they had rights to walk by the fields, woods and streams, so the purchasers could enjoy the pleasures of living on a farm.

Water Mills Survey 1970

Water mills were another class of building which we surveyed for the 'Countryside in 1970' celebrations and produced another fine booklet. The East Lothian water mill survey was carried out by Margaret Gilvray, a smart little girl, who was specially appointed for interpretative work in the County in 1970. She examined the forty-seven mill buildings remaining of the eighty-two shown on the 1854 6" Ordnance Survey maps. Thirty-four had been corn and meal mills and thirteen sawmills, waulk, bone or flint mills. The latter had been used to crush flints for the glazes used in the Prestonpans pottery industry. Six of the mills retained water wheels and some milling equipment and a further two had only water wheels.

Water Mills Conference 1970

Water mills provide a good entry point into the countryside with their riverside sites, their lades and tail races, usually a mill pond too, and a miller's small holding with his house and cottages all served by an access road. They are also examples of quite complex early craft machinery with all the workings clearly visible. So it seemed appropriate to organise a conference on "Water Mills and their Conservation" as another of the County's contributions to 'The Countryside in 1970'. The conference was held in the Marine Hotel, North Berwick, from 30 October to 1 November, when cheap boarding rates were negotiated. It was organised jointly with the Edinburgh University's Department of Extra Mural Studies and attracted some 50 people from all parts of the United Kingdom who left more knowledgeable and enthusiastic than when they arrived. Amongst the outcomes was the Scottish Mill Advisory Group set up in Edinburgh to help owners of mills, and to lobby the Secretary of State to assume guardianship of a large eighteenth century vertical water mill. At that time the Ancient Monuments Board only had a primitive clack mill in Shetland where the shaft of a small horizontal paddle wheel rested on the stream bed and turned the upper millstone directly above. As a result they took into guardianship New Abbey Mill, near Sweetheart Abbey in Dumfriesshire, which the owner, Charles Stewart, had drawn to the attention of our Scottish Mill Advisory Group.

Preston Mill, East Linton

After the 1948 flood, George Gray of Smeaton had given the seventeenth century water mill at Prestonkirk, East Linton, to the National Trust for Scotland who restored it with aid from the Rank Milling Group. In 1970 I persuaded him to donate the store and stable building alongside and we set up an exhibition in them. One room had a corn kist showing the different types of corn which could be handled, another had agricultural bygones and the third had a large historical mural painted by pupils of the Dunbar High School and indoor picnic facilities. Preston Mill is extremely picturesque with its single storey pantiled milling building, the detached circular drying kiln with conical pitched roof at an awry angle and mill pond which became home to a pair of our Muscovy ducks and their progeny.

West Saltoun Barley Mill

A much more historically significant mill was that at West Saltoun with its three storey slated mill building, its integral square kiln, and adjoining

East Lothian Water Mill

Plate LXV   East Lothian Watermills

The cover of the thirty page booklet presented at our Conference on 'Watermills and their Conservation',1970. It gave details of the ten watermills with some machinery which still existed in the County. 47 ruins were inspected out of 82 sites shown on the 1854 Ordnance Survey Maps. The National Trust for Scotland own and restored the seventeenth century Preston Mill after the 1948 flood and again in 1992.

cottages and stable, all in an L-shaped group with a fine miller's house some distance away.

This used the advanced milling techniques which James Meikle, a millwright, was sent to Holland to 'souse out'—an early industrial spy. The contract between him and Henry Fletcher of Saltoun Hall, dated 1710, still survives. It was the same Fletcher who had opposed the Treaty of Union in 1707 and who was a determined improver of his estates. His descendant, Captain Fletcher, told me how he valued the mill and had seen that it was kept wind and water tight. After his death, I upbraided his factor from an Edinburgh legal firm for neglecting it. When we met he asked why I was fussing over an old mill when he had a fine little panelled house at Ford which needed attention.

Plate LXVI   West Saltoun Barley Mill

The early seventeenth century water mill was designed to Dutch specifications. The three storey slated mill building to the left, the drying kiln with its cowl showing abuts it and the workers' cottages are alongside it. It was a tragedy that the machinery was stripped out of it but the buildings have been well converted into a comfortable house. Vernacular building at its best.

Ford was in Midlothian and so not my concern, but as Mary and I were looking for a bigger house I went to see it. It was 'A' listed, built in 1680, and L-shaped with a turret stair in the re-entrant angle. It had harled rubble walls, crow-stepped gables and a slated roof. It was built within its walled garden and was the quintessence of a seventeenth century Scottish laird's house. Mary had already been in the house. The ceilings were down, the skrim which lined the walls was falling off, the floors were badly worn and sagging, but it was in a better state than other houses we had been looking at and I remarked 'we could move in tomorrow', a phrase she has never let me forget. We acquired it with a little help from the factor, but it was not until after the 1956 October flood had passed through the house that we got the builders started and moved in during July 1957 just before our Jemima was born. We changed the colour of the walls from white by applying copperas lime wash—'Loretto colour' as we called it—but since then Loretto School has changed to a cement based paint that in no way has the quality of copperas—a tan colour which deepens with the years. I always think

Plate LXVII   Ford House

(a) Before Restoration
Built in 1680 and typical of its period with its entry door and staircase in the re-entrant angle. We were surprised to find a small doocot in the conical roof over the turning stair. The left-hand window in the gable which had been inserted was blocked up again and the original window into the front courtyard reopened.

that I was rewarded in this way for the watch that I was keeping over the listed buildings of East Lothian long before they had been formally listed.

This watch was not, however, sufficient to prevent the factor of Lennoxlove Estate, who had bought the adjoining West Saltoun farm, from stripping the machinery out of the barley mill on the assumption that the Estate owned it. It was an act of extreme vandalism, as he had been warned of its great historic importance by the retired blacksmith at East Saltoun, Mr Durie, who refused to do the job. The building still remains and it has since been converted into a good house, but what a tragedy, what ignorance, and what conceit! It made me lose all faith in factors.

Sandy's Mill

The most interesting of the mills surveyed was Sandy's Mill, its cottages and miller's holding, five miles down the River Tyne from Haddington, which had been the Gilmerton Estate Mill. It had been acquired for its water rights by Dr Dunlop of Stevenson House, who installed a turbine

(b) After Restoration
Sound and trim with its coat of copperas, white down pipes and gutters and grey window surrounds in place of the white and black of the original. It stands beside the old Roman road with its sheltering sycamore tree. Many Edinburgh travellers deviate for the pleasure of seeing the house. We floodlight it on high days and holidays as a gesture of thanks for a Historic Buildings repair grant. The weather cock came from Lasswade Old Church via a metal merchant's yard.

to generate electricity for the mansion house in the mill race. However he had seen the mill in operation turning out animal feed stuff and agreed at the Conference that he would keep it wind and water tight for future restoration and use as the Scottish Mill Centre. It was another integral mill with a square kiln and a complete range of buildings. Uniquely, it had a pearl barley mill where the wheels turned vertically alongside each other polishing the grains, as compared to the grinding action of the corn mill where the stones turned horizontally one above the other. I was a Trustee of the Brown Dunlop Country Houses Trust, but unfortunately after I left the County Council the new personnel in the Planning Department were not able to mount a positive scheme for a mill centre. Eventually the mill holding was sold to a small speculative builder who restored the cottages and converted the steading to a house for himself. The Trust, by virtue of their superiority, were able to see that the mill was not converted to a restaurant and the builder, on my advice, obtained a Historic Buildings repair grant for the mill building and is slowly restoring the machinery as a hobby. All is not yet lost.

The only other mill with some machinery is the Gimmersmill in

Plate LXVIII   Sandy's Mill

Another watermill which survives with its machinery and cottages. It is five miles downstream from Haddington and used to be the mill for the Gilmerton Estate whose tenants were required to have their corn ground there. It also has the distinction of having a pearl barley mill where the stones run vertically against each other to polish the barley, rather than horizontally to crush the oats and other grains.

Haddington to which the County Council gave a restoration grant. It has two water wheels, side by side, in the centre of the building, one of which generates 16.5 horse power.

Doocots

The large masonry stand-alone doocots had captured our imagination as I had never seen them before, having been brought up in Surrey, not a corn-growing county. Mary and Douglas Bailey, a colleague from Peterlee, who on the death of his first wife had moved up to Glasgow, carried out a survey of these buildings, fifty-seven in all, which was published in the Transactions of the Ancient Monuments Society in 1963. They classified doocots into 3 types. The earliest, beehive doocots, the shape of a straw beeskep with the stones corbelled into a central entry hole for the pigeons, such as can be seen at the Northfield doocot at Prestonpans. This was the first I persuaded the County Council to acquire and restore. The next, in time, was the lectern type with a one way roof pitched to the south and, typically, with entry holes between the upper half rafters, which rested on a crossbeam. A good example of this type is in the grounds of Preston Tower, Prestonpans, which was also taken into the ownership of the County

Plate LXIX East Lothian Doocots
(a) Beehive, Northfield. (b) Lectern, Pilmuir House.
(c) Tower, Bolton. (d) Interior of Northfield

The three types of doocot found in the County. All have projecting stone string courses
to prevent rats climbing into the doocot and doors that open outwards because of the
accumulation of pigeon droppings inside. Inside are 624 stone nesting boxes.

175

Council. The double lectern type has as many as two-thousand stone nesting boxes. The third type, later still in time, was the tower, or decorative doocot which came in various shapes. The County Council grant-aided the one at Johnstounburn, designed as a 'cottage orne', and another at Bolton, built as a circular tower with an elegant cupola, or glover, on top serving as entry for the pigeons. By 1975 the County Council was the owner of twelve doocots and the Town Councils had four others. I often had to use the old saying that 'to demolish a doocot would bring ten lean years' in order to persuade the owners to repair others. This prophesy no doubt originated from the fact that the rock pigeons, which inhabit the doocots, breed throughout the year and so provided fresh meat at a time before the introduction of turnips, when all except breeding cattle had to be slaughtered in November and salted down.

Mary and I had often thought we would like to farm Lady Kitty's Doocot, another tower doocot, which stood at the opposite end of the Nungate Bridge to our first house in Haddington. It would have produced eggs, young pigeons or squabs as they were called, and dung for our garden. The input would have been nil as the pigeons gleaned the surrounding fields. But such a weird notion found no favour with the Town Council who owned it. Years later I asked the County Ranger to farm the Luffness beehive doocot which was near his house at Aberlady to provide essential information on the husbandry of the pigeons.

Doocot Conference and Tour 1970

Again, as part of the 'Countryside in 1970' events the County Council organised a Doocot Seminar in the Council Chambers in Haddington, hearing first of this farming experiment and later of the architectural qualities of the doocots. This was followed by a lunch in the Tweeddale Arms at Gifford where we served pigeons' eggs as a starter, and pigeon pies as a main course, one lot made of the tender young squabs collected from the nesting boxes before they had flown and been fed only on their 'mother's milk', and the others made from tough wood pigeons which had been shot on the wing. These pies were as different as chalk from cheese. After lunch the coach toured round several doocots ending at the splendid circular tower doocot of Elvingstone House where Sir David Lowe had preserved the potence or revolving ladder which enabled the eggs and squabs to be easily harvested. I meet people who still recall this most revealing tour although I have not heard of anyone taking up pigeon farming yet. Perhaps it was the hard boiled pigeon eggs which put them off as the white of the egg turns transparent and not opaque as a chicken's egg, or the numerous fleas of which the Ranger complained. It is also perhaps a rather anti-social thing to do and in the sixteenth century the right to construct doocots had to be restricted

Plate LXX   Harbour Terrace, North Berwick

The eighteenth century warehouses, constructed of purple rubble stone were converted by Mary Tindall into flats. The Harbour is built on a rocky spit which divides
the East from the West Bay. It is the pivotal feature of the town and it was essential
that these buildings were retained. In the foreground is the crane which lifted the
storm-boards into the slot seen on the bull-nosed entry—that work dates from 1887.

by legislation to people owning a certain acreage of land so that they
did not feed entirely off other people's ground. The first information
leaflet we prepared was on the County's Doocots.

Harbour Terrace, North Berwick

There were two key projects in North Berwick which had taken place
earlier and had attracted much attention. The first was the restoration
of the large and prominent nineteenth century warehouses at Harbour
Terrace and the second was the restoration of the Lodge, the old laird's
house at the south end of Quality Street backing onto a fine park, both
of which were owned by the Town Council.

The Harbour Terrace, grain and potato warehouses, had been
converted to emergency housing before the First World War when the
County lost its valuable potato trade to Lincolnshire. They had lain
empty apart from their use as fishermen's stores for many years. They
are massive four storey buildings, built of the purple rubble quarried at
the foot of North Berwick Law and built on the south quay of the harbour.
The County Planning Department had organised a study to look into

their future, as they were falling into serious disrepair. Our proposals centred around a seafood restaurant on the first floor, with two floors of flats above for renting to the fishermen, and with their stores on the ground floor. I had interested Bill Garrard, the restaurateur of the Howgate Inn, who had introduced Danish Smorrebrods to Scotland. His wife, Buttercup, spent some time in Denmark that summer learning how they cooked their fish. The town badly needed a good restaurant, but the Town Council got cold feet—"What would happen if they invested all this money in a restaurant to let to Bill Garrard and he died?"—which he was not to do for another twenty years. "Take out a life insurance policy", we replied. However this effectively stalled the project until one day Mary was approached by William Toynbee of Dennis & Co, builders at Dalkeith, who was a fellow member of the Midlothian Valuation Appeal Committee. She prepared a scheme for flats for sale on the upper floors, leaving half the first floor in case anybody came along wanting to establish a restaurant. But nobody came, and so it was also converted into flats. Halfway through the project Mr Toynbee suddenly died, but the building was carried through to completion by the firm. The redevelopment was so stunning that it won her another Civic Trust Award and a place on the front cover of the Civic Trust Award Manual of 1972 in front of all the other awards in Britain. What pleased Mary most was that she saw it from the escalators at Heathrow advertising "Come to Scotland".

The Lodge, North Berwick

The Lodge, which was a crescent of houses round the original burgh market place, had been gradually bought up since the seventeenth century and made into the seat of the Dalrymple family. The Dalrymples had moved out to Leuchie in the 1920s and the Town Council had acquired it and roughly subdivided it into houses. The Planning Department with Alan Reiach & Partners produced various alternatives for its deserved community use, but none of them quite stacked up financially. However the National Trust for Scotland was persuaded to undertake its renovation under their Little Houses Improvement Scheme, although it was not a little house, with the help of an interest-free loan from the County Council, which later was converted into a grant. And so it remains, in individual private hands, all covered in National Trust for Scotland white harling. There is a passage through to the town park at the back with its flower beds, aviary and paths round a nice big field surrounded by large sheltering tree belts. It, too, has a small lectern doocot.

Stevenson House, Haddington

Further mention should be made here of Stevenson House near

Plate LXXI   The Lodge, North Berwick

At the other end of Quality Street to the Harbour is the Lodge, another Town Council property which was falling into disrepair. This view is from the garden side showing the plain sensible commodious building of the eighteenth century after its restoration for the National Trust for Scotland by Schomberg Scott, Architect.

Plate LXXII   Stevenson House, by Haddington

The south and bowed east elevations of Stevenson House with the old laundry wing to the west. The exterior gives no hint of the square inner courtyard with turreted circular stairs in its corners. The walled garden, open to the public, lies to the right of the house.

Haddington which Dr Dunlop's father, who lived at Seton House, had acquired before the 1939-45 War and which Jack Dunlop restored with Mary's help after the war. The Mansion House dates from before the seventeenth century and was built round a central courtyard with spiral stairs in each corner, although in the eighteenth century a new straight scale and platt stair had been inserted to the south side of the courtyard and connected to the four turret stairs by a first floor passage. Mary worked at Stevenson for many years converting the laundry wing for Jean Ronaldson and the coach house for Isobel Dunlop, Jack's two sisters; the steading for Julia, his daughter; the garden cottage for letting to members of the National Trust for Scotland; and modernising the other estate cottages. Jack asked me to be a Trustee when he set up the Brown Dunlop Country Houses Trust to own and run the estate and to ensure that it was passed on to succeeding generations in good order. He and his wife, Betty, gave a succession of twenty-five Christmas concerts organised by Isobel, a composer, with young musicians, many of whom later made their names in the London concert scene. They were the most wonderful occasions.

Jack also gathered together a small group to import French wine by the barrel, which we then bottled in the commodious cellars at Stevenson. The high point perhaps was the importation of Taylor's port, Quinta Bargellas 1962, which Jack and I shared—180 bottles each at a cost of ten shillings and two pence a bottle which included the cost of corks but not the labour of scrounging and washing 360 bottles.

Stevenson was a marvellous house and although Jack never entered into local politics he gave me very wise advice. The walled garden which he replanted is open to the public and Stevenson is a model of how a mansion house can be kept alive, even though he and his sisters are now dead.

Prestongrange Beam Engine

I was able to introduce into the list of buildings for the County several industrial buildings. The prize here was the giant beam engine steadily pumping water in the Prestongrange Colliery. Arriving as I had from the East Durham coalfield, I was fascinated by collieries and charmed by the ramshackle buildings which had accumulated at Prestongrange over the 250 years of its development. The beam engine was made in

Plate LXXIII Beam Engine, Prestongrange

The technical drawing we produced of this fine engine, the last in Scotland. The north gable, third from the left, shows the doors which once gave onto aerial platforms so that the pinion could be greased. The drawing bottom right shows how the cast-iron beam was strengthened by a truss, the drilling for which was done by a portable steam engine. The drawing does not show the turned wooden banister to the stairs, replaced by Moray House Teacher Training Centre.

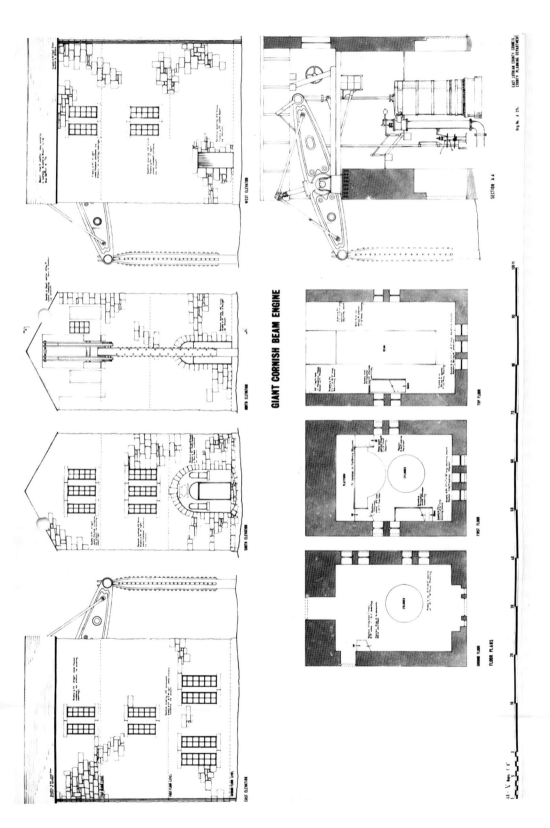

GIANT CORNISH BEAM ENGINE

WEST ELEVATION

SECTION A-A

NORTH ELEVATION

SOUTH ELEVATION

EAST ELEVATION

TOP FLOOR

FIRST FLOOR

GROUND FLOOR

FLOOR PLANS

EAST LOTHIAN COUNTY COUNCIL
COUNTY PLANNING DEPARTMENT

181

Cornwall in 1872 and installed at Prestongrange in 1890 to enable the lower seams of coal to be worked in the great coal boom years. Here it had been nodding away for 60 years, night and day, at the rate of three and a half strokes a minute, raising 650 gallons of water a minute.

Similar beam engines survive, not in Cornwall where they were developed for the tin mines, but in the pristine water pumping stations in southern England. The Prestongrange engine as unique because of its battle scars. It had been strengthened by a truss mounted on the top of the beam for which the manuscript calculations still exist. The pump rods were of 23 inch square Oregon pine weighing 105 tons and operating 24 inch pumps at three levels. The engine had two mishaps in 1916 and 1938 when the 10 foot piston in the 70 inch diameter cylinder broke, cracking the base and the cylinder itself. The base was recast on both occasions, but in 1916 the cylinder was recaulked with red lead and linseed oil and clamped with cast iron rings and set screws which can still be seen. After the second mishap a more elaborate mend was made with a dovetail joint cut into the cylinder wall and a copper strip inserted. The beauty of these old steam engines is that all this history and their method of working is visible. It has three working valves for letting in the steam at the head of the cylinder, which pulls up the beam and rods so working the pumps down the shafts. Another valve lets out steam at the bottom of the stroke into a condenser and then an equilibrium valve. It was a great thrill to discover below the floor of the engine house two further floors which housed the cataract mechanism that controlled the timing of the valves. This consists of two wooden boxes moving one inside the other at the end of the equilibrium rod. To go faster the operator merely bored another hole in the inner box, to go slower he merely plugged up a hole.

At that time there was no provision for listing industrial machinery but the building itself, of massive squared bull-nosed blocks of masonry and its elegant timber stair with turned balusters, quite justified its listing. When the colliery closed in 1964, and the demolition gangs moved in, I reminded the National Coal Board of its status as a listed building. So it was left standing in splendid isolation as the other colliery buildings all round it were demolished and it was revealed to the public eye for the first time. Its slated roof suffered in the 1968 storm and as it was of little concern to the National Coal Board I recommended that the County Council should acquire this corner of the Edinburgh Green Belt, and its great beam engine, which should be the centre-piece of an historical site commemorating the seven centuries of mining industry in East Lothian. The tale of this and of David Spence is told at more length in Chapter Twelve, the Development of Tourism.

I very much regret that I did not also have the beehive pipe kilns listed as well. The colliery had mined clay, as well as coal, and there were twelve beehive kilns and a three storey moulding shed for making fireclay pipes, chimney pots and a range of decorative salt glaze ware. These continued in production after the colliery was demolished—but were later demolished 'overnight'. I confess that it was this bitter realisation that I had lost a visible reminder of Prestonpans' early involvement with ceramics that led me to appoint Dr Eamon Hyde, an architect-trained industrial archaeologist, to my staff in the Regional Council rather than an architectural historian. I knew that I would get plenty of advice on architectural matters from the voluntary bodies—but there were few people at that time who were interested in industrial plant and buildings.

Prestongrange had a great history and it was, indeed, the first recorded coal working site in Scotland, mentioned in a charter given to the enterprising twelfth century Cistercian monks of Newbattle Abbey. It had seen also the introduction of many engineering innovations in the nineteenth century including hydraulic power, as recorded on the visits of the Institute of Mining Engineers. Much of this history has been revealed by excavation on site.

In no way could the site convey any idea of the work of a miner or the technology needed to win the coal. In reality it was just an archaeological site with a single giant beam engine. But it had been recognised by the National Coal Board as the Scottish Mining Museum and a substantial collection of steam machinery had been gathered in by David Spence.

Lady Victoria Colliery, Newtongrange

When the Lady Victoria Colliery at Newtongrange closed in 1981 I persuaded the Lothian Regional Council to assume responsibility for it. It was an 'A' listed building and probably the finest surviving nineteenth century colliery in Europe. It was complete with its village alongside it, all built by the Lothian Coal Company in the last decade of the nineteenth century. Three Councils, Lothian, East Lothian and Midlothian, agreed to take over and fund it as a twin-site museum, connected with Prestongrange by a tourist trail leading past other reminders of the mining industry, and the whole forming the Scottish Mining Museum.

Lady Victoria is a magnificent industrial monument complete with its winding engine house and winding engine; eight Lancashire boilers which provided the power; an extensive pithead; coal washeries; and twenty-two rail sidings which passed below the buildings between rows of brick arches holding up the pithead floor, with all its processing equipment to sort and clean the coal before being tipped into the wagons beneath. It was held by the National Coal Board on a 99 year lease from the Lothian Estates. I persuaded Lord Lothian to give the Council

a 25 year renewable lease at a nominal rent, although I think he thought me a little mad. I also persuaded Albert Wheeler, by then risen to be Scottish Area Manager from an apprenticeship at the Lady Victoria, to forego the scrap value and give the buildings as they stood to the Regional Council.

Dr Eamon Hyde and Jim Catherwood, both on my Regional staff, set about restoring the buildings with the aid of over 100 unemployed youths engaged under the Community Programme. After 1983, running of the museum ceased to be a Regional Council function and so the Scottish Mining Museum Trust was set up in 1984 by the Regional Council and the two District Councils. There was a great party to mark the handover and former boilermen volunteered to fire a boiler and the 2,400 horse power winding engine turned again under steam. I was later appointed Vice-Chairman of the Trust and it looks as if the National Lottery Heritage Fund will provide the millions of pounds necessary to restore it completely and make it both a great visitor attraction, and a worthy monument to the many hundreds of thousands of Scottish miners and their hard hard work over eight hundred years.

Newtongrange Mining Village

The significance of Lady Victoria Colliery was enhanced by its large village of Newtongrange. The earliest houses were being demolished by the National Coal Board as they became empty under the terms of their 99 year lease. The Regional Council was loath to see the waste of these 900 good houses, and so with part of my departmental Heritage Fund I arranged with the Lothian Estates to acquire the land and properties at 127-31 Fifth Street. The Council took over the four derelict houses from the Coal Board, made them wind and water tight, devised plans and negotiated grants for their modernisation, and sold them on to restoring owners. This example encouraged others, including Lothian Estates, Castle Rock Housing Association and some occupiers, to do likewise, and so the village of Newtongrange was saved and later defined as a conservation area by Midlothian District Council. It is a rare combination of a nineteenth century colliery and colliery village surviving in Europe. It is a fine counterpoint to the glories of Edinburgh's eighteenth century New Town whose wealth was in part founded on the exploitation of the Lothian Coalfield.

Plate LXXIV   Lady Victoria Colliery, Newtongrange

The 1900 pit-head buildings are in the middle of the photograph, below them the vast National Coal Board Area Workshops and across the road, the A7 Edinburgh to Carlisle, the Headquarters of the Lothian Coal Company and what remains of the pit head baths, canteen and laboratories.

Lothian Building Preservation Trust

It was only after I had retired from the Lothian Regional Council on 19 March 1983, that former colleagues asked me to become the Director of the Lothian Building Preservation Trust. This was the first of the regional building preservation trusts to be set up in Scotland and we prepared the first 'Buildings at Risk' register. It was based on the list we had always kept in East Lothian. This was later extended by the Scottish Civic Trust with a grant from Historic Scotland to cover the whole of Scotland.

The cause of the neglect of many of the buildings at risk arose from the attitude of the owners, who were not very responsive and were often very unresponsive to an approach from the local planning authority, but the Trust had more success as we followed up the cases. The other task of a building preservation trust was to act as an agency of last resort restoring buildings which were too far gone to be restored by their owners or private developers.

There were two buildings in East Lothian which I had always wanted to see restored. The South Lodge at Broxmouth Park whose owner, Robert Hope, had not been responsive to my approaches as County Planning Officer, owing to our dispute over the cement works, but he succumbed to the charms of our first chairman, George Russell, WS, OBE. He gave us the property, and a handsome donation after the gateway had been vandalised. It was an attractive two-storey lodge with a pyramidal roof, a high panelled upper room and fine gate piers built in the early eighteenth century. It was important that it should be restored, both because it was very prominent on the southern approach to Dunbar and because its restoration would be a symbol of faith in the eventual restoration of the landscape that was being torn up by the cement works quarry and, further along the coast, by the construction of the nuclear power station.

Bankton House, Prestonpans

The other building was Bankton House at Prestonpans which was burnt out for the second time in 1967. It had been the house of Colonel Gardiner who had died heroically at the Battle of Prestonpans in 1745. It was built about 1720 and designed symmetrically, the south front being the same as the north and both gables very similar. These gables were capped by curly whirly skews and skew-puts after the Dutch manner. It had five floors of which two were in the high slated roof. It had all the virtues of Scottish building, with battered walls for solidity and worked stone only being used for margins, string courses and cornices, the rest being economically built of rubble, lime harled and painted with copperas. The main house was supported either side by a straight thirteen feet high wall ending at the east end with a three storey

Plate LXXV Bankton House, Prestonpans
(a) Before. (b) After Restoration.

This handsome house, built about 1720 and the home of Colonel Gardiner who was mortally wounded within sight of it during the Battle of Prestonpans, 1745, was restored by the Lothian Building Preservation Trust in 1995 by Nicholas Groves-Raines, Architect, and divided into four houses. To the north is old parkland, to the south a newly planted orchard.

house which had vanished and at the opposite, west end, by a tower doocot with a pyramid roof. For twenty-five years it had stood a ruin. Many attempts to interest people in its restoration had all fallen through and so the Trust decided to have one last attempt to restore this beautiful and historic house. It was in full view of the new Tranent Bypass and stood there as a reproach to all of us.

I persuaded the British Coal Board to give the ruined house and fourteen acres surrounding it to the Trust and managed to raise over £760,000 of public money to help finance the restoration. This was completed in July 1995 in time for the two hundred and fiftieth anniversary of the Battle of Prestonpans that September.

In return for all this public funding the Trust created public walks through the parkland and restored the doocot, using its undercroft for a small exhibition on the Life of Colonel Gardiner and the Battle of Prestonpans, told from the point of view of a common soldier. The doocot, containing 834 nesting boxes, has been fitted with a potence and is open to both the pigeons and the public. The land to the south has been planted up as an orchard with 142 fruit trees, mainly varieties of Scottish apple, which is not only an easily maintained landscape feature, but recalls the many commercial orchards which flourished in Prestonpans in previous centuries and were grubbed out for housing schemes.

This quite stunning restoration with its lime harling and lime wash using an admixture of 10% iron sulphate (copperas) to give its glowing pale golden colour, finally completed the transformation of this once terrible area of old collieries and coal washing and storage plant at Meadowmill to be described in Chapter Nine. It makes a contribution to the history of Scottish architecture, and its restoration has had a great influence in raising the local morale of this mining town. The old village of Preston now has a group of four fine houses and a Mercat Cross that show the development of Scottish domestic architecture from the fifteenth century up to the age of William Adam in the first half of the eighteenth century.

8

AGRICULTURE AND FORESTRY

Historic Legacy • Exemption from Planning Control
Tree Preservation Orders • Wartime Experience in Austria
Maintaining Tree Cover • Ancient Woodlands
Control of Afforestation • Dutch Elm Disease
The Need for Planning Control of Forestry
Central Scotland Woodlands Project
Agricultural Initiatives • Food Factories • Open Air-Markets
Whitadder Reservoir 1970 • Megget Reservoir • Pentland Hills

The beauties of the East Lothian countryside arise from the high
standard of its cultivation, from its fine mixed woodlands, from its
mansion houses and their policies, the charm of its small towns and
villages, its rubble and pantile cottages, and from its legacy of interesting
buildings from the past. It has an attractive variety reaching from the
coastline, with its dunes and golf courses, through the rich arable farms
of the coastal plain, to the mixed livestock and arable farming of the
River Tyne Valley and finally to the smooth horizons with the sheep
and grouse moors of the Lammermuir Hills.

Historic Legacy
This beauty is largely due to the efforts of the eighteenth and nineteenth
century landowners and their tenants. It was in that period that the
landscape was formed, the land was drained, fields enclosed with hedges,
tree belts and woodlands planted, and the farm steadings, houses and
cottages built. These farms were then let on nineteen year leases, as
compared with the previous annual lets, thus giving the tenants an
interest in their continued fertility.

The Hopetoun Monument on the Garleton Hills was erected in
memory of the fifth Earl of Hopetoun by his grateful tenantry. It is a
potent reminder of the real gratitude that tenant farmers then felt for
their landlords who had invested so much in the land and provided the
farms on which they could earn a good living. They, in their turn,
developed the art of careful husbandry.

It is a most delightful County in which it was a privilege to work
for twenty-five years. It was often said that I treated the County as if I
was an eighteenth century improving laird and indeed that was a part

I would have been proud to play. But I stated, more realistically, in the Recreation Report 1971, that as there was no modern counterpart for these wealthy eighteenth century landlords, beneficent changes could only result from the fruitful co-operation between the local authority, the landowners and entrepreneurs.

Exemption from Planning Control

The Town and Country Planning (Scotland) Act 1947 made little direct provision for country planning except that planning was not limited to towns and their peripheral area, as in earlier Acts. It was to embrace the whole County even though the countryside tended to be treated as a residual area to the towns. Agriculture and forestry were 'permitted development' and so planning consent was not required for agricultural land use changes or for the erection of buildings, as was required of urban developers. We therefore rarely saw farmers in the planning office and socially they kept themselves very much to themselves.

Tree Preservation Orders

Planners had more contact with foresters who consulted us informally and, gradually over the years, more formally. We also had the power to intervene by making Tree Preservation Orders. These are absurdly misnamed as one cannot preserve a tree, but they did require the owners to apply for consent from the County Council if they wanted to fell, lop or trim the trees in order that the public interest, in retaining or replacing them, could be considered. It was the usual practice to make these orders only when the trees were under threat but this always led to conflict. The County Council made nineteen tree preservation orders with twelve more pending as part of our study of each settlement, well before any question of their felling arose. This early action enabled agreement to be reached on the trees and woods which were of such importance that the County Council should be consulted on their management. Landlords were concerned about their liability should trees, subject to a preservation order, fall and cause damage, so the County Council undertook to inspect the trees regularly. This would exonerate landlords from claims, which had to be based on negligence.

The Council itself owned various woodlands, which it fell to me to supervise, and so we began to understand the ways of the forester. The County Council employed Mr Butt of Scottish Woodland Owners to manage their woodland and carry out our planting schemes. In the early days, we had much difficulty in persuading Mr Butt to give more weight to amenity rather than commercial values and there is still this element of conflict in a forester's mind.

Wartime Experience in Austria

Foresters were always welcome in the planning office and I had a high regard for them from my experience at the end of the war. I was commanding "B" Company of the 5th Northamptonshire Regiment in the closing stages of the Italian Campaign. The day after VE Day we were suddenly ordered to commandeer vehicles and to get up over the Dolomites into Austria as fast as possible to race the Soviet army coming down from the north-east and the American army moving in from the north-west. What a journey, without maps or any other support, but we made it and captured the bulk of the German army marching home from the Balkans in the Tamsweg valley, 50 miles north of Klagenfurt. As the Germans crossed a hump-backed bridge we made them dump all their small arms in the river and then opened the field gates on the south side of the road, one after another, and shepherded them in. At the end of the day we had 20,000 prisoners—all the 'odds and sods',as we called them, of the German army—the construction companies, communication workers, Luftwaffe personnel, dental corps, press corps, etc. "C" Company had a whole SS division in an adjoining valley. Being Germans, they soon organised themselves and we sent them into Italy to salvage their lorries and bring back rations from their abandoned dumps. They provided me with an encampment of six command vehicles and a Luftwaffe staff of interpreters and secretaries. They did not have much tentage and they had to make what shelters they could in the fields in the rather chilly month of May. They had soon stripped the local sawmills and were cutting trees from the forests on the hillside to make dug outs and shelters. About the fifth day of this organised chaos a small man, very smart in his breeks, green tweed jacket and hat with a cockade of feathers in its ribbon, came into my headquarters, clicked his heels, saluted smartly and announced that he represented the Royal Austrian Forestry Service, the oldest in Europe, and that the indiscriminate felling of state trees had to stop. I agreed with him but asked him how he proposed that this should be done, as I was well aware that it was quite beyond the power of my company of some 110 men. He said that he would mark out a cutting zone where the Germans could cut trees, but nowhere else. This was eminently sensible and it worked out well. I was greatly impressed that it was a forester, not a burgomaster, sawmiller, farmer or state functionary who had first raised his voice in protest. It was a forester, with a concern for his forest and a long-term plan for its management, that had the courage to take on this formidable mass of military people. I often saw the same concern in the foresters who came into my office.

Maintaining Tree Cover

Both farmers and foresters work to different agendas, more influenced by national policies on subsidies and grants than by land use considerations. It was, however, national and county policy that agricultural land should not be used for other purposes and that the existing tree cover should be maintained. It was the County Council who enforced this policy, as both the Department of Agriculture and the Forestry Commission officers were too ready to make exceptions on behalf of 'their customers'. Farmers were always wanting to sell off bits of their fields for housing, and the landlords were wanting to fell and grub out shelter belts to increase their arable acreage, which the County Council resisted with only partial success.

A celebrated victory occurred over Blinkbonny Wood by Gladsmuir, after I had left the County. It was a rather neglected wood owned by the Forestry Commission, part of which I had identified as an overnight camping site off the A1, and one of our tourist development proposals. The purchaser, after selling the Norway Spruce as Christmas trees, wanted to grub out the remainder and use it for more cultivation. The granting of a felling licence was objected to by the District Council and eventually upheld by the Secretary of State. The wood remains, partly in the ownership of the Woodland Trust and partly of the District Council, although its use as an overnight camp has not yet materialised.

Ancient Woodlands

East Lothian has two of the earliest hardwood plantations in Scotland dating from the seventeenth century, which I considered of equal significance to buildings of that date. They should not be felled to make way for plantations of quick growing coniferous trees, which were all the fashion. These magnificent old oaks and beeches were of little timber value but had resulted in a rich community of plants and had great scenic and psychological value. This argument is now accepted at national level and the Scottish Natural Heritage is charged with defining these ancient semi-natural woodlands and the Forestry Authority in safeguarding them.

It all started one day in May 1970 when the County Council served a Tree Preservation Order on Yester Old Woods which contained magnificent old beeches, one of which was the tallest in Britain. It proved to be a long tussle with Tillhill Forestry and in the end the County Council was persuaded to withdraw the Tree Preservation Order in favour of a Management Plan, on which it was to be consulted every five years. The other case was Gilmerton Old Wood by Athelstaneford. Mr Goodenough, a forest officer from the Commission, reminded me recently that I had argued that the large oaks there should not be felled but allowed to die gracefully amongst their offspring naturally regenerating around them. And so it has been.

Plate LXXVI   Yester Woods
Yester MansionHouse is at the top of the photograph with its walled garden and stable
block to the right. The private avenue can also be clearly seen. The Woods which
surround it still contain some of the earliest planted trees in Scotland.

Control of Afforestation

A more difficult decision was the question of afforestation in the
Lammermuir Hills where the value of their heather for grouse shooting
and sheep grazing saved the beauty of their soft contours from
afforestation and we managed to keep planting off the skyline. The
Hopes Reservoir catchment area was also one of the areas saved from
afforestation, although we advocated planting in the eroding gullies.

To follow up these efforts, I wrote an article for the Town Planning
Institute Journal advocating that afforestation should be subject to
planning control. I argued that it created similar problems to
urbanisation and that it could be controlled by similar techniques.
Afforestation usually presented a conflict with other land uses such as
nature conservancy, access, archaeological value and landscape interest.
It broke up the social and economic integrity of hill land where the
farmers depend on one another. A full grown wood is as large an element

in the landscape as a two storey housing scheme. It has similar, though lesser, demands on infrastructure—roads, drainage, fire fighting and often housing. It also has a harmful effect on water catchments, first causing flooding and later reducing the run-off. It can be controlled by the usual planning techniques—zoning, leaving areas unplanted, varying the density of the planting, selecting different types of trees to obtain variations in the colour and height, stipulating conditions for public access, and the safeguarding of monuments and other natural features. The counter argument was that planners were not qualified to exercise this control. That is now less and less true as many authorities employ foresters and landscape architects and more would be recruited if this duty was placed on them.

Dutch Elm Disease

The competence of planners was not questioned when it came to controlling Dutch Elm disease. As this hit Scotland the Forestry Authority turned to the Regional Planning Authorities to control its spread and limit the movement of felled trees. By that time, I was with the Lothian Regional Council and luckily had won the staffing battle to have an ecologist on my staff—Dr John Sheldon. As the City of Edinburgh's Director of Planning said he had no staff to control the spread of the disease and some 70% of the trees in the City were elms, I persuaded the Regional Council to take on the responsibility in the City and the Edinburgh Green Belt, rather than have a devastated City. We instituted an annual inspection of all the elms in July/August when we employed university undergraduates and drew up a map showing every elm tree in the City. The owners of diseased trees were asked to fell them over the winter and we gave them names of suitable contractors. If the trees were not felled and burnt by March we served a statutory notice and sent in contractors to fell them, charging the owners. In this way we limited the disease, which could not be eliminated, to 2% or 3% of the elms per year. Edinburgh must be the only city in Britain that still has plenty of these magnificent trees. I regret that East Lothian could not be included in these arrangements and its landscape is still disfigured by dead or dying elms.

The Need for Planning Control of Forestry

The case for planning control over afforestation seems to me to be unanswerable but has not been strongly supported by others. Scottish Natural Heritage pays out large sums of compensation under the Wildlife Acts to control it when it affects sites of special scientific interest, which would not be necessary under the Planning Acts under which no compensation is paid for refusal. However the forestry interests are gradually putting their house in order, employing their own landscape architects, instituting consultation procedures and formulating codes of practice which are resulting in more congenial and beautiful forests. Regional planners in Scotland have, as part of their structure plans, evolved indicative forestry zones where afforestation should and should not take place, and have assessed the amount necessary to support a viable forestry industry. In the former Lothian Region the restricted areas were the Lammermuirs, Moorfoots and northern Pentlands while Central Scotland was the preferred area for planting.

Plate LXXVII   Central Scotland Woodlands Project

The cover of the feasibility study which initiated this project in 1978, fifteen years before similar projects in England. It starts with the words "The Study draws attention to the distressed condition of the central part of lowland Scotland". It concludes "that these unsatisfactory conditions need not and should not persist"and that "the means of change are seen to be the extension of woodland planting". The steering group for the study was led by Dr John Sheldon and the cover was drawn by Dr Eamon Hyde, both of my staff in the Lothian Regional Council.

CENTRAL SCOTLAND WOODLANDS PROJECT

Central Scotland Woodlands Project

To implement this I established the Central Scotland Woodlands Project in 1978 in association with Strathclyde and Central Regional Councils, seven District Councils, the Forestry Commission, the agricultural advisory services and the landowners' associations. It covers an area of 640 square miles, high and bleak, separating Edinburgh and Glasgow, and houses some 50,000 people who had worked in the abandoned mines. The objectives were to make the area more congenial as a place to live and to improve the environment as a spur for the attraction of alternative employment. It would do something to lessen the separation of the two big cities and would utilise low-grade land unsuited for agriculture. It was a low-cost initiative with a team of four people identifying planting opportunities mainly on publicly-owned land and getting it planted up. I was honoured in 1984 to be asked to plant the five millionth tree at Harthill. That is not a vast number by forestry standards but when spread over five hundred sites they will be making a substantial impact when well grown. This initiative preceded by a decade the similar initiatives for central English forests. I would like to pay a special tribute to the support given to me on this project by John Davies, the Forestry Conservator for South Scotland, without whom this initiative would not have taken place. I am glad that it continues.

Agricultural Initiatives

Agricultural landuse is entirely outside the planning system and is greatly dependent on the various subsidies provided by the Government to stimulate the production of food. During my time this resulted in more and more land going into cereal crops and less and less people being employed on it. This was a far cry from the previous century when landowners and farmers delighted in creating employment. There was little the County Council as local planning authority could do to aid the agricultural industry and the Department of Agriculture officials were resentful of any interference. But there were several matters that the farming community could not resolve by themselves, and which I remember trying to tackle with but little success.

The first was the water deficiency in the spring when transpiration usually exceeded rainfall and crops such as potatoes and soft fruit suffered. Farmers resorted to irrigation by pumping from the water courses, until stopped by the River Purification Board which required a minimum flow in the rivers and streams. I floated the idea of supplying public 'off-peak' water from the hill reservoirs which overflowed during the winter to a new reservoir north of the Garleton Hills where it could be distributed by the two Peffer Burns that flow west to Aberlady Bay and east to Ravensheugh Sands. The East Lothian Water Board, which was controlled by the County Council, maintained they had no power to do this as they were only authorised to supply domestic and industrial users, despite the fact that they supplied golf courses during the summer months! They also raised a technical problem that they could not have purified and unpurified water flowing through the same pipes. There was also remarkably little enthusiasm from the farming community, who would have had to enter into co-operative organisational and financial arrangements which were beyond them. They preferred to construct their own inadequate farm reservoirs or sink poor-yielding boreholes. This was a non-starter.

Food Factories

The assistance that the County Council as local planning authority could give to the agricultural industry was on the processing and marketing front. Here we tried a number of initiatives.

When the sugar beet factory at Cupar closed the industry had a problem in finding a 'break-crop', once the old crop rotations had broken

Plate LXXVIII Pencaitland Maltings

This is one of the largest maltings in Europe and shows the evolution of silo design from the original concrete ones to the horizontal shed in the trees to the left and the latest, the circular metal type. The County Council assumed responsibility for the trees which had failed when originally planted as they were eaten by rats!

down under the pressure to grow more cereals year after year. The solution in the 1960s seemed to be to grow peas and other vegetables for the frozen food market and here the County Council could have helped with its powers to provide factories. Discussions with farmers showed that those already growing vegetables were too wedded to selling in the fresh market to be interested in a new venture. A freezing plant was eventually established at Eyemouth to tap farmers in the Borders with no previous experience of growing vegetables and some East Lothian farmers joined in, but they had to be within half-an-hour's lorry drive to Eyemouth. It was initially run on a co-operative basis but eventually went over to the private sector. The County Council, reluctantly, decided that it could not build a factory for an Aberlady farmer to supply peeled potatoes for the restaurant trade due to its strong and harmful effluent which, before the coastal trunk sewer was constructed, would have gone direct into the Forth. Eventually the plant was built at Bo'ness and has flourished there, using East Lothian potatoes.

Another deficiency was a lack of animals on the farms which had always been traditional in East Lothian crop rotations, with cattle over wintered in cattle courts and their dung used to fertilise the fields. The two local slaughterhouses, run by the Town Councils of Haddington and North Berwick, and many small private slaughterhouses had been closed under the Public Health Acts and so a feasibility study was carried out by the County Sanitary Inspector, Jimmie Gibson, into the possibility of building a central slaughterhouse in Haddington to provide for both the local butchers and to revive the export trade that had flourished in Haddington before the Second World War. Again this was a non-starter.

One that did succeed was the establishment of a major maltings at Pencaitland. This was nearly lost to the County when the quite unsuitable site at the west end of Haddington, which William Baird of Glasgow had chosen without any prior consultation with us, was refused planning consent. But I managed to find the firm an alternative site at Pencaitland. It needed a good-yielding borehole to supply water at a constant temperature and the easy disposal of the effluent from their treatment plant. We thought they needed rail access, as they were malting imported as well as local barley. That is the explanation for the siting of the maltings on the high ground up against the railway line, which it was hoped, their traffic might save, but it was closed nevertheless. The maltings is now one of the largest in Britain producing malt to twenty-six different specifications for distilleries and breweries throughout Scotland.

Open-Air Markets

On a smaller scale we thought that the establishment of an open-air market in Haddington would not only have provided a market for small-holders and other fruit and vegetable growers and widened the range of vegetables available to the public, but would have enlivened the County Town. So when the County Council received the standard objection from the Association of Market Traders objecting to the County Development Plan making no provision for markets I went to Sheffield to discuss the practicality with their Secretary, who had an office over a pawnbroker's shop. He was flattered that a county planning officer had taken his routine objection seriously, but had to admit that open-air markets depended mainly on the clothing trade and his members would not travel to Scotland from their bases in the Manchester area, because they could not get there and back in a day. My experience of thriving markets in County Durham confirmed that, without this solid core of clothiers, a market would not attract sufficient custom to make it worthwhile for farmers and others to attend. The recent spread of open-air markets in Scotland is largely the result of the improvement in motorways and trunk roads. A thriving Sunday market was established on the disused East Fortune airfield in the 1970s, but Haddington retains its Sunday calm. It was also planning policy to encourage produce stalls along the Haddington-Pencaitland road for the sale of the soft fruit crop, but this has declined as the small-holdings were amalgamated and ceased to grow soft fruit.

Plate LXXIX Whiteadder Reservoir

A view from the north east showing the plantations which both sheltered Priestlaw farm and its in-bye grazing land, and transformed this large puddle of drinking water into a lake, as I put it. We designed a fishermen's cabin and jetty for their boats at the south end, and alders and willows were planted to provide for the fish. Landscape Architect: Dennis Thornley.

Whiteadder Reservoir 1970

My only opportunity to intervene on the supply side of agriculture occurred with the planning of the Whiteadder Reservoir in the Lammermuirs Hills which was the pet project of Thomas Gibb, the County Clerk. He was also the Clerk of the East Lothian Water Board and always dealt with their correspondence before dealing with County Council papers. I remember asking him once what was his greatest ambition for the County and his reply was to have every house in the County connected to the public water supply. He fell somewhat short of achieving this target, but it was not for want of stretching the economic criteria, for which I greatly admired him, and helped him make the case from our population projections. This is not likely to be the objective of the regionalised water boards in Scotland or the privatised boards in England and Wales.

The Whiteadder Reservoir required a Special Parliamentary Order and, as was the custom, included only the very minimum land required for the reservoir and what I called 'spitting distance' around it to prevent direct pollution. After the Water Board had acquired their land they had to get planning approval. The County Clerk thought this was a foregone conclusion, but I thought it was a good opportunity to do some catchment area transformation. The reservoir was taking the low ground, essential for wintering stock from two hill farms, and there was a good economic case for acquiring both farms, amalgamating what remained of the lower ground, resiting the farm buildings, and planting forestry blocks and shelter belts to improve the remainder of the land. The Clerk to the Board was staggered when he learnt, late in the day, that the cost for the accommodation works and building a new bridge and road into Priestlaw exceeded the value of the land by five times. My proposals then gained credibility, but it was too late to change. I think the Clerk to the Water Board regretted proceeding to the Order without first having gained planning consent from the Clerk to the County Council.

All I managed to achieve was the transformation of the reservoir into a lake with tree planting and proper facilities for fishing, not merely a very large puddle of drinking water with a dirty rim as the water level went up and down. Dennis Thornley, the landscape architect, was employed by the water engineers, Hill and Sons, both from Manchester, and a very sensitive job he made of it. However, he left me to fight for the heather finish to the dam face. The engineers were insisting on sowing grass across the steep face of the dam, which would have shown up as an unnatural green curtain, between the two heather-covered sides of the valley at the Hungry Snout. I considered they should be sown with a mixture of grass and heather knowing that eventually the heather would prevail. But there was no heather seed available commercially except for exotic garden heathers and so I persuaded Mr Mills, a retired Haddington seed merchant, to gather seed from the hillsides for us. Its germination was rather poor, but rather than give up, I insisted that divots of heather were dug from the hillsides and planted across the face of the dam to comply with the planning condition. Unfortunately the contractors went bankrupt before this was finished and it was left to time and nature to achieve a full heather face. Other minor successes were the achievement of a properly designed fishermen's cabin and jetty for the boats, and the elimination of all the "Egyptian" precast stonework on the buildings, which was the hallmark of the Manchester School of Water Engineers.

The Megget Reservoir

A similar problem faced me at the Lothian Region as vast sums of money had to be spent on accommodation works to rebuild all the farmhouses higher up the hill to make way for the Megget Reservoir but again, I was too late as the property deal had been done. Nonetheless I managed to persuade the Water and Drainage Committee to appoint a landscape architect to transform it into a lake and to provide proper facilities for the visiting public. Bill Cairns, the landscape architect, entered this reservoir for the first BBC Design Award and, to our astonishment, it was voted top project by the viewers. Few of them will ever make the trek to the Border hills to find it, but they just liked the idea of a water reservoir being done properly and on a large scale, in preference to the many other entries such as kitchen gadgets, a midget excavator and I forget what else.

Pentland Hills

The Lothian Regional Council designated the Pentland Hills as a Regional Park in 1986. This proposal had a long history, based on Robert Louis Stevenson's description of them as 'the hills of home'. The City of Edinburgh, together with Midlothian and West Lothian County Councils had made little progress with it, except for the creation of an artificial ski-slope at Hillend. It needed the strength provided by the Regional Council to carry it through. The Council then secured the agreement of the Army to give up their rifle range at Dreghorn, but we lost the public inquiry to turn them out of their Castlelaw range, although we ensured that they employed a landscape architect to modify their plans.

My objective was to give the Council an active part in the management of the land uses in the Pentland Hills. They were much loved and much used by the people of the region, but their landscape was visibly deteriorating through lack of investment and overgrazing. The Council gave the Regional Park a small annual budget to repair the dykes, replant and manage the woodlands and improve the path system. It established a ranger service, provided car parks and reception areas for information and developed nature reserves. Because of this recreational element it was put under the control of the Director of Leisure Services. I was horrified to find that the rangers spent most of their time escorting school parties on the northern slopes and were not known to the farmers and landowners, and so failing in the positive land-use objectives of the Regional Park. These could only be realised through persuasion and grant-aid to the landowners and through demonstration on the publicly owned land.

It was my ultimate objective that the Regional Council should increase their ownership by acquiring farms as they came onto the market and then re-letting them subject to conditions concerning land uses, animal grazing capacity, the limitation of muirburn and the reintroduction of traditional mixed-farming practices. We had seen such leases working very successfully in the Dutch Texel islands where such restrictive leases fetched on average some eighty-five per cent of the open market values. In this way the Regional Council could have played a major part in ensuring that the landscape values that so endeared the Hills to the region's population were enhanced.

To sum up, I confess that there is little to show from these interventions into farming and forestry, but I do believe that they demonstrate that there is a future role for planning authorities in the fundamental economy of the countryside. Although I would not go as far as Sir George Taylor, who retired from being the Keeper of the Royal Botanic Gardens at Kew to live in Belhaven House, Dunbar. He held me responsible, as County Planning Officer, for the hybridisation of primroses and cowslips along the North Berwick coast, which he deplored.

9

ENVIRONMENTAL IMPROVEMENT

Wartime Coastal Defences • Woodhall Bing
Prestongrange Motor Sports • Meadowmill, Prestonpans
Other Environmental Improvements in East Lothian
My Lothian Region Land Reclamation Unit.

The Town and Country Planning Acts gave local authorities the power to tackle wasteland and remove eyesores. By the 1970s, Government grants were made available to encourage them to do this. The main push came after the reform of local government in 1975 when the Scottish Development Agency undertook the full cost, and I set up a special team in the Lothian Regional Council to carry out an annual million pound programme of land renewal, as it came to be called. But this had been preceded by many small projects in East Lothian.

Wartime Coastal Defences

One of the earliest tasks was to remove the unsightly, and often dangerous, defences left from the Second World War. The wide beaches had been protected against invasion by double, sometimes triple, rows of concrete blocks at the dune foot. An ingenious system had been worked out by the Wemyss Landed Estate whereby every tenth block along Gosford Bay had been toppled seaward and the adjoining blocks toppled sideways into the holes each left. This removed them from view along the road, but it had the great disadvantage of disturbing the vegetation on the dunes and leaving a solid block of concrete in the dune, upsetting the water table and inhibiting the regrowth of dune grasses. Once exposed by the wind and waves, the sand eroded ever more quickly between the blocks, which were once more revealed. These now lay at all angles and were far more dangerous than in their original position, where they at least had some sort of foundation. There were many people who advocated lining these blocks up along the toe of the dunes to protect them from wave erosion. That would have been most unsightly and the waves would have scoured round and under each block while the grass, the natural protection of the dunes, would never have grown. Removal was the only sensible course and the money was available from the Scottish Office under the Compensation for War Damage Acts, but only for blocks considered to

Plate LXXX   Defence Blocks, Ferny Ness

A group of defence blocks solidly founded on rock left at Ferny Ness Point as a reminder of the folly of war. Behind the blocks is a mature stand of Sea Buckthorn—photographed in October with its orange berries just ripening.

be dangerous. Each winter I solemnly walked the coastline with Mr Shiels of the Scottish Office Water and Drainage Directorate marking these dangerous blocks. After several years, he insisted that we map all the blocks as he was beginning to think that he was paying twice for the same block, as well he might have been. Approval having been obtained, we let small contracts for their removal, either intact or broken up with explosives. This latter course was by no means easy, because we found that the wartime contractors had profiteered by casting old petrol cans and drums into some of the blocks to save concrete. A heaven-sent opportunity occurred to get two thousand blocks away to armour the steel caisson wall at Cockenzie Power Station, but the South of Scotland Electricity Board required us to deliver them to the site. We used four hundred to build up the land between Port Seton harbour and the swimming pool to make a fairground. These were founded on rock, arranged stretcher bond style, and have stood the test of time. It was also the time when tower cranes started to be used on building sites and we found contractors helping themselves to the blocks most easily reached from the roadside to act as counterweights. Some groups of blocks were left where they were sited on rocky headlands such as Ferny Ness and Hummel Point at Gullane as memorials to the folly and extravagance of war. Along the eastern edge of Aberlady Nature Reserve every hundredth block was left to mark the boundary of the Reserve.

As well as the concrete defence blocks, an array of wooden poles had been cemented into the broad flat beaches to prevent enemy aircraft or gliders landing. These were only unsightly stumps by the time I arrived, but caused injuries to bathers and accidents to canoeists and sand yachts, so we dug them out.

In the dunes themselves there were masses of rusting barbed wire defences. Those around the gun positions at Archerfield were removed by two International Conservation Work Parties, led by Swedes but including German youths, who all camped at Yellowcraig. That involved quite a lot of time and effort as we had to supply tents, food, transport and some entertainment. On their departure I inherited six attractive black and white kittens which had been found in a nest in the dunes, one of which, Keeling, Danish for kitten, became our house cat. I also received a complaint from Mr Reid, the local Councillor, that a volunteer had absconded with a shot gun that he had kindly lent them to shoot rabbits to vary their tinned rations. We never traced the rascal, a Londoner, so Mr Reid never got his gun back, which was a shame as the Councillor had done a lot to make their stay in his parish enjoyable as well as useful.

These were the programmes that occupied us in the early years. By the late 1960s it was the dereliction left by the National Coal Board, as they closed their collieries, which worried us and the County Council was stirred into action by the offer of 75% Government grant. The Scottish Development Department, under the persuasion of Professor Sir Robert Grieve, had at last realised that the economic regeneration of Scotland by new industries would never happen in a landscape dominated by pit bings, derelict land and dreary towns, the remains of the old extractive industries. Maurice Taylor, the County Planning Officer of Fife, had pioneered this environmental recovery and shown how successful it could be in attracting industrialists who were then on the move, due to the constraints imposed by the Labour Government on employment expansion in south-east England.

Woodhall Bing

It was on the Woodhall Bing, west of Pencaitland, where we got our first experience. It had been burning at the time of the 1940s blackout and the colliery had closed, largely because it was merely stoking up the bing as a beacon for enemy aircraft on the way to the Forth Bridge. The bing had been acquired by the Forestry Commission and there was a piggery using the old colliery buildings, as was frequently the

Plate LXXXI   Woodhall Bing, Pencaitland

Scene during the operations of spreading fine material over the burnt stone from the colliery. This was later contour ploughed and planted with trees and fertilised with sewage sludge. The trees in the background screen the bing from the west. In the Lothian Regional Council we trained up several young engineers as Landscape Engineers skilled in these massive operations.

case on old mine sites. The Forestry Commission had never done anything with the bing and were only too pleased to sell it on to the County Council. The pig farmer reluctantly sold some years later.

The bing consisted of two elements: a large conical heap eighty feet high, which was still burning, behind a belt of trees on the west, and a four acre slurry pond to the south into which fine residues from the washery had been settled—tweny-two acres in all. The coal slurry had been dug out from the pond and exported to power stations in Denmark, although one ship sank crossing the North Sea when this very fine, almost fluid, material shifted in the ship's hold. When we acquired the bing, the slurry pond was empty and it was a classic case of putting heaps into holes. The trouble was that the heap was so hot that it melted the fuel pipes and other less robust parts on the bulldozers as they worked amidst great clouds of dust. The heap filled the hole and left a fine south facing slope. There was no soil available on the site, so it was decided to plough the surface material and plant it with trees. I persuaded the County Sanitary Inspector to run his sludge

Plate LXXXII Woodhall Woodland

The woodland 20 years on, after its first thinning and inter planting with oaks. It has made a grand recreational woodland amidst the cultivated land all about it, with access along the Pencaitland railway walk from Ormiston and Pencaitland as well as a picnic site for those travelling by car.

lorries onto the bing and pump the wet domestic sludge into the ploughed furrows which ran along the contours. A good mixture of trees—alders, birches and Scots pines—were planted along the upturned material from the furrow, just as in an afforestation scheme. The tree growth was phenomenal as was the crop of puffballs. This was investigated by Edinburgh University Department of Forestry who discovered that the beneficial effect of mycorrhizal fungi which fastened onto the roots of the trees, enabled them to take up more moisture, phosphate and nitrogen from the sludge on this barren material.

I was under no illusion that the forestry would ever be economic, but such was the cost to the public purse of the engineering works, £3,600 an acre, that I considered it should become a public recreational wood, rather than be grassed down and sold off for scruffy grazing as was happening in Fife. As well as trees, we also planted brambles and hazels to provide a source of "food for free". We laid out car parking bays, both shady among the old trees to the west, and sunny on the bing itself to the north. 'Just courting trouble' I was told, but I replied that it was a good and useful thing to provide secluded accommodation for courting couples. A tree house was also constructed and a slide for children, but even the best attention from the County Ranger could not keep those, or the honesty box for car parking dues, safe from vandalism. It was signposted as a picnic site but so unusual and so novel was the standard sign then that it was twice removed by collectors of these items. However the third replacement has stayed put. I visited the site recently after the woodland had been thinned and it is quite delightful as a recreational wood with glades and pathways running through it. But the sign of the barren hot spot at the very core of the bing is still there for those who know its history.

The Glencairn Colliery outside Longniddry was a small four acre site already made unsightly by car breaking. It led us to evolve a number of schemes which created basin-like hollows within which car breaking and other unsightly trades could be carried out unseen, behind surrounding tree-planted bunds.

Prestongrange Motor Sports

We also spent a considerable time seeing whether we could use derelict land sites to accommodate the growing demand for motor sports, which was beginning to cause trouble in the open countryside. The use of old colliery sites seemed, on the face of it, ideal for motor cycle scrambles and stock car racing with their well drained land and plenty of material to create the necessary hazards, dirt tracks and viewing ramps. The large coastal bing at Prestongrange seemed a good location and as the Edinburgh Speedway was being turned out of Meadowbank so that it could be rebuilt as the stadium for the Commonwealth Games we had a lot of discussions with their directors. In this we were encouraged by Katie Dawson, an attractive assistant County Clerk, who had some experience of motor sports. She later left fot the National Trust and then became Attorney General in Gibraltar. However nothing came of our efforts as nobody was prepared to put up the money to build the necessary facilities or to control a free-for-all sport for anything more powerful than pedal cycles. It was a hazard too novel for the County Council to get involved in.

Meadowmill, Prestonpans

The most dramatic of our schemes was at Meadowmill where forty acres of the utmost dereliction disfigured Prestonpans and marred the main road to Gullane and North Berwick. The main feature was the two-horned bing left by the Edinburgh Coal Company, who had had a central coal washery on this site. It was composed of the very fine waste from the washery. The rails and mechanism for tippling the hutches and the corrugated iron shelter for the 'boy' who had the miserable job of overseeing the operation, were still in place at the top when I first saw it. This was a common sight in County Durham. To the east was a disused coal stacking area crossed by rail sidings, one of which was the branch line round the east side of Tranent going to Fleets Colliery and another to the west going up the Tranent Coal Heugh. There was also a drift mine, a shallow angled shaft driven into the upper seams of coal that lay to the east and have now been worked by the open-cast method at Blindwells. To the west were the remains of Bankton Colliery, a 1920s sinking which had caused a great deal of surface subsidence and shattered the garden walls of Bankton House. The other main feature of the area was the flooding that occurred when the inland collieries stopped pumping water. This rose in the mines and then drained through old workings down to Meadowmill.

For centuries previously, the land had been the impassable marshy area which determined the course of the Battle of Prestonpans, in 1745. To prevent this water flooding the mainline railway, the National Coal Board had laid two large concrete pipes down the east side of the Prestonlinks Colliery mineral railway which discharged into the sea. Although these safeguarded the railway they did not adequately drain the site. There was also a further complication in that the fifty thousand tons of material in the two-horned bing had been sold to the Scottish Brick Company, along with many other similar bings in the Lothians. They had the right to work it at five pence a ton to make their rather inferior colliery bricks. At that time these were universally used for house building, and so the houses had to be harled to keep the bricks from spalling and to improve their appearance. Hence the vast estates of grey cement rendered houses which were characteristic of Scottish council house building from the 1920s to the 1980s. Private houses were dry dashed with Dorset pea or other small aggregate.

All in all it was a formidable combination of problems, but as luck would have it, a young engineer, George McNeil, a Musselburgh lad who had obtained a planning degree at Edinburgh University, applied to me for his first job. Subsequently he became Director of Planning for West Lothian District Council where he established a great reputation as a creative planner who would find a solution to the most intractable problems and yet had a strong historical and aesthetic sensibility. On the other hand, we had a landscape architect whose idea of rehabilitation was to return everything to nature with rounded natural looking forms. She constituted a great drag on the job until she left. A nice long ridge covered with straggly burnt-out grass was the last thing that was wanted and would have destroyed the physical features of the Battlefield of Prestonpans. What was needed were additional football pitches and here was the opportunity to provide them in a central position between Prestonpans and Tranent. It went some way to achieving Sir Frank Mears' idea of uniting these small mining communities into a social constellation which revolved round central facilities that none could afford on their own.

It was also a time when a group of local athletes were breaking world sprint records although debarred from the Olympics because they were considered to be professionals. I never really understood the position, having been brought up to think of Jesse Owens as the fastest man on earth, but these local boys won professional races in Australia and Europe and were local heroes. It would be making the most of their endeavours if there were local facilities which up and coming sprinters could use. The well-drained substratum, which could be provided by colliery waste, was essential to any running track.

The Scottish Brick Company was unwilling to allow their material to be spread over the large coal stacking area, thus complicating its recovery if it ever had to be used for brick making. There was a further factor in that the three pylon lines coming south from Cockenzie had turned a right angle to avoid the two-horned bing and this curious change of direction could never be explained if the bing had been totally flattened. Thus the present scheme was evolved with much of the ugly two-horned bing being transformed into the 'handsome green pyramid', and the remainder used to create an arena to the west utilising the lower slopes of the pyramid. A number of playing pitches were laid out and enhanced with a broom bank screen to the railway and an open view over the Edinburgh Green Belt to the Pentland Hills in the west. The Green Belt has recently been extended to include this now green but once grey, grey area through which the Tranent Bypass, the new Great North Road, passes.

I am glad to say that all this new landscape was in place before the road was built. The northern foot of the pyramid was planted with trees once the bing had been taken back, to prevent it slipping onto the railway as this danger had been highlighted by the Aberfan disaster. One disappointment was that the pyramid had to have a lower profile than the famous stone-built ones of Egypt as the material was so fine. Another was that grass overtook the coloured clovers which were planted on each face of the pyramid: yellow bird's foot trefoil (eggs and bacon) on the east face; white clover to the west; and red clover to the north. This was ecologically correct and if it had succeeded their roots would have produced the necessary nitrogen to sustain their growth. The south side was sown with grass as it was here that an artificial ski

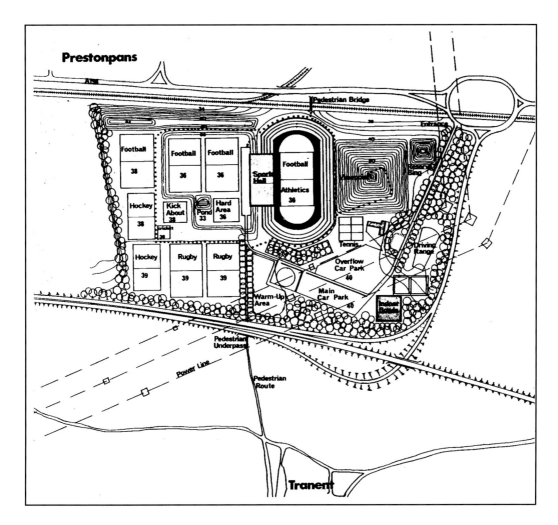

Plate LXXXIII   Meadowmill Sports Centre, Prestonpans

Our proposal drawing for the large central playing fields on the site of appalling dereliction left by the mining industry. The pitheap shaped into an attractive green pyramid which the locals thought would be a suitable burial tomb for their County Planning Officer. The sports hall was not placed centrally nor was the free flow junction provided initially for the North Berwick traffic, just miserable wee roundabouts.

slope for beginners was laid out to replace the somewhat hazardous runs that youngsters had developed with metal trays on the old bing. The summit was surmounted by a welded steel framework on which display boards were placed, some fifteen years later, to show the course of the Battle of Prestonpans. In the interval, they provided a wonderful objective for "Battles" between the youths of Tranent and Prestonpans.

In 1995 it provided the site for the celebration of the 250th Anniversary of the Battle of Prestonpans and it all looked very handsome with the restored Bankton House in the background.

There is a current concern that the flooding may once again occur when the Blindwells open-cast site is back-filled. However our reclamation works involved very thorough site drainage and leading the water away through a large rock-filled soakaway before discharging into the National Coal Board's concrete pipes under the railway. This should trap the silt that previously was building up in these pipes, and once they are cleared along their length to the sea outfall at Preston Links should prevent any flooding. As a result of this and other works the playing fields are wonderfully well drained and have never suffered from the impaction and ponding of so many reclaimed sites. They have now been supplemented by changing pavilions, a Sports Centre and indoor bowls rink, all helping to unite the three communities.

Other Environmental Improvements in East Lothian
While I was still with East Lothian we undertook many smaller grant-aided environmental improvement schemes. Among these were improvements with grass and paint round Cockenzie and Dunbar Harbours, the floodlighting of Aberlady and Whitekirk churches, and the clearing and regrading of the footpath of the old historic railway up the Coal Heugh in Tranent, although I never achieved the laying out of a geological transect of the coal seams and rocks of the Lothian Coalfield which I wanted to incorporate along the new footpath. The old mill

Plate LXXXIV   The 250th Anniversary of the Battle of Prestonpans

The Battle was fought over this land in 1745. The access road is on the line of the first railway in Scotland, constructed in 1722. Traces of it can still be seen between the dykes in the fields to the north. It was therefore a fitting place to hold the anniversary celebrations of the Battle with 'troops' from Captain Loudon's regiment. The course of the Jacobite campaign is told on the top of the handsome green pyramid.

Plate LXXXV   Gothic Folly, Abbey Mains

When everyone thought this derelict useless building should be demolished, I reslated it as one of the County's environmental improvements. It had been built as an eye-catcher in the landscape round Amisfield House and although that was demolished there was no need to demolish this puzzling feature beside the A1.

ruins at the Linn, East Linton and West Barns, Dunbar were consolidated, but perhaps the most visible was the restoration of the gothic folly beside the A1 just east of Haddington which was reroofed and made secure. It was one of the landscape features, an eyecatcher, seen from Amisfield Park with its high battlemented gable facing the demolished mansion house. It had never been inhabited and everyone thought that it should be removed and were astonished to see a little old grey lady appear at the blind painted window. I had heard that this character often appeared in Glasgow tenements before the war, but it was not liked by the East Lothians and so she had to be painted out.

Another work was the fencing off and planting with lime trees of the waste site on the north side of Market Street, Haddington which had suffered from the first bomb jettisoned on Scottish soil at the beginning of the Second World War. There is still not sufficient prosperity in Haddington to justify a row of new shops and so the trees still hold the street line there. The programme included much other tree planting and the restoration of Doocot Park in North Berwick. Another project was the improvement of the mile and a half embankment along the southern edge of the A1 between East Linton and Ninewar. This embankment had no doubt been thrown up when the railway was built in 1843 at the behest of the then Earl of Haddington to hide the passing of trains from his mansion house at Tyninghame. By the 1970s the roadside was unkempt and weedy as British Rail workmen never looked over the bank, concentrating instead on the rail track, which for many years was their prize winning length. British Rail were not prepared to allow us to plant trees in case, in their maturity, they might fall across the line. The solution we came up with was to plant the bank with privet. This shrub is mainly associated with the dreary clipped hedges planted around housing schemes because of its cheapness. When left to grow by itself it has a fine flourish of white flowers and an intoxicating smell. We could not find enough plants in Scottish nurseries and so imported plants direct from Holland. They have been a disappointment as the plants took a long time to establish and were slow to produce flowers, although I notice they are improving each year. There have, as yet, been no complaints from the trunk road engineers or police that drivers on the A1 are being intoxicated!

All these small schemes kept us busy and happy working on the ground and leaving behind visible improvements which we hoped raised the spirits of the people, residents and visitors alike.

My Lothian Region Land Reclamation Unit

When I moved to the Lothian Regional Council in 1975 I was keen to establish a Land Reclamation Unit in my department to carry on this good work and extend it throughout the Region. The Director of Highways argued that as so much engineering was involved it should be done in his department which at the time was short of road construction work, but I managed to fight him off saying that it was basically a land use problem which requiring imaginative solutions and a thorough understanding of landscaping works, of which his department was woefully ignorant. I had however to take one of his engineers to head the unit. He was an utter disaster and had to be got rid of—the only case in my career.

A unit of some 15 people was built up and we trained up a new type of young landscape engineer. The principles we followed were to make the sites largely recreational woodland, maintaining the high points for their great views and as a visible reminder of the generations of labour involved in the creation of these enormous heaps. A good example is the reclamation of the two old colliery bings, the "Emily" and the "Gore" at Gorebridge in Midlothian, which were essential preliminaries to the residential expansion of the town. It is now nicknamed the Gorebridge Alp. The "Ramsay" bing at Loanhead was also treated in a similar way to provide great views out over the Lothian plain. The problem here was a large precision engineering factory,

McTaggart and Scott, requiring dust free conditions in old buildings at the foot of the bing. Midlothian County Council had not been prepared to risk this reclamation, but with constant water sprays and a £15 million insurance policy, all went well and the sale of the coal slurry from three ponds, one built on top of the other, greatly reduced the overall costs. At Bathgate and Armadale in West Lothian we created town woods and at Addiewell we had the good sense to do nothing to the old shale bings, which were supporting a great variety of unique vegetation. It was a most rewarding programme and at least allowed me to get out of the office and get mud on my boots, after spending so many hours with them under the table arguing with my colleagues and hammering out the Lothian Region Structure Plan with my staff and the Government agencies.

10

RESTORATION OF GULLANE DUNES

Dune Conservation Study Group 1970 • Dune Management Procedure
The 1930s • Wartime Experiences • The Threat to Muirfield
Dutch Experience • Re-creation of the Foredune • Woodlands
Sand Winning • Sea Buckthorn

Chapter Two describes the richness and variety of the County's coastline and the steps the County Council took to open it up to the public and to assume responsibility for its management in fulfilment of the third principle of the County Development Plan to make provision for the legitimate recreation needs of the Region. This was a major task, as by 1975 the County Council owned, leased or managed 21.78 miles of the coastline and a further 8.25 miles was owned by the Burgh Councils—30.03 miles, or 71% of the County's coastline of 42 miles.

Dune Conservation Study Group 1970

Much of the managed coastline was backed by sand dunes and these were the lengths, greatly used and much enjoyed by the public, which presented the main problems. I set out our experience in a bound and illustrated report entitled *'Dune Conservation, a Twenty Year Record of Work in East Lothian'* which not only gave details of our methods, but of their costs and the income received. This was circulated to the Dune Conservation Study Group held in North Berwick in April, 1970, as part of our activities for the "Countryside in 1970", which I jointly directed with Dr Derek Randall of the Nature Conservancy Council. It was attended by fifty people from all over the United Kingdom. The outcome from this Study Group was agreement on Twelve Precepts for Dune Management. These were circulated with a Report of the

Plate LXXXVI A Twenty Year Record

This was the cover of our Twenty Year Record of Dune Conservation and shows the whole story at Gullane. In the foreground, brushwood fences to trap the sand and prevent continued stripping of the old dune. A little higher, marram grass is successfully established in the wider area where we had to spread nets to stabilise the sand and erect spur fences to stop the wind gougeing the sand behind the new foredune. This curves away to the left with its covering of sea-lyme grass. At the top of the picture is the Muirfield championship golf course.

Proceedings which ran into three editions as other local authorities and river boards began to manage their dunes seriously. One result of the Conference was that I was asked by the Northern Ireland Office to advise them on their dune management problems (The Troubles had started and they were exercising direct rule). I asked Jim McCarthy of the Nature Conservancy to accompany me and we had people from Stormont and Queen's University, Belfast, with us. It took three days to tour all the coastline, and an enjoyable and boozy expedition it was. The Northern Ireland Office got our advice very cheaply.

Dune Management Procedure

Our management procedure back home was to gather together on each site in the autumn all the County Council and Burgh Council officers involved to discuss the needs and the problems revealed during the summer, and to evolve plans for remedial works or other improvements during the winter. These could involve amending the bye-laws; resting parts of the grass car parks to allow the grass to recover; improving road access; providing diversionary activities to prevent too heavy trampling of the dunes; safeguarding rare plants; providing more information; improving the lavatories; and the fixing of next season's car parking dues to help meet the costs. We had a second annual meeting, after the spring high tides, to determine what works had to be done on the dunes as a result of the winter storms and to review what each of us had achieved by way of getting Committee approval for the works agreed at the autumn meeting. We involved the local Councillor if he was available, and I remember all the meetings as happy, positive occasions with a hot lunch thrown in.

The 1930s

The Gullane dunes were my main concern on which I will concentrate here as they illustrate most of the problems and the solutions we evolved. These dunes had been leased to the County Council in 1931 by the proprietors of the big houses on Hill Road overlooking the bay whose feus extend to High Water Mark. The land to the east up to the Muirfield boundary had been donated to the County Council by the Biel and Dirleton Estates. It is some 104 acres above High Water Mark and the fine sandy beach, below High Water Mark, stretches nearly a mile. The mineral rights and rabbit trapping were reserved to the feuars and the estate—a normal legal provision which subsequently caused us many problems. In 1936 the County Council obtained a private Act of Parliament to enable it to pass bye-laws, to build lavatories and to manage this area whose visitors, by the charabanc load, had grown beyond the ability of the feuars to cope. A series of photographs existed to support this private legislation showing a mass of black cars and charabancs. They also showed the start of the erosion on the forty feet high foredune as people clambered over it to reach the beach, and the further erosion caused by beach huts dug into the sea-ward face of the dunes. These invariably collapsed with the erosion of sand about them and were re-erected higher up the dune with the same consequences. It took many years to remove the last few huts remaining after the war, despite the demonstrable damage they caused.

Wartime Experiences

By far the greatest damage however had resulted from the use of the dunes, during the war, for training Royal Engineers in the recovery of military vehicles and tanks on the Normandy Beaches and the subsequent erosion by wind of the large foredune and the scouring of the marram grass ridges behind it. The County Road Surveyor, who had volunteered with many of his roadmen at the beginning of the war, had been captured in Crete and spent the rest of the war in prisoner of war camps. He had been put in charge of coastal protection after the war and spent the £1600 compensation using Italian prisoners of war to carry out remedial works. His efforts had merely accentuated the destruction of the foredune and I found a great expanse of bare sand sloping up from the High Water Mark to the very edge of the Muirfield Championship Golf Course. The sand was only held here and there by large tussocks of old marram grass and these were being excavated by Messrs Dobson, the local coal and gravel merchant, who was supplying the beautiful white sand to Edinburgh plasterers. This was a real disaster area.

My wartime experience was very different to the County Road Surveyor's as I had motored with the 2nd Camel Corps Battalion of the Sudanese Defence Force 800 miles across the sand sea between Wadi Halfa on the Nile and Kufrah in Libya. This oasis served as the base for the Long Range Desert Group and later the embryonic S.A.S. who, by their hit and hide tactics, did great damage to Rommel's supply lines when the British Army was digging in at El Alamein. In the meantime the 2nd Camel Corps, driving armoured cars plated up on Ford chassis in the railway workshops at Omdurmann, were chasing the Italians out of Jalo and patrolling the oases. This experience at Kufrah had taught me how blown sand behaves and shown me its great power to submerge plantations of palms, gardens and houses standing in its path.

The Threat to Muirfield

That there was a similar threat at Gullane was indicated by the inundation of the old St Andrew's Church at the west end in 1639, when it was abandoned, and another parish church built at Dirleton. The County Clerk, who lived in Gullane, was oblivious to this threat as

Plate LXXXVII Gullane Beach 1963

It shows the inhospitable beach with no dunes and the buckthorn planted along the rear bank to prevent its erosion. It was from this deplorable state that we set ourselves the task to create a comfortable happy beach for the future, as it had been before the 1939-45 War.

he had never visited the dunes, only the golf courses. As far as he was concerned the County Road Surveyor had done his best and if the sand blew onto Muirfield Golf Course it was an Act of God. I remember warning him that this would not be much of a defence in a court of law, faced with the talents of the Scottish Bar who comprised a large part of the membership of the Honourable Company of Edinburgh Golfers at Muirfield. I suggested that he had better let me have a go and, if my methods worked, he promised that he would support proposals for a full scale restoration scheme.

The County Council had no park staff, only the grave diggers who were put at my disposal when they were not digging graves. I started with them in the autumn of 1955. The first thing we did was to protect the rear bank, which was being eroded by the wind, with sea buckthorn transplants, so preventing further desertification and controlling access to the beach. The next was to check the supply of blown sand by rebuilding the old foredune which followed the high tide mark. This we did with sea-lyme grass, *Elymus arenarius*, a grass with a tough sword-like leaf of a blue-green colour. It was more tolerant of salt water than the traditional marram grass, *Ammophilla arenaria*, which has a slighter curled yellow-green leaf, which is its way to prevent excessive transpiration.

Dutch Experience

Mary and I had spent a holiday in Holland where the maintenance of dunes is a matter of life and death and is carried out by a Government department. We spent two days in Kennemerduinen, a large coastal park established by the three cities of Amsterdam, Rotterdam and The Hague. The Dutch showed us how they used wind to build up dunes with staggered fences but they had the added advantage of being able to fence people off the dunes while this was going on. The Park Director, E C M Roderkerk, a retired colonial man, had developed a whole series of diversions to hold the visitors back from the beach and foredune. The paths all zig-zagged past attractive features such as playgrounds, mazes and ponds, cafes and camping sites, so that few people eventually reached the beach. He had a splendid diorama exhibition hall and an adjoining bird and mammal hospital. He was an inspiring man, who asked us to vet the English translation of his guidebook; but his English was so bizarre that we had to largely rewrite it. He had his own problems, which were not ours, as the park was used as an underground water reservoir for the three cities, pumping Rhine water into the dunes in the winter and out of them in the summer. His trees and vegetation were dying as a consequence of the stress of this constant change in the water table and he was powerless to prevent it.

We tried to apply the lessons thus learnt in Holland to Gullane but the Council were not prepared to vote the money to restrict the public access or, as they put it, to commercialise the area with our proposals for a camp site and the hire of day huts. They were prepared to limit the numbers by not allowing the overflow car park to be used on peak days and by laying it out instead as a diversionary pitch and putt golf course, thus reducing the annual vehicle numbers from 24,000 to 19,000 cars. I had argued that just as cinemas had a fixed capacity, so had the beaches, and similarly, the public had to find somewhere else to go or something else to do, when a beach had reached its capacity. As we were opening up other beaches in East Lothian there was plenty of choice. They also approved of children's play areas being cut out of the buckthorn stands. To reduce litter we provided plastic carrier bags printed with a map of the alternative beaches on one side and an explanation of the dune conservation works on the other. It was one of the earliest printed plastic bags, now so common. Their supply with the parking ticket did much to reduce the litter and the danger from broken bottles left behind in the dunes where our son, Ben, had been so badly cut. This generated a lot of respect for our work.

Re-creation of the Foredune

All these measures and the growth of the foredune established confidence that I knew what I was talking about and the County Clerk honoured his promise. The County Council accepted my recommendation to employ David Skinner, a landscape architect, to produce a scheme and to let a contract for the work which he estimated would cost £6-8,000 and take 10 to 15 years to complete. The old tarmac pathway to the beach, which faced directly into the prevailing wind, was removed and a new zig-zag path, constructed of railway sleepers, led through the buckthorn to the beach with crossing points on the foredune marked by large black plywood diamonds on old telephone poles. These pathways were paved with straw, always in plentiful supply in East Lothian. The foredune which had begun to accumulate around the sea-lyme grass was raised by hammering in sawn boards, shoulder to shoulder, with 25% spacing between them to allow the sand through. Astonishingly, these boards were cheaper than brushwood, when we started. After two years, when they were submerged by accumulated sand, we had no money to put in another line further back, as the Dutch had taught us to widen and deepen the dune. We therefore put a chain round the original boards and pulled them up higher. This was a bad economy. Although we quickly got a high twelve feet dune it was too steep and too near High Water Mark and so liable to wave damage. To get over this problem we allowed the public to walk along the top of the dune and to sit on the back of the dune which faced south and so was very popular. The wriggling and sliding of human bottoms had the intended effect of broadening the dune. On the seaward side we used brushwood fences at right angles to the prevailing wind and 8 metres apart to gather summer sand blown along the beach and rebuild the toe of the dunes, as at Longniddry.

The flat valley behind the foredune was divided into compartments and planted with marram grass. As this area was still being stripped of sand by the wind plunging over the foredune, we covered the sand with fishing nets from Stewarts, the net manufacturer in Musselburgh, suspended on fence wire above the sand. The nets were seconds and cost threepence a square metre. And so this area of blown sand was stabilised and the public were kept off it. Before the war the area had been called "Happy Valley" and was a dune slack fed by water from the water table which rises within the dune and then filters out at its base. I am still looking for this to occur again when the dunes are higher. The work was done by an agricultural contractor, Mr Livingstone, whose hardy labour force was out working in all weathers

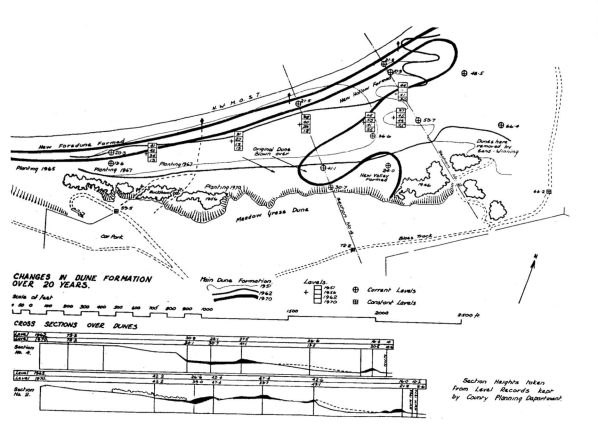

Plate LXXXVIII   Dune Movement 1951-1970

This drawing was included in the Twenty Year Record showing the changes from levels
kept in the County Planning Department. The crossing points on the new foredune
are marked by the black diamonds which in reality were large plywood boards mounted
on telephone posts.

and we got cheap rates as they worked when there was no agricultural
employment available.

The critical areas near Muirfield involved some bulldozing to
link up adjoining tussocks of grass to obtain aerodynamic shapes which
would be stable and could be thatched with brushwood and planted
up. On the seaward face we planted sea-lyme grass and inland marram
grass, thus effecting a two-tone finish which I recall was then a popular
way of painting cars.

Woodlands

Some time previously I had persuaded the Forestry Commission to
lease some 40 acres of dunes at Jamie's Neuk to the seaward end of
Muirfield. I had hoped that this would supply an endless source of
brushwood but the trees never grew well and I was never forgiven by

Plate LXXXIX The Situation in 1970
(a) Menace and (b) Measures

Photograph (a) shows the blown sand dunes menacing the Muirfield Golf Course top
right. Top left shows how the wind was breaking into the established dunes in the area
we persuaded the Forestry Commission to plant up.

This photograph shows the measures we took to prevent the sand at the shoreline reinforcing the advancing dune and to build up an aerodynamic shape which would eventually unite the old tussocks of marram grass. This blow through can be seen in the aerial photograph at the top of the beach.

the Commission's officers for selling them a pup. We also, as a fail safe precaution, planted two belts of lodgepole pine *(Pinus contortus)* near the Muirfield boundary. It caused some controversy as it was considered that the trees when grown would alter play on the second fairway. A compromise was arrived at—to stagger these belts, thus creating a "wind hazard" where a small water course led onto the dunes. I have not heard how this has affected play, but it settled the controversy.

Sand Winning
Another problem arose from the continued winning of the sand under the owners' reserved mineral rights which were robustly defended by Rear Admiral Brooke of Biel, whose uncle had given the land to the County Council. He won several annual extensions to the planning consent to work the sand, subject to conditions about the direction of working, thatching and planting, which were never carried out by Messrs Dobson, who had the lease, as the last thing plasterers wanted was bits of brushwood or roots of marram in their lorryloads of beautiful white

sand. The planning consent was finally refused when the Rear Admiral no longer wanted to face the journey from Dorset to meet the Sub-committee and argue his case, which had become more difficult year by year, as the dunes were stabilised. I rather missed our annual encounters with the old sea dog. We later used the lorry roads that Dobson had laid into the dunes to set out car parking areas for the periodic Muirfield Open Golf Championships and so got a little income to offset our expenditure. Signs of these battles and the half victories can still be seen in the dunes.

On the reorganisation of local government in 1975 the responsibility for the Gullane Dunes was moved to the newly introduced Leisure and Recreation Department of East Lothian District Council. This was largely composed of administrators and the park superintendents from the Burghs. The last thing they wanted to do was to spend winter days on the dunes, out of their warm offices or greenhouses, so there was a period of discontinuity which did not help the dunes. The Dutch had taught us that the battle with the sea and the wind is continuous and endless. However the position has been stabilised and, while it is not yet back to the pre-war 'Happy Valley' days, the dunes are much enjoyed and Muirfield is no longer threatened with engulfing sand as was Kufrah Oasis.

Sea Buckthorn

The sea buckthorn saga is well worth recording. It is an attractive, hardy deciduous shrub, (*Hippophae rhamnoides*), with grey-green summer foliage, bright orange winter berries and fearsome thorns. It occurs naturally from the sandy seashores of Scandinavia to the stony mountain tops in Asia Minor. It was introduced to Britain in the eighteenth century as a handsome garden plant and there were well-established clumps of it along the East Lothian shore. It is a quite excellent shrub for fixing the sand as it spreads by rhizome roots running out from the parent plant forming dense impenetrable clumps. It is also very useful for crowd control and we used it, both dead and alive, for fences which no one fancied crossing because of its vicious thorns

I first transplanted it onto the dunes at Gullane to hold the southern bank and was most disappointed when it showed no signs of berrying which it does at an early age. One day a botanist from Gibraltar Point in Lincolnshire, where there are vast stands of buckthorn, showed me how to sex the plants. We then started planting male plants within the stands, one male to approximately ten females—and so we got our berries.

Some years later, I was greatly concerned to see seedlings of sea buckthorn growing in the Aberlady Nature Reserve where the birds must have carried the seeds. It would have been a disaster if the fine wild blowing marram dunes and orchid slacks had become buckthorn thickets. We therefore not only got volunteers to dig out the seedlings on the Reserve but also started a male eradication programme at Gullane. This was no easy task and we clearly failed, as a most magnificent winter display of berries can be seen at Gullane. The local people call it "the Baked Bean Bush" as the berries cluster so thickly along the branches. They provide a veritable feast for migrant birds such as waxwings and fieldfares during the winter.

But this is not the end of the story as we found that the thick stands of buckthorn were harbouring rabbits. Due to the vicious thorns dogs would not go into the stands, so we had to cut two metre wide fire lines through the stands at ten metres intervals. These were cut straight up and down the dunes at right angles to the prevailing wind to avoid windblow and enable us to shoot the rabbits. But we soon found that these lanes were being used by the Hearts Football Club to strengthen their players' thigh muscles by running up and down them. This caused further erosion, so that the lanes had to be blocked top and bottom to prevent that use. The Planning Committee were quite mystified, never knowing whether I was asking for money to plant or to remove buckthorn, but by then we were beginning to show impressive results and so they left me to it. I made a rule that we should in future only plant buckthorn where we could control its outward spread by mowing.

It was not until I had left the County that I learnt that the juice of the buckthorn berries was greatly valued and was being imported from Russia and Finland to sell at vast prices in health food shops. The problem was how to pick the berries without getting torn to bits by the thorns. I asked my nephew, Dr Ranulph Glanville, who had married a Finn, to investigate and he had made for me a press with long handles and a bottle attachment which enabled one to press the berries on the stem without picking them. I am working on their marketing just now, but out there I have planted a fortune for the beach-combers of East Lothian did they but know it.

11

THE COUNTY RANGER SERVICE

The Countryside (Scotland) Act 1970
Type of Man • Archie Mathieson • Terms of Employment
The Suit of Clothes • Bulletins • Second Ranger - Catcraig
Third Mounted Ranger • Innerwick Centre
Annual Reports 1974

With all this work going on at Gullane and along the length of the East Lothian coast and our tourist development proposals to open up alternative spots inland, it was essential that the County Council increased their manpower to look after them.

The Countryside (Scotland) Act 1970

This Act empowered local authorities to employ countryside rangers and initially provided 75% grants to cover the cost of a ranger service. The County Council had previously funded a seasonal warden for the Local Nature Reserve at Aberlady Bay, but the Act provided the opportunity to establish a wider County Ranger Service, which would not only promote the public's enjoyment of the areas of wild land and beaches coming into County Council care, but also play its part in safeguarding wildlife throughout the County.

For instance, there had been the occasion when George Waterston, the Scottish Director of the Royal Society for the Preservation of Birds, who came to live at Humbie Mill, asked the County Council to protect an active badgers' sett. It was in a wood near him which was being clear felled and he clearly thought that the County Council should do something about it. We secured the retention of trees round the sett, but we had no idea of the relative importance of this sett or the numbers or location of others. Later we were able to get our Ranger to find this out.

I often claim that East Lothian's was the first County Ranger Service, although the first ranger was actually appointed by Renfrewshire County Council for their Muirsheil Country Park, but he had a more limited role.

Type of Man

There was considerable discussion with the Countryside Commission for Scotland over the type of person to be recruited. The Commission wanted to establish a service of young university graduates after the example of the American National Park Service. I wanted a more mature practical countryman in the mould of a gamekeeper, who would put down roots and get a thorough knowledge not only of the County but of the people visiting it. I had had two experiences of young graduates. The first was in the Swiss National Park in the Engadine which Mary and I visited after an International Union for the Conservation of Nature Conference in Lucerne. Here our party was sitting down and looking aghast at an eroding hillside with the pines browsed down to bushes, the edges of the newly widened road left bare, a wild stream carving out a great boulder gulley and not a bird or beast to be seen, but we were being plagued by insects. "Mr Tindall, you must not swat insects you are in a National Park", so spake the young guide from Zurich University which managed the Park. It was only when we moved to another area, just recently leased by the Park organisation, that we saw the rich variety of wildlife of the Swiss Alps. The Swiss professors had taken their philosophy of non-intervention to absurd lengths on the land their Society had owned for forty years with appalling results.

The other experience was on our own foreshore at Aberlady Bay where along its southern boundary at Kilspindie there are good mussel beds. The seasonal warden got into a fight with a small party of regular visitors, who had gathered mussels and were boiling them over a fire in the rocks, which was against the bye-laws but not against common sense. The warden not only lost his authority but also potential allies to help him in his main duties of protecting the nesting birds and plants. I was determined that the County Ranger would not be like this but would be user-friendly, in the terms of the jargon that was just coming in.

Archie Mathieson

We received a great many applications for the job but Archie Mathieson was the outstanding fellow from my point of view and quite won over Tom Huxley, the Countryside Commission staff member on the appointment panel. Archie was forty years old, born in Ayrshire where he had been an apprentice carpenter, had done a stint as an under-gamekeeper, some National Service, and after that had worked for the Post Office both as an outside linesman and as an inside installation engineer. He had a fine soft accent, a nice turn of phrase and a rich knowledge of country lore. A friend had told him of our advertisement saying that if he got the job he could earn a living at his hobby—nature study—and so it turned out.

Plate XC   Archie Mathieson

The first and finest County Ranger, looking much the same in 1997 as he did in 1970 when I appointed him, and showing the same enthusiasms. Photographed against the sea-lyme grass on Longniddry Bents, wearing our brass ranger's badge with an engraving of a tern flying over a beach.   Designer: Hamish Macdonald of my staff.

Initially he and his wife, Ann, a trained nurse, and two children were housed in a council house in Aberlady but later the County Council leased two farm cottages at Craigielaw Farm overlooking Aberlady Bay. The County Council adapted these to provide him with a house and a small office and specimen store and he was given the use of two stables in the farm steading for the care of injured birds and mammals. He lived happily there until he retired in 1990.

Terms of Employment

His terms of employment were that he had to work a forty one hour week, the same as other Council manual workers, but had no fixed hours. Like a gamekeeper he had to be out when he sensed trouble, he had to be out and about during the evenings and at weekends and he had to attend all emergency call-outs without overtime pay, but he could sleep in and be away during afternoons. He had to carry out small fencing and maintenance repairs on the public open spaces in his care; he was to lay on a programme of guided walks and talks to school and other groups. He had to keep a daily log of his hours and activities and any incidents or wildlife sightings. He was to get a knickerbocker suit each year, as game-keepers do, and have a Land Rover which he could drive for personal use within the County as I believed that the more this service was publicised the better, even if it was in shopping centres or on housing estates. The presence of his

Land Rover with fire brooms fastened on its roof was a very visual warning to the public of the fire hazard in our dry springs.

I had some difficulty in getting these terms of employment agreed by the County Council. The Convener at the time, a farmer, said that they were a recipe for 'turning a good man into a lazy rascal'. However I promised that an Annual Report would be submitted to the County Council detailing the work that was done and the hours worked each week. These showed that year by year he worked regularly in the summer a sixty hour week, much in excess of the hours required from manual workers.

In 1975 the County Ranger Service was taken over by the Department of Leisure and Recreation in the East Lothian District Council. The Director was an Education administrator who was aghast at the situation and required that Archie Mathieson be accessible during Council working hours and that he be paid overtime just as the school caretakers were and should not have a Land Rover. However he did not modify his conditions of employment and so Archie continued his evening and weekend patrolling and put in for overtime. This greatly swelled his weekly wage packet but soon 'bankrupted the Service'. When I heard of this I paid him a visit as I did not want him to think that I had short-changed him during the five years that we had worked together, but I found an unhappy man burdened by routine paperwork, without the freedom and room for initiative that I had given him and that he had so successfully and happily used.

The Suit of Clothes

The provision of the suit of clothes also presented a great problem to the County Council as none of their other employees, apart from the uniformed services, the police and firemen, were provided with clothes. But there was a precedent—Betty Black had secured a waterproof coat for the rent collectors, who at that time called from house to house in all weathers. I toyed with the idea of getting a bale of tweed especially designed and woven for the East Lothian Ranger Service as had been the custom of the old estates, but I realised how badly that would have gone down in the local press. If I had known that in five years there would be not just one ranger, but five, I think that I would have chanced it. What I did have made was a fine brass badge, two inches in diameter with an engraving of a tern flying over sand and sea and sky and the proud lettering round the rim "East Lothian County Ranger Service". Twelve of these were made and issued to temporary summer workers who were also enrolled into the service. Problems arose with the knickerbockers as the patrolling on the sand dunes resulted in phenomenal wear on the wool stockings which Ann, Archie's wife, was not prepared to continually mend and so he was given trousers instead.

I was also insistent that the Rangers should not patrol alone like policemen, but must talk and walk with everyone they met. Thus a wonderful rapport was established with regulars and visitors alike. The Ranger also had to post up on our land dated bulletins informing the public of natural events such as the arrival of geese or the flowering of plants. In this way the presence of the County Ranger Service was made apparent although the Ranger himself might have been at the other end of the County. Archie developed an ability to sketch the distinguishing features of birds and other natural phenomenon to illustrate these bulletins. It was articles based on them that we got the Haddingtonshire Courier to publish weekly under the heading "Where to Go". This weekly series has continued for twenty five years and I am glad to say that since Archie retired he has been paid for them. His daily logs of wildlife sightings give the most wonderful data base from which to compile these articles and to let people know what they should be looking out for week by week.

Second Ranger—Catcraig

The County appointed a second ranger for the coastal lands at White Sands and the east of the County. He lived in the restored calciner's cottage with a stable at Catcraig. Lime burning had been a continuous process and so there had to be a cottage and stables for the horses that carted the limestone from the reefs below the high tide mark and from the quarries, to be loaded into the top of the kiln. The large semi-basement, which no doubt had sheltered quarry workers and carters, made a good muster room for school parties. However the house had five apartments and the ranger was unmarried thus a scandal blew up and filled the correspondence columns of "The Haddingtonshire Courier" for several weeks. But, as we replied, Rangers could be married men with children as Archie Mathieson was and we were preserving a bit of industrial history.

Third Mounted Ranger

A third ranger was appointed for the lands at Tyninghame which later became the John Muir Country Park. The problem here was that the River Tyne separated the two halves of the public land and it was quite a roundabout journey by road between them. The sensible thing seemed to me was to have a horse which could ford the Tyne, swimming if necessary, instead of having the usual Land Rover. The mounted ranger was very popular with children and both the capital and running costs were infinitely cheaper. The only difficulty which emerged later was that the ranger spent so much time looking after the horse that he had little time to patrol and so this unique innovation had to be abandoned after my time—a great pity. A fourth ranger was then appointed for the western part of the County, the Railway Walks, Woodhall, and Prestongrange.

Innerwick Centre

The east of the County contains an enormous wealth of interest, natural, historical and recreational, which was little known. So that it could be adequately enjoyed the old school at Innerwick was turned at my instigation and with the advice of Mr and Mrs Brooks of the Kildrogan Field Centre into a small Field Studies Centre run by the Education Department. It could be both a day and an overnight centre and the County Ranger Service was available to help with school parties. We prepared an attractive booklet which gave details of the many excursions that were possible and of the history of the locality. In particular it told of Alexander Somerville, born in Oldhamstocks in 1811, who wrote his *"Autobiography of a Working Man"* in 1840 dealing with the agricultural conditions which eventually drove him off the land into the sawpits of Edinburgh where they sawed by hand the joists and scantlings for houses in the New Town. He then joined the Scots Greys and his radical views led to him receiving a hundred strokes with a cat o' nine tails—the last man of the British Army to be flogged. The symbol of the Centre was the wild dog rose. I was very pleased when it was continued by the Lothian Region Education Department in 1975 as an Outdoor Education Centre.

Annual Reports 1974

I have before me both the County Ranger Service's Annual Report and the Aberlady Bay Nature Reserve Report for 1974. This was the first year that the full-time warden at Aberlady had operated under the County Ranger Service although seasonal wardens had been employed since 1969. The County Ranger Service Report recorded for the benefit of the incoming District Council the main responsibilities of the service as 'The Care of the Countryside and the safety and enjoyment of the people who use it'. The 1974 Report records the programme of weekly 'Rambles with the Ranger', on Tuesday at Aberlady Bay, Wednesday at Yellowcraig and Thursday at Barns Ness, which attracted 367 participants. In addition the Ranger Service had guided 16 school outings, 27 adult groups and had made 9 visits to schools and given 33 talks and slide shows to adult groups in the County. They had led conservation volunteers on 46 occasions, collecting litter, tree planting, scrub clearing and path-work. This was a mammoth education programme which must have interested many people in their natural surroundings. The Service had discovered a rarity—the great crested newt nesting in the old Markle Quarry. The report recorded that the

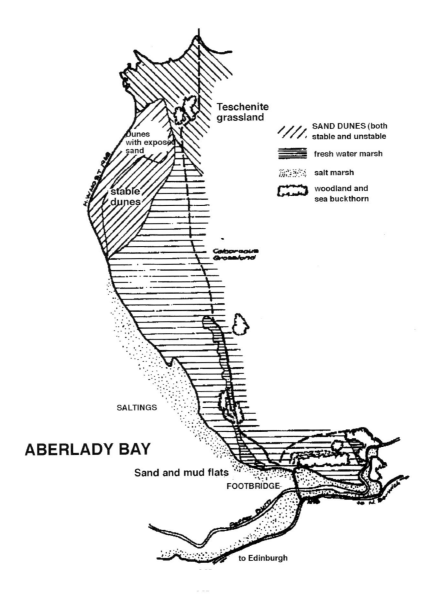

Teschenite
grassland

Dunes
with exposed
sand

stable
dunes

Calcareous
Grassland

SALTINGS

ABERLADY BAY

Sand and mud flats
FOOTBRIDGE

to Edinburgh

ABERLADY BAY NATURE RESERVE
Distribution of Plant Communities
(Boundaries of the Communities are only
approximate and have been sketched in from ariel photographs

Plate XCI   Aberlady Bay Nature Reserve

The Aberlady Bay Management Plan, prepared by Dr Michael Usher for the Planning
Department, contained this map which shows the seven plant communities that make
the Reserve such a rich place, not only for birds but also for plants. The main access
is across the wooden bridge over the Peffer Burn. The Nature Reserve continues to the
west along the south side of the Aberlady Bay where there are interesting geological
exposures north of Kilspindie Golf Course.

Rangers had cared for five injured kestrels, four of which survived and were released back to the wild and many hundreds of sea birds from an oil spill in May which had mostly died. I felt the Service had to respond to the public who brought in injured birds and animals and not merely put them in the bucket, when the finder had moved off. It records the signing of the Access Agreement with the Tyninghame Estate for the John Muir Country Park on 18 December 1974 and the start of the conservation on the Ravensheugh Dune with parties from a Girl Guides' camp. However the main bulk of the report consists of a month by month record of wild life findings.

The Aberlady Bay Report 1974 records that some 12,000 people visited the Reserve and that 10 plant, 8 bird and 2 mammal species were added to the Plan list prepared for us in the 1960s by Dr Michael Usher, who is now the head scientist at Scottish Natural Heritage. The main bulk of the report describes the fortunes of the 170 bird species seen on the Reserve. It had been a bad year for the six tern varieties that had tried to nest on the sand spit, the nests being robbed by egg-hunters, washed out by storms and submerged by blown sand. This was disappointing, but as a result forty people had volunteered to stay overnight in the hide during the incubation period the following year. Unfortunately these annual reports were not kept up by the District Council but the basic log books which record wildlife throughout the County as recorded by the rangers were and are available.

I concluded the 1974 County Ranger Service's Annual Report, writing that it was much to the credit of East Lothian County Council that they had initiated this new local government service which had been greatly valued by the public, resulting in a widespread general appreciation of wildlife. It had seen a marked reduction in litter and vandalism on the publicly-owned land and the countryside in general. There is now a knowledgeable public in East Lothian, who get much pleasure from studying wildlife, and will not idly allow its diminution.

12

THE DEVELOPMENT OF TOURISM

Scottish Hotel Design • Local Authorities' Role
Changing Tourist Trade • County Strategy
Pencraig Serviced Lay-by • Bilsdean Serviced Lay-by
Information Laybys • Archaeological Trail
The Promotion of Dunbar • Castlepark Coach and Sports Centre
The Proposals Flounder • John Muir • His Birthplace
His Writings • The John Muir Trust
John Muir Country Park
Caravans and Camping • Yellowcraig • Barns Ness
Spread of Tourism to the Mining Area
David Spence: Curator Mirabilis • Pencaitland Railway Walk
Haddington to Longniddry Branch Line • Lengthening the Season
Guide Books

The idea of tourism as an industry was hard to put over in Scotland during the 1950s and 1960s. It was regarded as an extension of the hotel and bar trade—demeaning, low-paid, temporary work, in depressing old buildings or scruffy temporary ones with garish signs and drunken proprietors. Clearly, there was scope for its development in Scotland and in the County. This development was largely stimulated by grants from the Scottish Tourist Board, but it made little attempt to educate the hoteliers in visual matters.

Scottish Hotel Design

In the early 1960s the typical tourist development was a large flat roofed function room, like a shoe box, tacked onto a baronial country house hotel. Although the Board's 'Taste of Scotland' culinary campaign got surprisingly good results, in improving catering and giving tourists distinctive fresh Scottish food, it was such a pity that they did not take a similar initiative with the design, furnishing and decor of hotels as a condition of their grants.

It was always difficult for the local planning authority to take much part in the design of these buildings or their interiors. This was partly due to the restraints of the licensing procedures, as the hoteliers first sought a licence from the Licensing Court before applying for planning consent. If plans were adjusted in any way to meet the planning requirements they had to re-apply to the Court six months later, and it was partly because hoteliers were in a good position to canvass the elected members who seldom refused consent. Planning had no control over the furniture and interior fittings, which were universally dreadful. Only in the case of 'The Harvesters', a newly opened country house hotel in East Linton, were we able to influence the design of the basement bar as it was a listed building. The attractive dark purple stone rubble of the walls was exposed, the ceiling was lined with pine boarding, there was reed matting on the floor and wood benches round the walls. The walls were hung with cart horse leather collars and their distinctive tines, and other horse harness as East Linton was an agricultural centre; not a binnacle lamp in sight! It looked very good and I never heard that the lack of plush carpets and upholstery detracted from the sales of beer.

I also remember trying to persuade the entrepreneur who first acquired the disused smithy and carpenter's shop at Pencaitland, which the Winton Estate had built next to each other, to try something different. We suggested he should leave the smithy as it was, with a floor part beaten earth and part wooden sleepers for the re-shoeing of horses, and the scatter of tools and half finished work; merely serving whisky and beer as a blacksmith might have done from a capacious cupboard to his friends seated on wooden benches. The forge would provide heat. In the carpenter's shop, simple meals would be served to people sitting at a long board table. This would have been a low-cost solution and I considered a great attraction, as, for instance, Bannerman's Bar in the Cowgate, Edinburgh, later became. But he was not the sort of man to take the risk and we got the usual high-cost, safe, carpeted arrangement with some smithy tools tacked to the walls. This pub-restaurant never really took off and it has passed through many hands and many refurbishments since.

Local Authorities' Role

The difficulty of promoting the tourist industry is that it depends on a great variety of impressions perceived by the visitor and touching on all aspects of their visit. In 1962 the Scottish Development Department issued Circular 2/1962 requiring all local authorities to prepare Tourist Development Proposals, and the Civic Amenities and Countryside (Scotland) Act gave planning authorities new powers and grants for all the multifarious provisions which are necessary to attract visitors, and lengthen their stay.

I remember spending many happy evenings with Eric Crosbee, an architect planner in the Scottish Development Department, who had worked for Sir Frank Mears and was much of the same mind as myself. He had worked on the Circular and the map notations which were adopted by the Ordnance Survey and are still used. We were joined by David Skinner, the freelance landscape architect, who we were using at Gullane dunes. We met in his office to assemble a travelling exhibition for the Scottish Branch of the Royal Town Planning Institute to demonstrate by plans and photographs the range and quality of tourist proposals that were being provided elsewhere in Britain. These were mounted on eight plywood doors which were first shown at the 1961 Study Group in Braemar and then circulated, wrapped in their old grey army blankets, to county towns throughout Scotland. I wonder where these boards are now?

Changing Tourist Trade

East Lothian had a headstart in all this as the third principle of the County Development Plan was to make provision for the legitimate recreational needs for the region. Perhaps I should explain that the word legitimate was inserted by the County Clerk. I often wondered what was going through his mind.

North Berwick and Dunbar both had a major stake in the industry with 12 per cent of their employment in the tourist trade. The nature of their tourism had changed, as before the war both places attracted families for long holidays in owned or rented houses. Up to 1940 a weekend sleeper coach, attached to the midnight train from King's Cross, stopped at Dunbar and was de-coupled at Drem Station and terminated in North Berwick, bringing husbands and weekend guests to these seaside golfing resorts. This custom gradually faded away, the holiday houses were subdivided into permanent homes and the tourist trade became one of overnight and day visitors. Longer holidays were spent abroad in Spain and along the Mediterranean.

The County Planning Committee set up a Tourist Development Sub-committee under our Chairman, Provost McNeil, to which they co-opted the Burghs' tourist officers and a number of hoteliers and shopkeepers. Mr Togneri of the Lothian Hotel, Dunbar was made the Vice-Chairman—a very charismatic second generation Scottish Italian. I serviced this Sub-committee who advised the County Council on the measures they should take to promote tourism and to encourage hoteliers and others to join in. I remember their meetings with great pleasure.

County Strategy

The County's aim was twofold, first to spread the benefits of tourism more widely throughout the County and then to extend the tourist season, as many of the hotels had pathetic bed occupancy rates down to a third. The strategy was to promote the A1 as an International

Tourist Route up the east coast and so avoid tourists being diverted by the M6 to the Lake District and the west coast of Scotland. Within the County, this strategy would have the advantage of diverting traffic from the A198, the busy coast road to North Berwick, towards Dunbar and the beaches we were opening up to the public beyond. This strategy would spread the benefits of tourism through the heart of the County, would boost Haddington and lead visitors towards the charms of the Lammermuir villages and foothills. The increased traffic would strengthen the case for the improvement of the A1 at a time when all the Government's money was going into road schemes in the west of Scotland. Such improvements would increase the flow of tourists all the year round.

The County got no help in promoting this strategy from the road engineers of the Scottish Development Department, even though it was supported by their planning division whose officers no doubt had the same difficulties with their road engineers as I had with my County Road Surveyor. The road engineers stated that they could not give preference to any of the three roads that led across the Border: the A1 at Berwick-upon-Tweed, the A697 at Coldstream and the A68 at Carter Bar, which carried about equal volumes of traffic. So they divided their improvements, mainly straightening out bends, to all three routes. We had made common cause with Berwickshire and Northumberland County Councils to promote the A1, but the engineers were not prepared to concede anything. The County's only way of implementing their policy was by publicity and by making the A1 the more attractive and friendly route into Scotland. Leaflets were distributed to continental ferry firms docking at Newcastle and Immingham to draw the visitors up the A1 and we made it more congenial by providing serviced lay-bys and overnight caravan sites. The trunk road engineers denied any responsibility for making this provision and, in fact, did their very best to scupper us from doing so by insisting on long expensive deceleration and acceleration lanes leading into and out of the lay-bys.

Pencraig Serviced Lay-By

However a loop off the old A1 had been left at the top of Pencraig Hill and, with the financial help of the Carnegie United Kingdom Trust and the Royal Automobile Club, we created the first serviced lay-by and picnic site. This adjoined a pleasant woodland, which was owned by the County Council. Pencraig Hill, at 600 feet above sea level, gives splendid views to the south over Hailes Castle nestling in the River Tyne valley, and to Traprain Law and the Lammermuirs Hills beyond. A minute's stroll up the hill from the lay-by, we built a stone viewing rampart on the top of the boundary dyke to command the panoramic view to the north, of North Berwick, the Bass Rock and the great estate

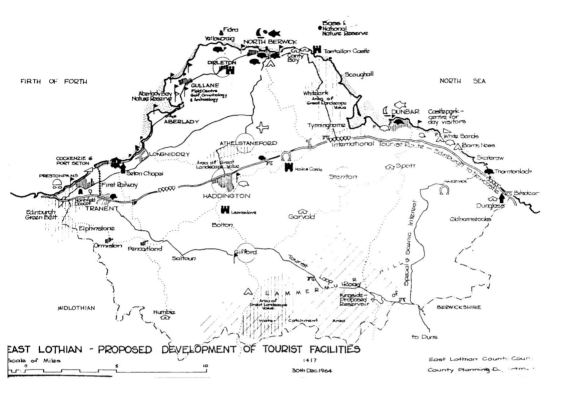

Plate XCII   Tourist Development Proposals

This map was submitted to the Secretary of State in 1965. The facilities are shown in
the standard notation and are largely self-explanatory. It shows the existing development
along the coastline to North Berwick and the proposed developments along the A1 and
around Dunbar in outline. The coast in between was designated as an Area of Great
Landscape Value with no developments. The south eastern part later became the
John Muir Country Park. The proposals for holiday huts, Danish style, in the hill
villages came to nothing as we could find no entrepreneur to finance them.

of Tyninghame. Russell Turner designed the melamine plaques that were let into the cope of the rampart describing these views. For those wanting a longer break in their journey, a narrow path was led across the top of the quarry into the woodland, where rides were cleared and bluebells planted.

All this was innovative enough in the 1960s, but perhaps even more innovative was the design of the public lavatory. In the past all public lavatories in Scotland had been built as little pavilions with separate entries for men and women. Each had a small entry hall, or lobby, with on the male side, an urinal and wash hand basins and a pair of water closets with penny in the slot brass meters. A somewhat similar arrangement pertained back-to-back on the ladies' side. In between there would be a broom cupboard for cleaning and often a room for the janitor. Their external appearance was usually slightly Japanese, with hipped tile roofs and panelled walling lovingly designed by a junior in the engineer's offices. In my time I managed to have two such pavilions demolished and was determined that I would not follow this model. I reverted to an earlier type, that of the privy at the bottom of the garden. A simple building with a door that you opened and there was both water closet and wash basin in a small space, no entry lobby, no hallway in which to be embarrssed—merely enter, close and bolt the door behind you. I intended that the back-to-back privies should be used by either sex, but public opinion forced me to allocate one to men and one to women. These two privies were stone built off the line of the front dyke with a mono-pitched pantile roof and a window over the door frame—as simple as simple could be. It was looked after by an old man, who climbed the hill each day from East Linton and seemed happy to spend a lot of his time on a seat in the sun yarning with the visitors.

The other features of the lay-by were our paired information boards. One carried the one inch to the mile coloured Ordnance Survey map of the County. The other was a drawing describing the significance of Traprain Law, both geologically and in pre-history for on top had been the large Iron-Age town of King Loth, who ruled the Lothians. The board also invited the visitor to turn off at the next town, East Linton to the east and Haddington to the west, for refreshment and accommodation. The Royal Automobile Club provided their standard emergency telephone and later we stationed our tourist accommodation caravan there. We tried to keep lorries out of this lay-by during daylight hours so that it could be enjoyed by the tourists but this was opposed by the road engineers. The lay-by is now rather commandeered by lorries which have presented problems as they turn blind across the carriageway to gain access from the east.

For several years we had to provide an annual report to the Carnegie Trustees on the use of the lavatories although the only statistics

Plate XCIII Pencraig Lay-by

(a) The rampart look-out which gives a great view to North Berwick and the Tyninghame coast. To the south a good view of Traprain Law and the Lammermuirs. Let into the cope are boards describing these views and the points of interest in the adjoining towns. To the left, the path along the top of the quarry leads to the bluebell wood.

(b) The pantiled privy showing the path to the look-out point and the walk to the wood. This serviced lay-by attracted much publicity as well as many clients. Would that other main road lay-bys had such facilities and were in such interesting situations.

we had were the number of toilet rolls used or stolen. However they were universally liked and I never had any complaints except that they were on the wrong side of the road for visitors arriving from England. But many used them all the same.

Bilsdean Serviced Lay-By

We got on the right side of the road with our second serviced lay-by at Bilsdean just at the boundary with Berwickshire, where road improvement works enabled us to squeeze in a lay-by up against the high railway embankment. The County Council acquired a narrow strip of raised ground where people could picnic and admire the long views of the Berwickshire coastal cliffs and be thrilled by the trains passing 'over their heads'. There the County Council built an information kiosk and sales point flanked by two privies. It was intended to be let during the season for the sale of sandwiches, etc, but this was never followed up. It remains unstaffed as a useful stopping point with lavatories open 24 hours a day, 364 days in the year—not New Year's Day. An attractive little walk was laid out through tunnels under the railway to the hamlet of Bilsdean with its three high bridges, now four: the first is an eighteenth century single high-arched masonry bridge which the County Road Surveyor wished to close and take off the list of public highways instead of just repairing the iron balustrades. The second is the Victorian railway viaduct on four stone arches, and the third is a reinforced concrete bridge of the 1930s which had to be replaced by the fourth—a new steel box girder bridge in 1994. These all make dramatic leaps over the deep Dunglass ravine, each embodying the construction techniques of the era in which it was built. I was never able to find a conservation group who were prepared to construct a devil's staircase down the side of the picturesque tree-filled ravine and through to the coast. Perhaps one day!

Information Lay-Bys

As well as these two serviced lay-bys there were a number of places where vehicles had pulled off the road and made informal lay-bys, which might or might not be regularised by the next road surfacing operation, without the extravagant acceleration and deceleration lanes demanded by the road engineers. The General Billboard and Posting Company was at that time promoting free-standing advertising panels for urban sites. I persuaded John Baillie, their Edinburgh manager, to erect pairs of these panels, not vertically but horizontally, landscape fashion, in these lay-bys. My department provided a poster for one panel describing the historic features and activities occurring in the view to be seen and the charms and tourist facilities in the next town. The company sold advertising space on the other to local hoteliers, shops and garages

Plate XCIV   Dunglass Three Bridges

Now there are five with the 1930s reinforced concrete bridge having to be replaced by a steel one. In the foreground the single arch masonry bridge (1798) which the County Road Surveyor wished to close instead of repairing the parapet. The railway bridge is in the middle and, out of sight, the earliest bridge down by the shore is at the foot of the ravine.

along the route. This met to some extent the demand of local businesses for main road publicity, without the proliferation of disfiguring signboards, but required people to draw into the lay-bys and get out of their cars to read them. It worked for a time, but Mr Baillie found it tiresome collecting the many small payments as compared with the ease of billing big corporations, such as Guinness or Shell, for use of the firm's hoardings, so he eventually gave it up and donated the panels to the County Council. We similarly had neither the staff nor the tradition of exacting payment from small businesses and so filled the second panel with the one inch to the mile coloured Ordnance Survey

The Tyne Valley

The strip of country spread out in front of you to the south is typical of the rich well-wooded farming land of the Tyne Valley. Looking down across the arable fields in the foreground the course of the river Tyne is marked by the trees on its banks, it has a footpath along most of its length and is much improved as a trout river   (Permits: Main, 87 High Street, Haddington).

The river traverses the whole County from its source high up in the Moorfoots south of Edinburgh, passing through the village of Pencaitland, the magnificent Burgh of Haddington and further downstream tumbling through the rocky Linn at East Linton and on past picturesque Tyninghame Village to the sea. In the past it powered many water mills and of these, five remain to this day, the Poldrate and Gimmers Mills in Haddington, Sandys Mill which you can see to the right, Preston Mill and Tyninghame Mill Preston Mill has been restored by the National Trust for Scotland and is open to the public where the miller will show you how the corn was milled in the eighteenth century. The Tyne also passes many fine mansion houses, Winton Castle; Saltoun Hall; Lennoxlove by Haddington, which is open to the Public every day July to September; Stevenson House whose yellow walls and chimneys you can see; and Tyninghame House.

The most prominent feature in the foreground view is the great volcanic mass of Traprain Law, which has a notable iron age settlement on its summit. Beyond the river the land rises gently at first, then more steeply in a series of long rolling foothills typical of a glaciated countryside, to the sheep grazings and grouse moors of the Lammermuir Hills. Ground down and rounded off by the passage of the ice, these hills have no notable peaks, but along the gently undulating line of the watershed it is possible to pick out Newlands Hill 1387 ft., Bleak Law 1508 ft. and Lammer Law 1733 ft.

Haddington

Do not miss Haddington, the finest surviving example of a late eighteenth century town in Scotland. The streets are divided by the Town House with its spire; elegant bank buildings line Court Street; the High Street has continuous elevations of buildings of architectural interest.

Plate XCV   Lay-by Board

An example of the information posters that we designed for the lay-bys on the A1 to entice travellers to explore the County. This board was on the south side of the road. On the north side was a poster describing the farming and extolling the charms and hostelries of East Linton.

map of the County. These, together with our interpretative posters, were annually renewed, using the good old cheap bill-posting technique of flour and water paste. Morayshire, the county which in statistical terms was closest to East Lothian, copied these boards and they subsequently have been taken up by the Scottish Tourist Board in a rather formalised way like a trade calender but without the interpretative poster, which was the distinctive East Lothian hallmark.

Archaeological Trail

Once tourist traffic was moving along the A1, the problem was to spread its benefits to the hillfoot villages. In 1973 the County Council had appointed a part-time archaeologist, Helen Nisbet, to survey all the field monuments in the County, interest the landowners in their preservation and secure where possible rights of access for the public. Her survey was built into our planning control information system, but it also led to the creation of an East Lothian Archaeological Trail—a motor trail which led into the Lammermuirs where the majority of the hill forts are situated. It was a booklet of some 30 pages describing ten sites along a route of some forty miles starting from Dunbar. This booklet has proved the most popular of all our productions with five reprints to date. The first stop on the trail was at White Castle Fort above Garvald where the Abbot of Nunraw Abbey allowed access to a very complete small hilltop Iron Age fort near the moorland road. Here we created a small lay-by and installed our usual interpretative board explaining the layout of the fort, how the people lived in it and their daily lives as far as is known. This and other monuments were marked by "concrete mile stones" into which were cast the words 'East Lothian Archaeological Trail' and the number of the station. The second station marked the Snail's Cleugh settlement, a fine pear-shaped hill fort, dating from the first or second century A.D. on the north side of the Whiteadder Valley. The land along the valley bottom below the dam was laid out as a picnic site and is very popular when the sea haar makes the coast unwelcoming.

Garvald and Gifford were the take off points for the roads looping over the Lammermuirs and through the Whiteadder Valley, and were the main beneficiaries of the increase in visitors. Public lavatories and children's playgrounds were provided in both villages for visitors and locals alike. The hoteliers responded with extensions and fuller services. Mr Muir at the Goblin Ha' Hotel in Gifford set up a pony trekking business which provided a grand way for visitors to explore the neighbourhood.

The Promotion of Dunbar

The other reason for promoting the A1 as an international tourist route was to help stimulate Dunbar, and open up the coastline east of the town and the splendid Belhaven Sands to the west to public access. This would take some of the pressure off Gullane and North Berwick. It would also help check rural depopulation in the eastern parishes. One of our earliest tourist promotions was that of sand-yachting on Belhaven Sands, by the removal of all the wartime obstructions sunk in the beach. Young farmers welded up these wheeled yachts and participated in the competitions and the beach was long enough and wide enough to provide good sport, but the craze died out, replaced by sail boarding.

Dunbar in the 1950s and 60s was sorely in need of a boost, and some would say it still is. It had a wide High Street, full of struggling shops and ruinous closes. It has fine coastal parks with excellent recreational facilities. It has a capacious harbour and the picturesque remains of a castle. It also had a little-used army barracks on the cliff top at the head of the High Street behind Lauderdale House which had great potential.

Plate XCVI   Dunbar

Castlepark Coach and Sports Centre
The opportunity to realise this potential came in 1958 when the barracks, last intensively used as an Officers' Training Centre during the war, were declared redundant. The Scottish Office proposed to use it as a borstal for young offenders. This damnable proposal was eventually fought off and resulted in the County Council acquiring the barracks and in my attempt to develop it as a centre for touring coaches in the summer and sports coaching in the winter. Our proposals were simple. Coach parties were being turned away from most 'respectable' resorts and hotels. At the barracks we could welcome them, provide a lounge and dining rooms for their sustenance in the barrack blocks with dormitory accommodation for youth parties on the upper floors and posher residential accommodation in the adjoining Lauderdale House. The Town Council would organise voluntary guides to show parties round the town, thus benefiting the shops and inns. A daytime wet weather club would be established in the old gym down by the

248

harbour for the day visitors, caravanners and those staying in bed-and-breakfast accommodation. In winter, the buildings could accommodate groups for sports training holidays on the excellent frost-free grounds with coach transport provided by the Scottish Sports Council, which at the time was encouraging such establishments.

The drab appearance of the tarred barrack square was to be overcome by making a virtue of it through the acquisition of four 25 pounder field guns. These cost the County Council £25 each plus £25 for their transport from an Ordnance Depot outside Nottingham. The guns were in full operational order but without their breech blocks and provided endless entertainment for children of all ages, traversing and raising their barrels until they got rusted up by the sea air. I was accused in the press of defiling the memory of all the artillery men who had used these guns during the war. However I was fireproof because as a subaltern in the Rifle Brigade my carrier platoon was part of a 'Jock Column' which, with a troop of South African gunners and its 25 pounders, raced across the Western Desert to hold the Ageila gap in February 1942. I remember the terrifying noise of Rommel's blitzkrieg as it advanced at dawn through the gap and our valiant gunners firing over open sights in the vain attempt to halt them, before we had to

Plate XCVII   Dunbar Artillery

The 25 pounder field guns were acquired to enliven the barrack square. Great playthings for children of all ages! Behind are the two storey barrack blocks which were to be used for the reception and catering of coach parties and on the first floor as dormitories for sports coaching groups. But this never came to pass and they were subsequently demolished, after my time.

race back again to El Adam, south of Tobruk, and eventually to El Alamein. Anyhow, these four guns at Dunbar were not sold to Third World countries to continue their deadly purpose.

The Proposals Flounder

This whole tourist initiative floundered when the Dunbar Town Council was not prepared to give the catering rights in the old gym—renamed the Victoria Ballroom—to Mr Harwell, a well known outside caterer with whom I had reached agreement to run the Coach and Sports Centre. It was not approved because the local rugby club wished to use one of their own members to do the catering for their dances. It left me with a fifteen year struggle to make the Barracks pay and play some other part in the development of the town's tourism.

The two large stables, one stone-built and slated for the cavalry horses, and the other built of corrugated cast-iron for the artillery horses, were let to Willie Dale, the farmer at Lochhouses, to house his collection of vintage cars which were subsequently housed in the Myreton Motor Museum. We also let out accommodation for scuba divers which was just coming in and has since flourished in Dunbar. The barrack-room blocks were more difficult to let, but Spaniards came to the rescue and established a scampi factory employing 50 people in two of them—an early example of the commercial acumen of the Spaniards who have since won so much of the United Kingdom vegetable trade. Lauderdale House was let as temporary offices, first to Belhaven Breweries and then to the South of Scotland Electricity Board and lately to John Hume Robertson, our M.P. We set up Robert Hughes in the coal depot and he has since developed a major haulage business and it gives me pleasure to pass or be passed by his lorries on the road.

Their tourist development having failed, Dunbar got a boost from the building first of the Cement Works, two miles south of the town, and later of the Torness Power Station, six miles to the south. The construction workers inhabited the B and B accommodation and this led to some house building and a substantial rise in the resident population but did little to restore the town's fine buildings. The town had to wait 20 years for the Dunbar Initiative to be set up by the District Council, long after the Town Council's demise. The economic conditions of the 1960s and early 70s were not such as to lead to risk taking by private enterprise or local authorities. Dunbar certainly lacked bright sparks or people with a long term vision. They were contented with life in a comfortable, decaying town. Subsequently they lost their last chance of tourist development as the three large hotels went out of business and became derelict. After my time, even their beautiful rock-cut bathing pool was closed and cleared away; the barrack blocks, stables, and the guard-room were demolished, leaving only Lauderdale

House to close the view up the High Street. This was converted to housing, not the public use it warranted. A large hi-tec leisure pool was built on the cliff top and the square covered with grass. What a failure of civic design!

Hopefully this downward trend may be reversed by the legacy of a Dunbar 'lad of parts', who emigrated to America as an eleven year old in 1849. He did not bring back large pots of gold as did Andrew Carnegie, his contemporary, but developed a whole ecological philosophy and a way of looking at nature and human life as 'hitched to everything else in the Universe' which may yet save the World and Dunbar.

John Muir

In 1966 Bill and Mamie Kimes came over from California to see the birthplace of John Muir. They were the bibliographers of John Muir who in 1913, a year before he died, had published the first volume of his autobiography *"The Story of My Boyhood and Youth"*. The first three chapters told of the first eleven years of his boyhood in Dunbar before that glorious evening of 18 February 1849 when, as he wrote: "I and David were at Grandfather's fireside and solemnly learning our lessons as usual, when my father came in with the news, the most wonderful, most glorious that wild boys ever heard, 'Bairns', he said, you needna' learn your lessons the nicht for we gang to America the morn". *'The Story'* then goes on to describe the hard hard work of a pioneering family in Wisconsin up to when, at the age twenty-six, he left: "one university for another, the Wisconsin University for the University of the Wilderness". This is not the place to repeat his story which is now becoming well-known, but merely to say that by the time of his death in 1914 he had made a reputation as the first ecologist, was credited with being the father of the National Park system in America and had left collected literary works of some twenty volumes. None of these was available in Scotland nor even in the National Library of Scotland. He was unknown in Scotland although he was proud of his Scottish descent and had never hidden it from his fellow Americans. John Muir is sanctified by his life, his writings and his philosophy by the youth of America, a hero for our times.

How right I was to repatriate this long-lost son to his homeland as part of the County's celebration of "The Countryside in 1970". Russell Turner organised an exhibition in Dunbar of Muir's life with stunning black and white photographs of Yosemite National Park by Ansel Adams. These were donated by the Sierra Club which John Muir had founded in 1892 to help with his campaign for National Parks. This exhibition made Dunbar aware of the stature of its most famous son. In 1976 the East Lothian District Council was searching for a name for the Country Park it was proposing to establish over land I had negotiated round the

Plate XCVIII   John Muir

Born in 138 High Street, Dunbar on 21st April 1837. Died Los Angeles 24th December 1914.
Father of the American National Park System and 'green' philosopher for our time. There are plans afoot for a centre in Dunbar to spread his message in Europe.

mouth of the River Tyne. The Earl of Haddington, understandably, did not want it to be called Tyninghame Country Park foreseeing coach loads of people arriving at his mansion house expecting tea. Ian Fullerton suggested that it should be called "The John Muir Country Park" for it was where Muir had roamed during his boyhood, bird nesting and enjoying "the marvellous singing and soaring of the larks".

However, before going overboard on our new-found hero, I thought he should be checked out as the Americans are prone to great hyperboles. Mary and I took the opportunity of a holiday in America to visit our son Benjamin, who was on a year's exchange with the University of Pennsylvania at Philadelphia. We flew with him to California to see the national parks Muir had founded, talk to people in the Sierra Club and visit Martinez, where the large Italianate house in which he died is a National Monument. We were received by the Martinez City Council and I was given the freedom of the City. They were delighted to make the link with Dunbar and a modest exchange of students has taken place ever since as well as a growing pilgrimage of Americans to Dunbar.

His Birthplace

Graham Duncan, who had succeeded me as Director of Planning in East Lothian District Council, managed to secure John Muir's birthplace at 138 High Street. It was the top, second floor, flat in an eighteenth century building in a property owned by Mrs Hawryluk which she had applied for planning permission to turn into a fish and chip shop. This would hardly have been appropriate to John Muir's memory. So he arranged a deal whereby the Council restored the building with the ground floor used as a photographic shop by Stephanie, her daughter, who would live on the first floor flat. The top flat would be leased to the District Council and be open to the public as a small museum which Mrs Hawryluk furnished with bygones of the 1840s. There was also a video programme telling the story of John Muir, born in these humble circumstances and risen to the height of an American hero. Not only had his birthplace survived but all the features mentioned in "The Story" were still to be seen and in my lecture to the Sierra Club I used photographic slides of them all. I photographed the Castle, the Earl of Lauderdale's garden, the High School, the railway station, the broken bottles on the garden walls, his grandfather's house, and the lettering on the shop fronts from which he had learnt his alphabet and of course the rock pools, the wild lands and the smooth cultivation. The only two features I was not able to photograph were his first school on Devil's Brae, which had been cleared to make way for Victoria Street down to the new harbour, and No 140, later the Lorne Temperance Hotel, where the Muir family moved as they outgrew the flat. This had been rebuilt as Smith's the Bakers, but the garden behind, which Daniel, his father, had tended as if it were part of the Garden of Eden, was still there. I never worked out whether my American audience admired this heritage or pitied the lack of progress over 130 years.

His Writings

On our return from America I persuaded the National Library of Scotland to acquire a set of Muirs' complete works and to put on a public exhibition of John Muir's Life. The Canongate Press were persuaded to republish "*The Story of My Boyhood and Youth*" for which they asked me to write an introduction. Later they published "*My first Summer in the Sierras*" for which Chris Brasher wrote the introduction. At the opening of the exhibition I gave all the guests a potted seedling of the *Sequoia giganteum*, the great Californian redwood, known in Britain as the Wellingtonia, raised from seed gathered by the Kimes in the Mariposa Grove which John Muir had protected. I hope in years to come to see these trees rising above the houses in Edinburgh's elegant crescents. Some years later to mark the Centenary of the Sierra Club I received a presentation gift of 100 seeds which had been taken to the moon and back by the astronaut, Neil Armstrong, a great fan of John Muir's, and a grove of redwoods were planted in Tyninghame.

The John Muir Trust

Quite separately, the John Muir Trust was established in 1988 to safeguard wild places in Britain. I was asked to be a trustee but declined and suggested they appoint my son Benjamin whose passions were mountaineering and the love of wild places and whose imagination and natural abilities would serve the Trust well. The John Muir Trust is now supplementing the efforts of the National Trust for Scotland in its care for places of natural beauty but in place of the National Trust's emphasis on visitor facilities, which has for many marred its custody, the John Muir Trust emphasis is on the conservation of the place and working with its inhabitants for their own sake. The Trust has the Prince of Wales as their Patron and has been most successful in raising money and to date have acquired some 35,000 acres of the best wild land in Scotland.

The John Muir Trust has maintained a link with Dunbar and has an annual gathering in the town to mark his birthday on the 21st April 1837. At one of these birthdays Don Bracewell, an outdoor educational adviser with the Lothian Regional Council, dressed up some primary school children in Victorian costume and they posted letters they had written to all the World's Heads of State telling them of John Muir and asking what their countries were doing about saving wild land. We were all flabbergasted and delighted at the response they received. Out of this was born the idea of a John Muir Centre in Dunbar to propagate his philosophy. The idea was hijacked by the District Council who proposed to establish a visitor centre in the John Muir Country Park— more recreational than educational. This raised a storm of protest as it was so contrary to all that John Muir stood for. It was abandoned by the District Council and the Dunbar John Muir Association was founded to produce an educational and proselytising centre in the town itself. This was a dream until the National Lottery encouraged the Association to proceed with their ambitious plan which could put Dunbar on the map, not just as a seaside town, the castle town of Black Agnes, the Cromwellian battlefield or indeed as the Scottish source of cement, but as an International Centre for the Protection of Wild Lands of the World and the Careful Use of the Globe, the message that John Muir was the first to spread.

John Muir Country Park

The County has no mountainous land. Its wild land is best seen in the shore round the mouth of the Tyne where the forces of wind and sea continue to fashion the land and men's endeavours to reclaim land for

Plate XCIX   John Muir Country Park

The southern half of the Park showing the broad beach and the hooked dune called
Spike Island as it was once separated at high tide from the land. The main course of
the Tyne is at the bottom of the picture and across the river the trees come down to
the rocky shore.

agriculture have been thwarted. It is this wild land where John Muir roamed as described in *"The Story of his Boyhood and Youth"* and it has been rightly named after him—The John Muir Country Park.

It came about this way. After the dispute concerning the roadway to Tyninghame Links described in Chapter Two had been resolved, I considered that the County Council should establish public rights of access to the coastal land as well as the right of way. Provisions for this were contained in the Countryside (Scotland) Act 1970 although they had not been much used. This put some financial liabilities on the County Council, not just for fencing and other works, but also, it was argued, for insurance and loss of value. In the end these could not be justified and public access has caused no damage which has been subject to a claim.

The Tyninghame Estate however did not own the foreshore and so we had to lease this from the Crown Estate Commissioners who were by this time trying to re-assert their rights all round the Scottish coastline. This meant that we had to map where the foreshore started and over several chilly days we pegged out and surveyed the Low Mean Spring High Water Mark according to the tide timetables. On the Belhaven Sands the coastline was accreting and Spike Island was now no longer cut off by the tide and so was included in the Tyninghame Estate Access Agreement rather than the Crown Estate Commissioners' lease. We also acquired land at Linksfield from the estate for a car park and subsequently the small pine plantation to the north. In all, it amounts to some 731.5 hectares and was duly designated a Country Park as provided for in the Countryside (Scotland) Act 1970. It is the only country park in the County as I never wasted time in designating Country Parks at Gullane, Yellowcraig or White Sands acquired prior to passing this Act, although they readily met the criteria.

Caravans and Camping

The two aspects of tourism that did flourish in the 1960s and 70s were caravaning and camping. Dunbar and North Berwick both had established cliff-top sites with regimented layouts and close cut grass and were very conspicuous with their pale coloured vans. Similar sites were typical throughout Scotland and England. Both sites have now been cleared. The Dunbar site was shifted to Seafield by the old clay-pits between Belhaven and West Barns. The site was planted up in my time and the ponds, once septic from tipped refuse, cleaned up. It enabled this bare site to accommodate caravans without creating much of a local uproar or introducing a cheap note on this main entry to the town. The North Berwick site was moved back behind the Rhodes Steading and sited on the former limestone quarries which had been filled in.

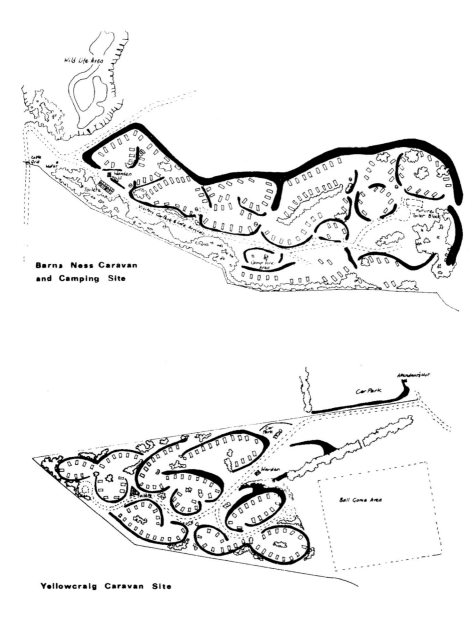

Plate C Caravan Sites
(a) Yellowcraig (b) Barns Ness

Caravan and camping sites had previously been laid out along military lines. These two sites established a new model with kidney shaped enclosures for twelve to eighteen vans ringed by earth banks or hedges. This encouraged camaraderie amongst the caravanners and increased the wild flowers and bird life which were much appreciated. The Yellowcraig site was laid out in association with the Caravan Club; the Barns Ness site in association with the Camping Club of Great Britain and Northern Ireland. Landscape Architect: Morris and Steedman.

The traditional regimented layouts were quite unsuited to our coastal lands and so we took a new approach to their layout and management. The County Council arranged 25 year leases with both the Caravan Club at Yellowcraig and the Camping Club of Great Britain and Northern Ireland at Barns Ness. Both sites were designed by Morris and Steedman, landscape architects.

Yellowcraig

The Yellowcraig site was the first to be developed. It was surrounded by grass mounds so that from the outside the caravans appeared 'hull-down'. Internally the site was divided into kidney shaped enclosures with brushwood fences, into which the old scotch dog roses or buckthorn hedges were planted. The enclosures each contained fifteen to twenty vans which was thought to be the optimum number for caravanners to strike up holiday friendships. The enclosures greatly increased the privacy of the caravanners and also the wealth of wild flowers and bird life that could be seen from their vans. The site received a Civic Trust Award in 1969 and the following year was visited by the Queen. She was so impressed with the site and the Caravan Club wardens, Squadron Leader and Mrs Hidden, that she enticed them away to run the caravan site that was being laid out at Sandringham. I was very sorry to see them go for they had done a lot introduce caravanners to the charms of the County. The site became so popular that we had to limit the length of stay to three days during the popular months.

Barns Ness

The Barns Ness site was more open as there was less material for the earth ramparts. The interior partitions were made of buckthorn hedges. It was screened from the future limestone quarrying by a coniferous shelterbelt, managed by the Scottish Committee of the Camping Club of Great Britain and Northern Ireland, and there was a more communal spirit. I designed a wigwam with a movable canvas cover and a barbecue site for weekend parties. It was opened by the Secretary of State for Scotland as it was the first project to benefit from a grant under the Countryside (Scotland) Act 1970. These two sites set completely new standards for caravaning and camping.

Another attractive caravan site was established in the large walled garden at Gosford House and operated by the Caravan Club. It was the County Council's policy that no caravan site was approved where the only casual recreation was either trespassing or driving out. Thus the Gosford garden site was only approved on the condition that caravanners had the right to walk through the woods and round the ponds at Gosford. The two coastal sites, of course, had the beaches and the dunes for the recreation of the caravanners.

We had proposed to boost the visitors to Haddington by another walled garden caravan site in Amisfield Park where the large eight acre garden where its columned and domed corner pavilions could have been put to good use, but nothing came of this.

We established a series of small overnight caravan pull-ins along the A1: at Thorntonloch, at East Linton, at Monksmuir, where there was already a small site, and at the Tranmere, a site behind the petrol station at the east end of Tranent. The proposal for a site at Butterdean Wood by Gladsmuir has not yet been realised.

We also considered various caravan sites near Ormiston for the travelling people, as the gypsies were called, but at that time the problem was not pressing. It was not until I got to the Region that I laid out, after quite a lot of trouble and controversy, the first official Travelling People's Site at Duddingston in Edinburgh. East Lothian now has a site at Smeaton.

Spread of Tourism to the Mining Area

We also spread the benefits of tourism to the mining areas in the west of the County. Our most ambitious proposal was the establishment of the Scottish Mining Museum at Prestongrange. This was already mentioned in Chapter Seven dealing with the rescue of the Giant Beam Pumping Engine and the other industrial archaeological remains. But this section deals with how we turned it into a modest tourist attraction and the debt owed to David Spence.

David Spence : Curator Mirabilis

I made a bargain with David Spence that I would promote Prestongrange as a historic site for the Scottish Mining Industry if he would be its Curator. It was he who had first shown me the Giant Beam Engine in 1951 and as pit manager had a survey drawn of the whole colliery before he was promoted to be Group Manager for the East Lothian Coalfield. All that remained of his colliery in 1968 was the Beam Engine and the Power House which still had the electricity sub-station for the miners' houses at Prestongrange. This was broken into one night and the vandals cut the cables, not realising that they were still live. They escaped with their lives but burnt the roof off the building. I persuaded the chief engineer of the Scottish Brick Company to use the insurance money to replace the roof. Over the years David Spence filled it with a fine selection of early machinery which is still there. It should be named 'The David Spence Gallery'.

David Spence had been born to a miner's family in Tranent and had gone to work at the age of fourteen at Glencairn Colliery alongside his father just before the miners' strike of 1926. He was a small stocky man and had a good brain and a great personality. He studied and

**Plate CI   David Spence,
born 1900, died 1985**

A very typical picture of a pitman
although he rose to be an Area Manager.
He is wearing his pit helmet with the
primitive miners' lamp which he
treasured. They were only used in
collieries with no risk of explosion.

passed the various exams and on nationalisation he was the manager
of Newcraighall Colliery from where he moved to Prestongrange and
later became Group Manager. He was a great favourite at the Scottish
Headquarters of the National Coal Board in Edinburgh. He had the
great ability to get consistent and loyal work from volunteers, both
male and female, whom he gathered round him at Prestongrange and
who devoted Sunday after Sunday to the conservation and exploratory
work. It was indeed industrial archaeology as the whole site had been
covered with cinders and blaes and this had to be scraped away leaving
the foundations exposed in "Abbey Style", as we joked. One of the
features revealed was the sooty area where fires were kept burning to
draw the foul air up the pit before the days of pumped ventilation.

One of our difficulties was that there was so little left on the site
to explain what a colliery really was like and so we set about assembling
some of the missing plant. David was most scornful of the small winding
head stock frame which was given to the collection and now stands
over one of the earlier shallow shafts beside the road. When
Newcraighall Colliery closed he was determined to get its winding engine
and with the volunteers we spent many hours taking it apart and moving
it to Prestongrange, where it still awaits assembly. All this activity
soon attracted wider attention and we had our glory day down in London
as a finalist in the BBC's Chronicle Annual Award, where we competed
resplendent with white heather from David's garden in our buttonholes.
We won! This gave a great fillip to our endeavours. The County Council
then provided David with "a brusher", the pit name for an odd-job
man, to help with the maintenance. A railway preservation group,

'The Prestongrange Society', was established to work the various pug engines and other steam equipment gathered on the site one weekend a month. There were other plans, which I hope will be carried out eventually, to cut a drift mine into the bank to the south of the site, to construct a wooden ladder shaft and erect a replica horse gin—as used in the fourteenth century and consisting of a horse harnessed to a large wheel roping up the baskets of coal.

In due time, David Spence lost his wife and then his old Labrador dog and said that all he had left was this colliery. By then British Coal had made him the Historical Curator of Mining Machinery in Scotland. He jokingly said that I was worse than the old coal owners and I had thirled him to the colliery. He was there every day inspiring visitors with his reminiscences and his passion for the coal industry and furthering the cause of industrial archaeology. By 1975 we had 10,000 visitors a year. David's only other recreation was bowling and his holidays were spent touring with a group of friends playing bowls throughout Scotland.

Pencaitland Railway Walk

The County Council was the first in Scotland to acquire a disused railway line in 1965 and exploit its recreational value. This was the old Smeaton to Gifford line from the County boundary at Crossgatehall through Ormiston and Pencaitland to West Saltoun with the branch line to Macmerry. The final stretch from West Saltoun to Gifford had already been sold by British Rail to the adjoining landowners and so was not available, although its formation still remains. There was a great deal of fuss in the Committee about this purchase, as the Council was taking over the legal burdens of maintaining the bridges, the fences, the drains and all the other minor engineering works along the route. British Rail had spent very little on their maintenance over the preceding years and the farmers, despairing of the procrastination of British Rail, had in effect assumed responsibility for them. However it was thought that if the County Council owned it, farmers would be at the Councillors to insist that the County Council carried out these old legal obligations. In fact that never happened and the lines have proved attractive, level, well-drained walks through the countryside for people on foot and on horseback. We prepared a management plan for the walkway, its embankments and cuttings, which, I remember, specified three types of treatment: one, the traditional controlled burning of the vegetation, another the coppicing and encouragement of natural regeneration with the provision of nesting boxes, and finally, bare areas where trees were to be planted. On the lengths where there were double lines, one was reserved for horse riding where pony clubs and riding schools were allowed to erect jumps.

This railway line had served many collieries along the route and where the sidings took off we erected concrete 'tombstones' naming the colliery, the coal company, the seams worked, the peak numbers of miners, the dates of its opening and closing and any recorded incidents. This information was inset into the cast concrete moulds using cork letters. The entry points to the railway walk were provided with small car parks and marked by old railway signals which we obtained through Graham Duncan's father, who had worked with British Rail. One great disappointment was when I lost my argument with the County Roads Committee to keep the stone-arched bridge which carried the Pencaitland to Ormiston road, A6093, over the railway. It was demolished and the rail cutting filled in, so straightening the road and reducing highway maintenance but losing some of the magic of the walkway and presenting a possible accident hazard to the walkers. Nevertheless the walkway gives great pleasure to local people with its wealth of wildlife and its intimate views of the countryside and one meets an increasing number of Edinburgh people walking along it.

Haddington to Longniddry Branch Line

Later the County Council acquired the Haddington Branch Line from Longniddry with a view to providing facilities for the Scottish Railway Preservation Society to run their collection of steam trains, which at that time were in store at Falkirk. This steam railway would have given a fine *"Little Red Engine"* journey through the countryside and would have been a great tourist attraction for Haddington as are the Great Little Railways of Wales. But the proposal raised great objections from the residents of the new houses at Somnerfield Park in Haddington, who did not want it in their back yard (NIMBY). They first complained of possible soot nuisance and when we overcame that objection by moving the engine shed nearer the bypass, they objected that they would not be able to get their children to bed in the evenings for watching the trains go by! In the light of this parental weakness and continued opposition by the Town Council, the County Council decided not to proceed with it. The Scottish Railway Preservation Society later established their headquarters at Bo'ness and the Haddington line became a walkway.

Plate CII   Pencaitland Railway Walk

The Information Board which was erected at the various access points to the railway walk. This was available to walkers, cyclists and horse riders. I was always conscious of the attraction of "Food for Free" available along the route. On closer inspection I see that this edition was prepared by the District Council after my time but it was drawn by Margaret Montgomery of my staff, and follows closely my design.

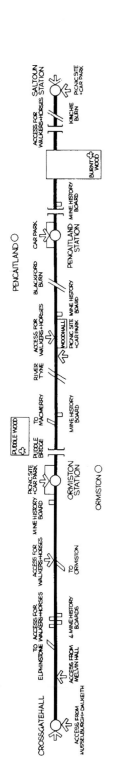

CROSSGATEHALL — ELPHINSTONE WALKERS+HORSES — TO ACCESS FOR — MINE HISTORY BOARD — ACCESS FOR WALKERS+HORSES — PICNIC SITE + CAR PARK — ORMISTON STATION — PUDDLE BRIDGE — TO MACMERRY — MINE HISTORY BOARD — RIVER TYNE — ACCESS FOR WALKERS+HORSES — WOODHALL PICNIC SITE + CAR PARK — MINE HISTORY BOARD — BLACKFORD BURN — PENCAITLAND STATION — MINE HISTORY BOARD — CAR PARK — BURNT WOOD — ACCESS FOR WALKERS+HORSES — SALTOUN STATION — KINCHIE BURN — PICNIC SITE + CAR PARK

ACCESS FROM MUSSELBURGH-DALKEITH — ACCESS FROM MELVIN HALL — 4 MINE HISTORY BOARDS — TO ORMISTON — PUDDLE WOOD

THE WALK

The 12km (7.5mile) walkway along the old railway line extends from the old railway station at West Saltoun through Pencaitland and Ormiston to a car park at Crossgatehall. The 5/acres of land were acquired to ensure public use of the ready-made level path which passes through otherwise inaccessible parts of East Lothian. Walkers, cyclists and horse riders can enjoy views of farmland and former mining areas that the motorist never sees. Most sections of the walkway are suitable for wheelchair users. There are connections to Whitecraig and Musselburgh by way of the River Esk from Crossgatehall.

The Railway Walk is managed by the Department of Leisure, Recreation and Tourism through the Countryside Ranger Service.

Coal mining in the area dates from about 1841. The Railway Walk fringes the East Lothian Coalfield which is an outlier of the much larger Midlothian Field. All the pits are now closed and only remnants of a once flourishing industry are visible from the Walk. This is a 4-4-0 tank locomotive class D5 designed by Dugald Drummond, the last passenger tank engine designed for the North British Railway Company. It was withdrawn from service in 1929.

THE RAILWAY

The history of the railway is linked to coal-mining rather than to passenger transport. The section of the line from Ormiston westwards to Smeaton, was opened in 1867 by the North British Railway Company. The remainder of the Walk from the junction at Ormiston to West Saltoun follows the line built in 1901 by the Gifford and Garvald Light Railway Company, at a cost of £100,000. The service continued until 1844, purely for goods traffic, the passenger service having been withdrawn in 1933. The closure of the line was due to the shutdown of all mining works in the area. It is generally believed that the railway was conceived too late, was poorly planned and badly run.

GIFFORD STATION IN 1927

THE NATURE

The trackside is actively managed to encourage a richer variety of wildlife than is found in the adjacent land. Left undisturbed for many years, it is now an important haven for wildlife. For example, over 90 species of birds have been recorded.

Scrub provides food and cover for hedgerow birds such as the finches and warblers; themselves prey for the hunting sparrow-hawk. As it matures and woodland develops, other bird species become more common.

Similarly, hawthorn and wild rose give way to oak and ash. Apple, rowan, sycamore, cherry, pine and willow can also be observed.

Open grassy banks are managed for their wildflowers such as cranesbill, knapweed, wild strawberry and vetch. These attract butterflies, bees and hoverflies; whilst the grassy ground cover provides a home for mice and voles.

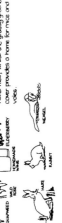

Lengthening the Season

Thus we spread the benefits of tourism through the County, but we were much less successful at lengthening the tourist season as hotel after hotel closed. Nature study however is an all-year-round activity and many people come to the County in winter to see the geese at Aberlady Bay, to Yellowcraig to hear the seals singing and, curiously enough, to the ash lagoons at Musselburgh where a great variety of ducks and waders can be seen. Cockenzie Power Station has conferred an added bonus with its wasted hot water providing excellent sea angling off the walkway. These interests, together with the more intense use of the golf courses, draw people who benefit restaurants and local businesses throughout the winter.

Guide Books

Good guide books are essential to attract tourists and extend their stay and make it more enjoyable. We produced in all twenty-five guides and leaflets. County guide books had been produced before my time by the Simmoth Press and other firms in Dundee, balefully cobbled together from gazetteers and financed by the advertisers. After recasting the Haddington guide book to show off its architectural qualities, I recast the County guide book as four car drives: two out from Edinburgh, along the A198 to North Berwick and along the A1 to Dunbar; and two back to Edinburgh, one along the foothills of the Lammermuirs passing through the attractive hill villages, and the other over the Lammermuirs to the Whiteadder Valley and back through Gifford. They were written to interest visitors and residents alike in the many features of natural and historic interest, and told of the efforts the County Council had made to conserve them. As the County Convener proudly said in his introduction: 'Visit East Lothian and see the Difference'. Harry More-Gordon, the artist, designed colourful covers for the guide books and we used Tom Scott for the photographs. He was recommended to me by Colin McWilliam, but I was very doubtful when I first met him helping out in a photographer's studio/shop on Greenside Place, Edinburgh, where the main trade seemed to be providing photographs of visiting sailors and their girls taken behind wooden cut-outs in highland dress. However, he was the accredited photographer to the National Gallery of Scotland and thoroughly enjoyed the townscape and landscape work we gave him.

Today many planning departments have excellent in-house graphic designers and produce splendid literature, but these were pioneering efforts. The most ambitious was the East Lothian Golfing Handbook. Archie Weir, who was our public relations consultant at the time, and Frank Moran, the Scotsman golf correspondent, produced plans and descriptions of the eleven golf courses in the County printed

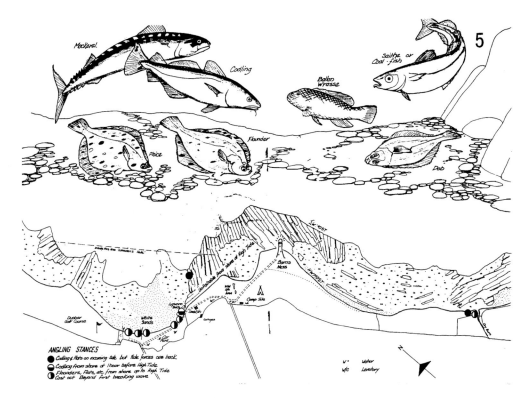

Labels in illustration:
Mackerel. Codling Saithe, or Coal-fish Balan Wrasse Plaice Flounder Dab 5

ANGLING STANCES
● Codling & Flats on incoming tide but tide forces one back.
◑ Codling from shore at 1 hour before High Tide.
◐ Flounders, Flats, etc. from shore up to High Tide.
◑ Cast out Beyond first breaking wave.

V = Water
W/C Lavatory

Plate CIII   Barns Ness Sea Angling

The Barns Ness booklet consisted of 17 pages and 11 illustrations covering the geology, the seashore fauna, the seaweeds, the plants and the birds as well as the Limekiln and Caravan Site. It was a complete compendium, written by experts, before the days of widespread field guides. Drawing by our Hamish Macdonald.

on re-cycled paper the colour and texture of a well kept green. It sold at 20p.

Substantial booklets were produced for Yellowcraig and Barns Ness. The Barns Ness booklet is a complete description of the site written by specialists. Archie Mathieson compiled a charming little booklet *Life on the Seashore* costing 10p, in the days when there were few other pocket handbooks dealing with shells and the small creatures to be found in the rock pools.

I was also proud of a free leaflet which we arranged jointly with a postcard publisher who used and shared the cost of the colour plates. There was a dearth of good scenic postcards at that time. The five views which Russell Turner provided were of: Tantallon Castle from the sea, showing its cliff-top position with the high screen wall to the landward and defensible cliffs to the seaward; Dunbar Harbour empty but for the colourful lifeboat; the interior of Preston corn mill; Yellowcraig beach with a view to Fidra; and a gannet and chick on the Bass Rock, our major wildlife attraction. In other years, to encourage foreign tourists, we produced leaflets in Swedish, Dutch, French and

German and put them on the North Sea ferry boats. This was done not only to attract foreign tourists but to help with our conservation work. We found that there was nothing like admiration from foreigners to impress the local people. The Scandinavians especially appreciated all we were trying to do, as well as our cheap beer.

We always considered it worthwhile to produce leaflets for distribution by honesty boxes to explain all our main conservation projects—Gullane dunes, Longniddry foreshore, Pencraig picnic area, Prestongrange Historical Site and Beam Engine, Stenton, Oldhamstocks, Woodhall picnic site, the Dovecots of East Lothian and the Pencaitland Railway Walk. All this greatly boosted our reputation and the County's attractiveness to tourists and residents alike.

13

TRANSPORTATION

Relationship between Roads, Land Use and Planning
Tranent Bypass • The Edinburgh City Bypass
County Roads A198 • North Berwick Rail Service
Bus Services • Post-bus • Pedestrians
North Berwick Pedestrianisation Scheme • Car Parking
Parking Plan for Haddington • Accident Black Spots
Road Drainage • Dykes and Hedges • Traprain Law
Wild Flower Verges

I, like several other County Planning Officers, confess to having difficulty in working with the County Road Surveyor. Up to the passing of the Town and Country Planning (Scotland) Act 1947, County Road Surveyors had usually carried out the planning function under the Restriction of Development Act 1932 and administered elemental town planning by laying down road widening lines. In several Scottish counties, including Berwickshire, they took over the full responsibilities under the 1947 Act. They were really quite unfitted for this role with their rather narrow outlook and the rigidity of the engineering codes of practice by which they were constrained. In my case three of them were Aberdonians, who had been trained as railway engineers, which did not help. Their predecessor, Mr Calvert, who was the County Road Surveyor of East Lothian before I arrived and whom I never met, seemed to have been a road engineer with whom I could have worked well and whose road works showed great visual sensitivity. At the end of my time with Lothian Region I had a very good working relationship with Peter Mason, Director of Highways, a Yorkshireman, who thought problems out including their visual appearance, instead of throwing the rulebook at them. So perhaps it was not entirely my fault.

Relationship between Roads, Land Use and Planning
The position was clearly a difficult one, well expressed by the Right Hon. Lord Emslie, then a young advocate, who appeared for the County Council at the Development Plan Inquiry. One of the contentious issues was the widening of the Hardgate in Haddington where the County Road Surveyor was supporting the pre-war road widening lines. These

were equidistant from the centre of the road and so affected properties on both sides, thus ensuring maximum blight of property values and minimum prospects of actual road widening being done. Mr Emslie calmly told the County Clerk that, as it was a Development Plan Inquiry, it was not the view of the County Road Surveyor that he had to put forward, but the Planning Officer's views and these should take account of all the factors, including in this case the visual impact, the presence of listed buildings, the ruin of Bothwell Castle and the urgency of the works. The County Surveyor's opinion was only one factor on which I and the Planning Authority should exercise judgment. We must be seen to have taken all considerations into account. I was extremely grateful to Mr Emslie for this lesson which the County Clerk never forgot, and the County Road Surveyor never forgave. Tom Hewitson, the City of Edinburgh Planning Officer, was not so lucky as he was ordered to incorporate the City Engineer's disastrous inner ring road proposal in the City's Development Plan. It was not approved by the Secretary of State, while I achieved the modest widening and redevelopment of the Hardgate.

Plate CIV   Hardgate Road Widening, Haddington.

These new buildings line the west side of the Hardgate. I wanted 'genuine' stone designs for the two storey houses and the three story block set back was constructed of brick and harl. None of this would have been possible under the Highways Acts; it needed the Comprehensive Development Area powers of the Planning Acts. Architect: J A W Grant.

Tranent Bypass

The only major road proposal in the County Development Plan 1953 was the Trunk Road Authority's southern bypass of Tranent which had to be incorporated into the Plan. The line of the bypass severely restricted the residential expansion of Tranent to the south, which was the only direction it could expand because of the subsidence dangers (see Plate V). I managed to write into the Plan that the County Council's approval was conditional on the line being reviewed every five years in the light of the Burgh's housing requirements. If this line had been adopted the bypass would now be deeply imbedded in the Wester Windygoul and Carlaverock housing areas. As the years went by, it became quite apparent that the economic justification for building the bypass could be met only if a northern bypass was adopted to cater for the traffic flows on both the A1 and the A198 road to North Berwick. Luckily there was a fine, thoughtful, pipe-smoking engineer, Mr Macpherson, in the Scottish Development Department who accepted this argument.

The northern route for the Tranent Bypass had two disadvantages. First, it crossed an area of old coal workings at shallow depth, which would make the road fail the cost-benefit criteria and sterilise seams of coal that could be worked by open-cast methods. It was therefore agreed to extract the coal and restore the land to provide a solid foundation for the road, hence the Blindwells open-cast coal site. This decision was later incorporated as one of the principles of the Lothian Regional Structure Plan, namely that workable mineral deposits should not be sterilised by development, but extracted before it took place. The other disadvantage was that the bypass, which started in the east at Macmerry, would come off the high ground at Bankton and open up motorists' views of the unsightly two-horned bing and derelict coal stacking yards of Meadowmill. This appalling prospect was not a consideration that worried the trunk road engineers for one moment. It was left to the County to do something about it, and what we did has already been described in Chapter Nine.

The Edinburgh City Bypass

It fell to my department in the Lothian Regional Council to finally determine the overall alignment of the Edinburgh City Bypass All previous plans had shown it terminating at the A68 near Dalkeith. Its obvious role was to provide a southern City bypass connecting the A1, my international tourist route, in the east to the M8 and M9 in the west and the A90 (Forth Bridge) in the north. It would also link up all the principal roads radiating from the City. And this is how it was built. The resulting primary road network ensures quick and convenient road access within Lothian Region and to other parts of Scotland.

Unfortunately it was too late to change the route of the Musselburgh Bypass to lead it directly onto the City Bypass with a branch off to Leith, instead of the City Bypass being a branch off the Musselburgh Bypass. At one stage the Director of Highways even resisted the formation of a slip road for City Bypass traffic from the west turning north into Leith, because, he said, it was quicker for lorries headed for Leith to plunge through the western suburbs of Edinburgh. There was no question whether this was desirable. A further absurdity was the proposal to build the Millerhill section of the City Bypass from Sheriffhall on the A68 to Old Craighall on the Musselburgh Bypass, both dual carriageways, with a single carriageway, hence the roundabout at Sherriffhall. This absurdity was based on the argument that the traffic forecasts would not justify the additional cost of dualling the Millerhill section. I was glad to have saved the Regional Council this embarrassment. I also got the Bypass built under the A702 at Fairmilehead and under, rather than over, the Carstairs railway line at Wester Hailes and the Union Canal at Hermiston. At Wester Hailes an elevated road would have been as high as the flats.

Ironically, it was only possible to do all this as the City Bypass was not built as a Trunk Road, despite the fact that it linked up all the other Trunk Roads: the A1, the A68, the A7, the A702, and the A8; and is very much part of the national road network. The case for it being a Trunk Road was strenuously argued in the press and in the House of Lords by Lord Ferrier, but to no effect until 1996 when it was belatedly adopted as a Trunk Road, long after it had been completed. So it was designed and constructed by the Regional Council with an 85 per cent grant from the Government. I think it is all the better for it—certainly the landscape is.

County Roads A198

The Development Plan also proposed to relieve the traffic on the coast road, A198, by a series of village bypasses, of which only the Dirleton Bypass was built. These bypasses would not have reduced the coastal traffic and so I proposed a series of spurs and loops off the mid-road, B1377, which ran parallel to the main line railway. One loop would lead from Longniddry Station to Aberlady and then back to Ballencrief, and the road across Gullane golf course would be closed. Another loop would lead from Drem to Dirleton and North Berwick with a separate loop off to Gullane. The money was never available to carry out such a radical scheme, even if I had persuaded the County Council to adopt it.

North Berwick Rail Service

In 1963, during the Beeching era, British Rail proposed to close the

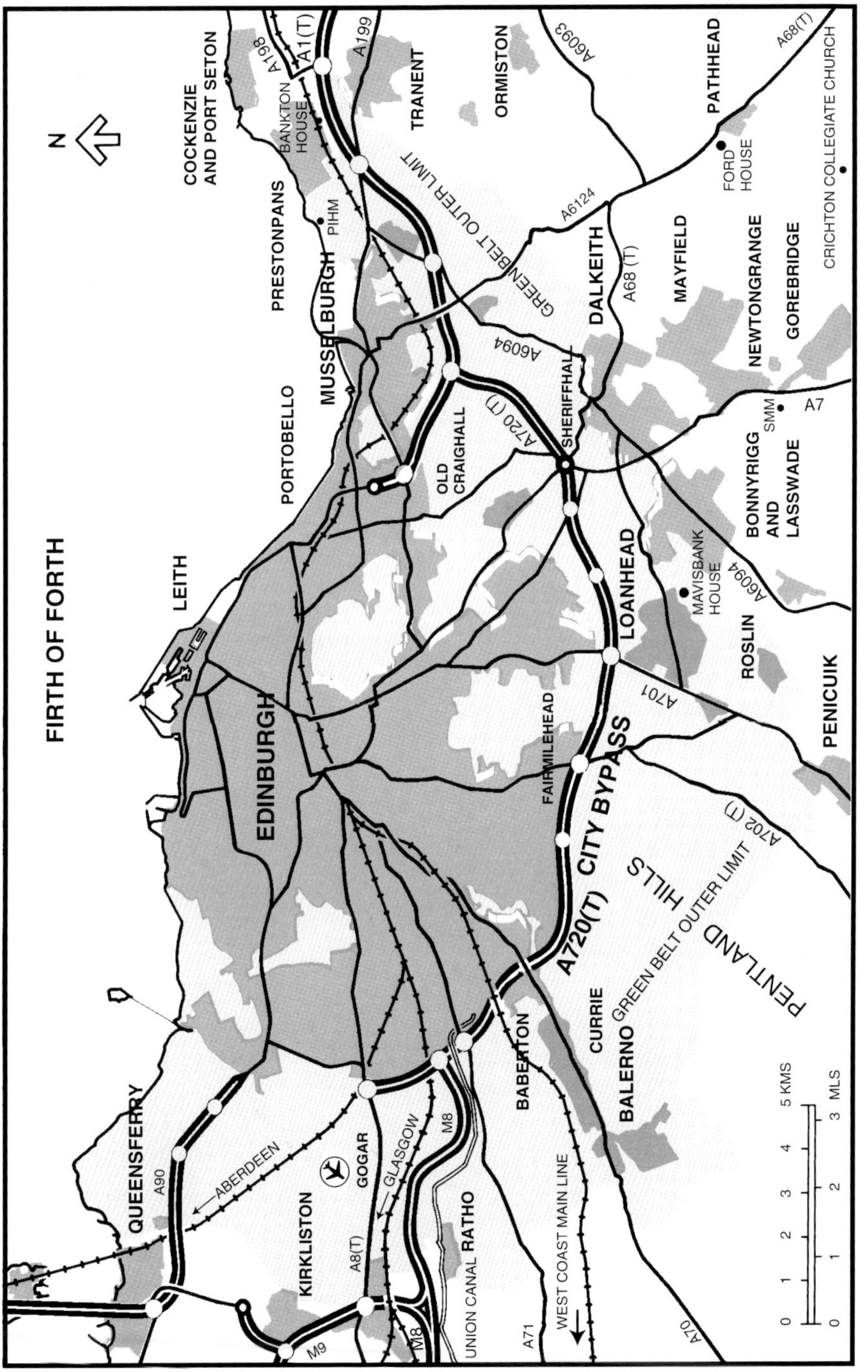

Edinburgh City Bypass and Other Main Roads

Plate CV   Edinburgh City Bypass

This drawing shows the Edinburgh Green Belt and the City Bypass linking up all the trunk roads approaching the City. It identifies those sections where I was able to prevent a number of absurdities proposed by the Director of Highways.

North Berwick branch line from Drem which had the townspeople up in arms. The County Council authorised me to employ Professor White of Newcastle University to provide the justification for keeping it open with the necessary public subsidy. He argued that the increased car traffic resulting from the rail closure would exacerbate congestion and delay for all road users in Musselburgh, and cleverly applied the Ministry of Transport formula to quantify the costs. Normally this formula was used to justify new road building but, turned on its head, it justified the retention of the North Berwick railway. As we predicted, rail traffic has since picked up and with electrification of the branch line made possible by a grant from the Lothian Regional Council, the future of the line is secure. It also attracted more passengers when the Regional Council persuaded British Rail not to terminate all the trains at Waverley, but to run some through to the Haymarket so that more Edinburgh offices and schools could be reached easily from the County. Many people now use the local stations with their extended car parks to travel into the City by train. It is these small measures which will have a cumulative effect on reducing congestion in the City and improving travel convenience for the inhabitants of the County.

It was also our determination that secured the listing of Drem station as a building of architectural or historic interest and ensured its preservation as a most attractive wayside station.

Bus Services

The County was quite well provided with bus services on the radial routes into and out of Edinburgh, but it was impossible to persuade Scottish Omnibuses Ltd to run looped services, for example Edinburgh—Haddington—Gullane—Edinburgh. There was also a shortage of bus shelters which the bus company said they could not afford. It is the waiting for buses which is the miserable part of travel by bus and I waged a forlorn battle for the 'heated seated bus shelter'. I built one at Macmerry Industrial Estate so that people who had put in a hard day's work, probably on their feet, did not have to stand in the bitter wind and rain for their bus home. But this shelter has now vanished. When I got to the Region I had more success with seated bus shelters, but none with the heated waiting room and kiosk which grace the bus terminals and busy interchanges that we saw in Switzerland.

Post-bus

The hill villages only had a weekend shopping bus service which was clearly inadequate for their inhabitants' varied travel needs. The Planning Department documented the needs of all the people in Garvald parish: university students wanting to get into Edinburgh, those wanting to attend clinics and surgeries, others going on shopping expeditions,

Plate CVI   Bus Shelter, East Saltoun

A seated village bus shelter converted from a wayside building provided by the Haddington Town Council to our design. There are other examples of wayside buildings being converted to shelters. That in the Hardgate, Haddington, was nick-named Fingal's Cave.

travelling to work, or joining a works bus in Haddington, a mother wanting to help her daughter on a farm, and some attending other appointments. We did this survey in our usual quick way by questioning knowledgeable people such as policemen, for it was in the days when the policeman lived in the village, or the district nurses who also knew a lot about the families and their travel needs and, of course, we checked up with the occasional family.

It was quite apparent that a forty-seater bus could in no way economically meet these varied needs but the post van, which then had to call twice daily for postal deliveries to the villages and the farms, was the ideal solution to the problem. A tradition had grown up of the postman doing messages, that is shopping, for outlying householders who were housebound, but they were strictly forbidden to give lifts.

Eric Crosbee had previously explored the possibilities of post buses in a chapter in the South East Scotland Survey and Plan. At the time there was a subsidy for new buses to improve bus company fleets and keep the vehicle builders busy and there was a discount on diesel fuel for their operation, both of which could apply to post-buses. So the time was ripe to promote the idea of a post-bus. We got a good

Plate CVII   John Mackintosh, M.P.

The Royal Mail post-bus service which still meets essential travel needs in remote areas throughout the United Kingdom was initiated by my report on the travel needs of the Garvald area which John Mackintosh, our Member of Parliament, promoted in Westminster. His deep understanding of rural life gained him many votes from the farming community and he left a safe Labour seat to John Hume-Robertson, M.P.

reception from the postmaster in Edinburgh, but it needed a political decision, so we approached John Mackintosh, our M P and on the basis of our report he persuaded the Minister of Transport in the Labour administration to set up three pilot projects in England, Wales and Scotland. Garvald was selected for the Scottish pilot scheme. All three were successful and so the post-bus service came into being, spread throughout rural Britain and continues to this day, despite the removal of the new bus subsidy. The County got two buses, one based in Haddington, the other in Dunbar to service Spott, Oldhamstocks and Innerwick. The post buses were not completely successful in meeting all the travel needs of the people as we could not persuade the postmasters to adjust the times of mail delivery to suit the travel needs. To do this the post bus had to be garaged not in the post town but in the furthest village. The post bus would then take the workers and students into the post town to catch the service buses to Edinburgh; then the postman would collect and sort his mail and start his round, taking with him any holiday maker wanting a walk in the hills or older people who had been rehoused off the farms in Haddington, wanting to spend the morning with their children still on the farms. During the morning delivery the postman would pick up people wanting to get to the post town for shopping or hospital visits, or to meet friends on adjoining farms. The postman would then return to the post town at lunch time and carry out his other duties. In the afternoon he would set off on his second delivery, taking home the shoppers, students and others before ending up in the village where he would be one more able-bodied man to help the community. Such an arrangement more or less fitted the majority of travel needs but it came up against the tradition of the breakfast time delivery of mail and the postmasters were not prepared to face the flak that they anticipated a mid or late morning delivery would occasion. We argued that if the reasons had been properly explained the irate majors and others might have been persuaded but to no avail. There was also the problem of housing the postmen in the villages but the County Council was prepared to provide accommodation for them. This shows how difficult it is to change ingrained customs and procedures of large organisations from the outside, even with the support of Parliament.

Pedestrians

Another disadvantaged class were pedestrians, that is all of us when we are not riding in cars or buses, and we got scant consideration from the County Road Surveyor. It was symptomatic that snow and ice were cleared and the carriageway gritted first before the pavements, where pedestrians were much more liable to serious personal injury than people cocooned in their cars. The County Road Surveyor's reply was that the frontagers were required by the Burgh Police Acts to clear the pavements in front of their property, but he made it no easier for them by ploughing the snow from the carriageway onto their pavement. The frontagers seldom carried out their responsibilities and he did nothing to encourage them to do so or to prosecute them for not doing it. One more meaningless rule from the book. I also wondered why the carriageways at junctions always joined each other on the same level and it was pedestrians and women pushing prams who had to step down and up at the kerbs. It was not until I got to the Lothian Region that we managed to change the practice. In busy shopping thoroughfares the pavements were carried through at the same level and the cars had to bump up and down into the minor road, thus showing the motorist that the priority lay with the pedestrians. How often too the carriageway was widened or straightened at the cost of the pavement but such operations within the boundaries of the highway were exempt from planning control.

North Berwick Pedestrianisation Scheme

Our worst case of pedestrian and vehicle conflict was in the narrow High Street of North Berwick, which could not cater for circulating traffic, service traffic, shoppers on foot and summer visitors. I set up a technical working party to examine the pedestrianisation of the street. It included Jack Burrows, a town planner from the Department of Health for Scotland, who later became the County Planning Officer for West Sussex, He was the only senior planner to "escape" from the civil service to local government and one of the few who returned to England

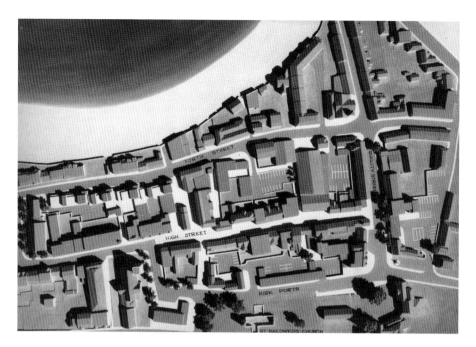

Plate CVIII   Pedestrianisation, North Berwick

Photograph of the model made by the Scottish Development Department to illustrate
the original proposal for making the east end of the High Street pedestrian only, shown
in white, creating a one-way system of Forth Street and Kirk Ports. It also shows how
all the shops can be serviced and parking provided for residents living above the shops
and the development potential that would make it viable. A large car park for shoppers
was provided on the lower slopes of the Glebe, just off the model bottom right.

from Scotland. A scheme was produced in 1960 and a model
constructed. It used Beach Road and a widened Kirk Port to cater for
motor traffic with service yards off them. The High Street was to be
closed to traffic from Quality Street, first as far as the Wynd and later
up to Bank Street as the traders realised that those on the pedestrianised
section might gain advantage over the remainder further west. A
financial statement was also prepared which showed that, if the
increased rateable value of the new frontage and back land development
was taken into account, there would be no annual deficit on the scheme.
Despite many public meetings, with opposition to the scheme coming
not from the traders but from car users, it was not finally overcome
until 1972 when the scheme was approved by the County Council. It
has still not been carried out. It was to be implemented as a
Comprehensive Development Area by the County Council under the
Planning Acts. This enabled the back land to be acquired for
development and so help meet the project costs, rather than a simple
road widening under the Highways Act which enabled the County only

to acquire the strip needed for the road works. Patience and persuasion are two qualities that the town planner must have. Clearly I had not enough of the latter, but the proposals have been taken into account in new development and its eventual implementation is a certainty. As a note-worthy scheme with its financial analysis, it was published in the Town Planning Review and presented at the Town and Country Planning Summer School in 1962.

Car Parking

Car parking was left to me to worry about as a land use matter, not a highways problem. The County Road Surveyor only imposed parking restrictions in order that moving vehicles were not impeded. His other contribution was to recommend that exaggerated car parking requirements were imposed on all new development. The County Planning Committee often ignored his advice until new legislation gave the Roads Authority a power of dictat over accesses onto public roads which complicated matters and led to some unfortunate conflicts. One planning condition we regularly imposed was that, where vehicle access was required off a main traffic route, the garden gates should be set back a sufficient distance so that a car could be pulled off the road without opening the gates. This can be seen working effectively in Dirleton Avenue, North Berwick where people had been in the lazy habit of parking cars on the carriageway or, worse still, on the narrow pavements during their lunch breaks instead of opening their garden gates and parking right off the carriageway.

Parking Plan for Haddington

I never solved the car parking problem in Haddington because I came up against a stubborn owner who would not sell his ground for access from Newton Port. However I left an approved plan for a service road and a large car park to the north of Market Street and Court Street to be carried out, again by comprehensive development powers. This proposal involved the movement of Dodds, the seed merchants, whose massive grain lorries had to back up a narrow vennel and caused lengthy traffic holdups in Court Street. I was anxious to see a supermarket established in Haddington as the town was beginning to lose shoppers to Musselburgh and the Asda superstore at Milton Road in Edinburgh. I encouraged William Low's supermarket chain to buy Dodd's premises, who then relocated just west of Haddington off the A1, where they still carry on their traditional business in new buildings. William Low was faced with adapting the three old frontage buildings, which were listed, and the seed warehouse at the back. This was done very successfully and the 10,000 square foot supermarket fitted very well into the fabric of the town.

The parking plan is being realised by slow increments but the detail is not as I would have wished it, with open space and car parking between the historic frontage buildings and the new commercial development to the north of the site hard against the Burgh walls. But I had learnt my lesson that retired planning officers must be content if their plans are implemented in principle. They cannot expect to influence the detail which evolves through the course of consultation with the public and negotiation with developers. The final outcome often turns on the personality and prescience of the planner involved, but more of this in the next chapter.

Accident Black Spots

As mentioned earlier, my department used to map all the accidents reported by the police to the County Road Surveyor who merely gave them a cursory look to see whether the condition of the road, pot holes, etc, were mentioned as the cause of the accident. This was seldom the case as the County roads were kept exceptionally well surfaced. Accidents were always attributed by the County Road Surveyor to the fault of those involved. I, on the other hand, took the view that there must be design faults at those black spots which experienced repeated accidents and such faults could and should be eliminated. He would have none of it. Accidents mainly took place at the busy junctions either on main roads, or, more worryingly, on the roads in housing areas. The latter were easily rectified by road markings, which indicated the road to have the priority. The main road junctions had to be examined individually but this was not done consistently until the Regional Council took over the highway function in 1975. The Scottish Office eventually accepted the planner's view that while individual accidents can always be attributed to driver error the Highway Authority must take some responsibility where there is a concentration of accidents. Our effort in keeping the accident black spot map up to date was fully justified.

Road Drainage

Another quirk of the County's roads was that the Surveyor took no responsibility for their drainage; arguing that he only had responsibility for the solum of the road and had a common law right to shed water onto the lower ground where it became the responsibility of the landowners. He would not maintain ditches even within the limits of the highway maintaining that these were also the responsibility of the adjoining landowners, as were the hedges. The owners did not think much of this and seldom cleared the ditches so that water flooded the roads and weakened their foundations. I suffered from the same attitude in Midlothian where our house at the bottom of the valley was lower

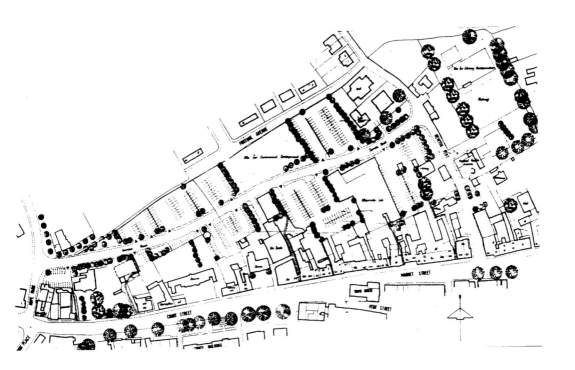

Plate CIX   Car Parking, Haddington

This was the approved plan for car parking in Haddington Town Centre which I left for my successors to carry out and which is now being done in stages. I considered it important that the Market Street properties should retain some vestige of the riggs, gardens and greenery.

than the carriageway, which had been built up over the years, with the result that water cascaded down the hill and flooded into our house. Fortunately by 1994 opinion had changed and the Regional highway authority installed a proper system of gullies and carrier drains on the hill at Ford to take the surface water into the river where it belongs.

Dykes and Hedges

It was the habit of the County Road Department to install the cheapest fence when they acquired new land to straighten corners or improve sight lines. The landowners went along with this as a more expensive specification, such as rebuilding the stone dyke or replanting a hedge on the new line, was counted as accommodation works and was deducted from the amount of financial compensation they were paid for the land taken into the highway. This habit was unsightly and broke the attractive flow of the countryside.

As planning authority the County Council insisted that utility companies—gas, water and sewerage—who were laying pipes across the countryside that required planning consent, repaired the gaps they created in the dykes or hedges to match what existed. It was not until I got to the Regional Council that I persuaded the Director of Highways that the cost of rebuilding dykes and replanting hedges, in fact replacing what was there, should be included in the cost of the road works and done as a matter of course and not paid for out of the owners' compensation. Other road authorities were doing this and I was particularly impressed by Cumberland County Council who were replicating quite ancient forms of enclosure such as ditch and mound topped with gorse in the Lake District National Park with great effect.

Traprain Law

The quarry at Traprain Law was the biggest eyesore and act of vandalism in the County that the County Road Surveyor was responsible for. The Law is crowned by the remains of an Iron Age fort, a scheduled monument on a large isolated volcanic plug rising from the cultivated land of the lower River Tyne Valley and prominently seen from the A1 road. The quarry was cutting progressively into the hillside, blasting away the fort's eastern gateway and ramparts. A vast array of workshops, garages, plant and road materials were strung out along the public road on its north side. There was a tarmac stone-coating plant and other oily horrors.

The Earl of Haddington periodically raised the question of this continued encroachment in the House of Lords, but all to no avail. The County Council was proud of its quarry and tarmac plant which, it was said, produced the cheapest road-stone in Scotland. I doubted whether this was true as the plant appeared old fashioned and its operation appeared chaotic, but there was nothing I could do except build up a fifty page dossier on the quarry. This I took with me to the Regional Council and the Director of Highways soon decided to close the quarry, rather than renew the ageing plant and face the continuing wrath of the amenity bodies. I failed, however, to persuade the Regional Highways Committee to carry out more than their legal obligations to redress the eyesore their predecessors had made. What I wanted was to have the lower parts of the quarry filled with dense baled refuse and sealed over. Access could then be gained to the hill fort through its original eastern gateway, and the upper walls of the quarry planted with climbing and hanging ivy. Perhaps this will still be done one day.

The Regional Council decided that they still required an East Lothian quarry, mainly as a means of controlling the price that the private quarry operators would charge for road-stone. A firm of civil engineers was commissioned to investigate and make recommendations. My preference was for the Markle Quarry which produced an attractive pale mauve coloured stone and was close to the A1, but hidden from

Plate CX Traprain Law

Ancient Monument v Road-stone Quarry. A distant view showing how the quarry has destroyed the eastern gateway to this Iron Age fort and is beginning to impinge into the upper rampart. It shows the string of plant and sheds lining the road which the Road Surveyor would never have allowed others to have. Beyond is the landscape and the smooth line of the Lammermuirs.

important view points in the County. I was delighted when the consultants, after a full investigation of all other sources, supported this choice and with them designed a diagonal cut into the hillside which minimised its immediate visual impact. Once the quarry was in operation and the stone chips laid on the roads, giving them a charming and distinctive appearance, they began smashing car windscreens as they were not binding well with the tar. As a result of public protest the quarry had to be abandoned at great cost and with red faces all round. After this mishap and a lawsuit against the consultants, it has been looked at again by an independent quarry master who was satisfied that if the quarry had gone deeper into the hillside the stone was excellent and it is now being worked again. Perhaps one day we will have attractive pale mauve coatings on the roads in the County in place of the dreary grey-black whinstone.

Wild Flower Verges

I must not end this diatribe on my relations with the County Road Surveyor without giving him full credit for co-operating with the Scottish Wildlife Trust in preserving distinctive wild plants growing in the roadside verges. The arrangement was that members of the Trust marked the floriferous lengths of verge with the initials 'SWT' painted on the edge of the tarmac and arrows marking the start and finish. That length of verge would not then be cut until after the wild flowers had seeded. This was the first such scheme to be introduced and has done much to add pleasure to drives through the rural parts of the County which we were encouraging tourists to take. The Director of Highways for the Lothian Regional Council extended the scheme to the whole of the Lothians and I think some other regions adopted it where the Scottish Wildlife Trust could muster sufficient volunteers to do the marking.

14

DEVELOPMENT CONTROL

Statutory Position • Prior Consultation • Open-ness
Visibility • Distinctiveness • Decisiveness • Uprightness
Public Local Inquiries • The Wimpey Appeal, Longniddry
Houses in the Countryside • Pantiles • Trees • Overhead Lines
Advertising Hoardings • Performance • Recording System
Annual Coach Tours • One Billion Pounds of Development 1979
Open-cast Coal Working • Fourth Natural Gas Pipe Line

This chapter might have been included earlier after the Development Plan chapter as it was through the control of private developers that much of the Plan was achieved. There was a constant flow of development applications and applicants through the office and it was their developments that fleshed out our plans. It was also a highly politically charged aspect of our work and we often got a terrible mauling at the monthly meetings of the Planning Committee and in the local papers to such an extent that Mary would not have them in the house for years. It was not put in earlier as this regulatory function is better known than the development function.

Statutory Position

But it is an essential, as the Town & Country Planning Act (Scotland) 1947 required, that consent should be obtained from the local planning authority for any change of use or development of land including engineering works. In making a decision the local planning authority (the Cities and County Councils) was required to have regard to their Development Plan and any other relevant considerations. No compensation was given for refusal of planning consent. The intention was that the sum of individual developments should add up to something worthwhile, implementing the land use provisions of the Plan and creating attractive towns and villages. I inherited from Sir Frank Mears' office in Edinburgh a series of maps which he called Progress Sheets. These recorded all the applications received and determined. Not only were they an excellent index but they also marked the progress towards the implementation of the Plan and identified the areas where pressure for development was building up.

The Act also gave applicants the right to appeal to the Secretary of State against the refusal or conditions imposed by the Planning Authority. This gave the Scottish Development Department a direct role in the whole planning process apart from the issue of circulars and planning advice notes for the guidance of the local planning authorities and of course the approval of Local Authority development plans. It was thus that the national planning considerations and priorities were filtered down to the local level. The British planning system was built up from the local level but steered from the national level. I rather fancy from what I read that planning authorities now await a lead from Central Government but this was not so in my day.

Prior Consultation

The difficulty with development control, as a process, is that it occurs at the approval stage and not at the planning stage. Plans for a development, prepared after considerable discussion with and at cost to the applicant, were submitted by the architect for approval. Our options were to recommend approval, with or without conditions; or refusal stating our reasons. The latter option was only available to us

Plate CXI   Newton Cottage, Pencaitland

We always treated this addition to an old pantiled cottage as an exemplar for others to follow. The ridge lines run through, the porch covers the change in level and the modern windows light the modern kitchen. Designed by Alan Reiach for Mr and Mrs Summers.

in the last resort as the County Planning Committee would not accept a recommendation to refuse unless we could show that we had offered alternatives to the applicant. They did not want to lose any development. We therefore encouraged applicants who thought of developing in the County to consult with us before they committed themselves and we put about our opinion that professional advisers: architects, surveyors, engineers and lawyers were acting irresponsibly if they proceeded to run up fees without prior consultation with my department. We had so much good and growing information on all aspects of land use, and were developing such strong views on what was right and wrong for the individual places, that to proceed with design work in ignorance of these was little short of negligence. We found that the better architects recognised this and appreciated that they had to both fulfil their client's brief and also meet the public requirements. Sadly the majority just carried on in the same old way. We soon learnt that it was impossible to teach old dogs new tricks and did what we could to see that they got no further work in the County. What we much preferred was meeting the developers before they had appointed their architects and giving them the names of three architects to choose from. This advice was generally welcomed by the private developer. It was considered at the time to be rather near the bone but followed the practice of the Royal Incorporation of Architects in Scotland who also gave the names of three architects when asked to advise on appointments. My particular regret was that I could never recommend the best architect working in the County—my wife. However word got around of her splendid facility with conversions and restorations, and it was not long before they were very visible in the County and set a standard for others.

This prior consultation took up a lot of time but it did make us look at each site and make up our minds what was desirable from a social, civic design or landscape point of view, without the distraction of looking at a set of proposals. It was then up to the architect to work out a solution that met both our vision and the requirements of their client. In fact we often found ourselves on the same side. Our interests were the same as the architects'—wanting a distinctive building designed for the site, of good materials and one that enriched the scene. We often supported the architect by inserting conditions in the consent which resulted in getting a better quality of layout and design, and an increased budget for the job. Perhaps it was this that led the Royal Incorporation of Architects in Scotland to make me an Honorary Fellow in 1990.

We did not publish any Design Guides as became fashionable in planning circles after the Essex County Council had produced theirs, preferring to spend time considering what was desirable for each site as it came up. For the larger sites we would prepare a planning brief, as it came to be called. No recommendations were made to the Committee without the site being visited and the applicant being met, if possible.

I had great difficulty with two architect-planners on the staff who would start tinkering about with submitted plans regarding window proportions, door details, etc. and getting on the wrong side of the applicants. I always considered that it was the things which were not shown on the plans which were more important. Very seldom did submitted plans give any indication of the height, appearance or materials of adjoining buildings, the design of enclosing walls and the levels of surrounding ground which were all essential to the creation of good neighbourly development. Traffic generation on larger schemes was usually ignored. Perhaps it was easier for me, not being an architect, to see the wood from the trees.

Open-ness

I required my staff to tell the applicant what they would be advising the Planning Committee. This was appreciated by the applicants and led to many useful revisions and agreements before plans came before the Committee. The Committee always insisted that we gave them a firm recommendation, one way or the other, on which they based their decision, but we could not always foretell which way the decision would go as we were continually trying to stretch the matters brought under planning control. The applicant at least had the right to know what we were recommending and attend the meetings of the Planning Committee which were open to the public.

My planning assistants attended the Planning Committee meetings to justify their recommendations although the County Clerk insisted that I signed each and every report. The assistant, therefore, had to voice not only his views but what he thought mine would be in the circumstances. If, beforehand, he was uncertain he would refer the application to me and we would visit the site together. It was only in the most exceptional cases that I dealt with an application from the start and the staff appreciated this. I only intervened in the Committee as a 'long stop' when they were clearly getting out of their depth or losing the argument. There was no specialisation within my department such as a conservation officer dealing with listed buildings or an enforcement officer, who in other authorities, was usually a retired policeman, to follow up breaches in planning control or failure to carry out conditions in planning consents. Each assistant had their own part of the County and was responsible for its listed buildings and for spotting when development had not been correctly carried out, turning a blind eye when necessary. This made for a reasonably happy staff who developed great skill over the years, particularly Jim Farquhar who came as a young lad from Falkirk, and although unqualified, raised himself up to be an Assistant Director and won the respect of many applicants and their architects.

Visibility

I always maintained that the result of development control should be visible to the public as they moved about the County and indeed we were often complimented that the hand of the planner was more visible in East Lothian than in most other counties. For instance, new building should be seen to be integrated well into their setting—not overlarge, their details in scale and materials appropriate. We always insisted that the extension to a building should be roofed in the same way as the original. This got us into awful tussles with some of the farmers who were being pressed to improve their farm cottages by the County Sanitary Inspector. In the 1930s these had been improved by adding a

Plate CXII   Petrol Filling Station Gullane

Petrol filling stations are one of the most difficult uses to fit into towns or villages. There are several examples of the difficulty in the County—Haddington, Gifford and Stenton but we were rather pleased with this Shell station at Gullane neatly fitted into the junction with Goose Green. The oak trees were retained, the stone wall continued along the front and even a little piece of public grass and seat provided. Two other good examples are at Aberlady, laid out by Mary Tindall, and the Shell Station at Newhouse, Dunbar (Plate LXIII).

lean-to building with a metal roof containing a bathroom directly off a kitchen. This was no longer acceptable and had to be rebuilt. It was more expensive to build a pitched roof and there were several indignant farmers who canvassed the Planning Committee members about this iniquity. But while those with influence got away with a flat-roof felted extension, our policy slowly became accepted and builders who were wanting to avoid all the hassle with the planning office submitted plans with pitched roofs. Now that these farm cottages are being sold off, I am occasionally stopped in the street and thanked by farmers who are getting much better prices for their cottages extended my way with a pitched roof.

A severe test of development control is how petrol filling stations are handled and East Lothian comes off quite well, with good examples at Gullane and Newhouse, Dunbar.

Distinctiveness

Probably East Lothian's most distinguishing feature was the distinctiveness of the development where elsewhere so many buildings were of a standard type. Jack Coia, a well respected west of Scotland architect, congratulated us at a Civic Trust Award ceremony in approving a modern flat-roofed house built in the grounds of the Old Manse at Gifford. Other authorities, he said, might well have insisted on a reproduction two-storey house in the Georgian style with disastrous results in scale and detail in that important conservation village. But we were satisfied with Ian Arnott's modern single-storey design which received an award. All was not so happy with a bungalow which had been a prize winner at the London Ideal Homes Exhibition and was submitted by Rear Admiral Brooke's daughter for a site near the conservation village of Stenton. It was a typical English hipped roof bungalow with external stone chimney feature, arched doorway, decorative stonework and red rosemary tile roof. Part of the boundary wall was to be taken down to allow it a view to the hills which made it more conspicuous. We framed a strong case for its refusal but it was "piped aboard" by the Admiral at the Committee Meeting with full naval aplomb. I subsequently used it to judge the reaction of new staff applicants as I showed them round the County. Some wondered, no doubt, why they did not get the job.

Decisiveness

Another necessity of development control is the swift initial response. One day I got a telephone call from a Texaco executive in London saying they wanted to come and see me about establishing an oil refinery at Yellowcraig, a site they had chosen off the coastal charts as the most suitable in Scotland. I remember telling them straight away that this

Plate CXIII   Ian Arnott's House, Gifford

This house was designed for his own family in the orchard of the old manse which is an eighteenth century listed building. I consider this contemporary design points up the qualities of the other far better than a 'period' imitation would.   Both are genuine responses to the needs and the materials of their day. It received a Civic Trust Reward.

would be quite unacceptable and gave them the telephone number of the Highland and Islands Development Board who were wanting to establish such industries along the Moray Firth. That was the last I heard from Texaco although Professor Sir Robert Grieve, the Chairman of the Board, later told me that Texaco told him that they had been refused planning consent by East Lothian. I kept this Texaco call to myself for many years but it shows the value of giving the decisive answer. I certainly saved the County from what could have been a disastrous development which would have ruined the whole coastline and the charms of North Berwick. I often wondered whether the Planning Committee might not have viewed it differently if Texaco had gone on and submitted a planning application.

Uprightness

I would like to record my astonishment and delight that so few professional planners were ever accused of accepting bribes. Many tens of thousands of pounds—millions in the cities—turned on the obtaining of planning consent. A number of administrators in the planning system were caught and of course Councillors were very liable to be influenced. Only on one ocasion was I offered a week's holiday in Rome, but as it had to be in the off-season, and I knew how awful that could be, it was not much of a bribe in return for recommending approval of a truly monstrous housing development.

Public Local Inquiries

The right of appeal put the local planning officers in the unique position of having to justify the advice they gave to their planning committees. Public Local Inquiries were set up by the Secretary of State to determine planning appeals. These public inquiries came more and more to assume the character of a court of law although the Reporters, as the civil servants charged with hearing the appeals were called, tried hard to keep the hearings informal. There was nothing to stop appellants being represented by advocates who introduced their adversarial techniques into the Inquiry procedure. No other local government officers had to justify and defend their day by day technical advice in this way so it gave us a higher standing amongst our other technical colleagues. Difficulties arose when the Planning Committee refused applications contrary to our advice. In such cases the Council was in a very weak position in any subsequent Public Inquiry, if the appellants asked what professional advice they had received and on what grounds they had rejected it. This class of appeal was usually sustained by the Secretary of State. The physical damage lay the other way, when the Planning Committee approved an application against our advice. There was no provision for third party appeals and so the development went ahead. The County Clerk, whenever he got drawn into a case, always quipped that I would be a rich man if I had received £10 for every time the Planning Committee had decided against my advice. I am not so sure, and as the years went by I would have not got much as the Committee began to trust me more, and I suppose, I was more attuned with their views. It was always a difficult line to draw but my opinion was that once the Planning Committee had determined a policy I must, as a professional, take this into account in framing my recommendations on applications. My Planning Committee, consisting as it did of independent members, seldom stood by the policies or the development plan and their decisons centred on other relevant or irrelevant considerations. My difficulty was in showing the public that there was some thread of consistency in these decisions.

I always took the view, and encouraged my staff to take the view, that an appeal and public inquiry were very much part of the planning process, a test of our policies and professional performance. I insisted that when our lawyers or junior counsel were involved they did not take an adversarial attitude but treated the appellants as rate-payers or potential ratepayers who paid or would pay for the planning service. But as time went on these inquiries required more and more preparation, effort and money from our always rather over stretched staff and budgets and tended to be seen as an unwelcome diversion from our main development tasks.

The Wimpey Appeal, Longniddry

I must admit I was very riled by losing an appeal by Wimpey against the Planning Committee's decision to refuse them consent for a very crass and poor-value scheme which they submitted for Douglas Road, Longniddry. I took a lot of trouble comparing their proposed houses to similiar ones built in the County. The comparative cost analysis per square foot of floor space was very revealing. While I cannot remember the exact figures, the houses Hart had designed and built for the County Council on similiar land at Longniddry worked out at say £3 per square foot, Jack Loudon's houses at North Berwick were £4, Bell's at Haddington were £4.50 and Wimpey's £5.20 per square foot. Wimpey's selling price was cheaper by a few hundred pounds but they were like the Wild Woodbine—cheap to buy but a very expensive smoke. They also had many design faults: there was no central heating, the chimney from the single fireplace was on an external wall losing a lot of heat which could have warmed the house, the plans were the same whether they faced east or west, north or south or whether they were on opposite sides of the road, and their large picture windows allowed one to see right through the house and often the next one behind. The houses had a poor relationship to their gardens and were way below the Parker Morris space standards which we were trying to uphold. They were also from Wimpey's stock range and the Committee, by this time, was concerned that if you came to East Lothian "you could see the difference" and we were trying to keep up the garden city character of Longniddry. Wimpey argued that their houses met the various bye-law standards, were well built, filled a place in the housing market, were approved by other planning authorities, and sold well.

I regret to say that the Reporter and the Secretary of State accepted these arguments as part of the drive to get more privately owned houses from the volume builders who at that time had the ear of the Conservative Government. I think that the Reporter considered I was stretching planning control to include quality and value for money, which I clearly was. Wimpey did slightly modify their houses as the result of our criticism. The houses were set back from Lyars Road so that they were not grimacing at the passing traffic and were only allowed pedestrian rather than vehicular access to Gosford Road thus trying to maintain the latter's pre-war quality. But, more importantly, they never submitted another planning application in the County while I was County Planning Officer. I notice that they are back in a big way now and the County is slowly being covered with these standard houses which are built all over Britain and make East Lothian less distinctive. I was always mindful of Lord Cameron's quip when he represented the National Trust for Scotland at the County Development Plan Inquiry in 1954. Referring to the proposed demolition of old buildings in the Hardgate in Haddington he asserted that I was in danger of making "Haddington indistinguishable from Hell, Hull or Halifax". I was determined that this accusation should not be repeated.

Houses in the Countryside

One controversial policy concerned housing in the countryside. There was a Circular from the Scottish Development Department deprecating this and saying that all houses should be grouped in villages. The Circular was tangled up with exceptions where houses were justified for agricultural purposes. I considered this guidance worked against our policy for checking rural depopulation and against what we knew many people desired. Therefore, in addition to having a list of old houses suitable for restoration which we plugged hard, we decided that private houses were acceptable on the following three conditions: that they did not take land out of cultivation, that they did not get access directly off main roads, and that they fitted positively into the landscape. We later added a fourth, that the site was large enough to pursue rural pursuits and to protect the property against noxious agricultural practices. My ambition was to see a lively populated countryside. My successors rather toed the Government line, although there are many waste corners which could be enlivened by a well designed house and outbuildings.

Pantiles

The County's vernacular buildings were mainly roofed with pantiles, which it was said, were originally imported as ballast in the sailing ships trading with Holland. However there were records of several clay pits in the County where they were made. Farm buildings and cottages were usually roofed with pantiles while slates, a rather more expensive and better material, were reserved for the farmhouse itself. I was particularly insistent that clay pantiles, which gave such a warm character to local buildings, should be used wherever appropriate. The Planning Committee did not always support me in this, especially in the early years when pantiles had to be lorried up from Dorset. Luckily, the Goxhill Clay Company started their manufacture in Yorkshire, nearer home. The only drawback is that their tiles are so dense and uniform that it will take a long time for them to weather, and they do not have the charm of the old hand-made tiles from the small local clay works. A campaign to save these old tiles was instituted but they proved difficult to re-use as they came from different local tileries and had no identity mark. It was hard to marry them up and make a uniform roof.

As the years went by and this policy stuck, I heard that builders were putting it about that my second initial stood for Pantile, and I was being referred to as Frank Pantile Tindall. However I noticed that more plans were coming in with clay non-interlocking pantiles and even more so after we served an enforcement notice on a new house in Belhaven; where, contrary to the planning consent, interlocking clay pantiles had been used. The Secretary for State supported us by dismissing the applicant's appeal and the roof had to be retiled with clay non-interlocking pantiles. Whoops, what a success!

Trees

Another mark of the planner is the well placed tree or trees. I was very keen on this and usually managed to persuade the applicant by the following argument. Trees planted now in the right place would grow more and more beautiful as the years went by, and this is more than can be said of his garden which would become a little less well-kept, of his house which would become more old-fashioned and of his wife who would become grey and more wrinkled. Only the trees he had planted would give him consistent pleasure to the end of his days. We got many trees planted with this advocacy.

One December, in a discussion with the Convener, Mr Rattray, a former factor of the Biel and Dirleton Estates who seldom spent the hospitality allowance which he was allowed, I suggested that he should give each of his council house tenants a Christmas present of a tree or a climber. This could have transformed the Council's drab housing areas but he did not take up the suggestion. Subsequently the idea of a free tree was taken up by the Central Scotland Woodlands Project and the Kirkliston Community Council have shown the visual improvement this achieves. As the housing schemes are being modernised more trees are being planted, but I have yet to see many virginia creepers.

Another feature which showed that planners had been at work was the fitting of new development behind old stone dykes and continuing them where necessary.

Plate CXIV   Overhead Wires, Macmerry

Despite its jolly name and attractive layout Macmerry was crucified by the A1 traffic and visually impaired by overhead electricity wires and telephone poles. All these were removed on the initiative of the County Council. The public quickly forget such eyesores existed and planners seldom get credit for their positive actions.

Overhead Lines

In the 1950s the South of Scotland Electricity Board had a fine programme of connecting up all farms in the County at a special standard charge of £400. The overhead electricity lines required planning consent and the Board's way-leave officer, George Campbell, was an old hand at coping expeditiously with the many applications. We jointly ran a score card. A retrospective consent, after a line was erected, incurred a penalty of 10 points which would be redeemed by the Board undergrounding a subsequent proposal. A change of route I thought necessary cost me points depending on the length. I gained points for speedy approval of proposals as submitted, while a lost file cost either of us 2 points. It was a rough and ready and most enjoyable way of proceeding and got the electricity network quickly extended with substantial improvements in its visual appearance. When the Board's area manager got to hear of it he was up in arms and stormed into my office demanding that each case should be dealt with separately on its merits, as indeed we were supposed to do. To satisfy him, I agreed, but few lines got approved without substantial resubmissions and delays and so we reverted to our points game and the network again grew rapidly. A few ugly lines were approved but I was fortunate in staying in the County long enough to make it possible to remove or reroute many of these errors in subsequent trade-offs. I also remember being invited to address all the Board's way-leave officers on the principles we followed for the routeing of electricity lines in the landscape. In any landscape the eye is drawn to certain views and these should be avoided by the lines. Multiplication and zig-zags were also to be avoided and changes of direction should be related to landscape features. Terminals should be sited close to buildings. Gaps cut in shelter belts should be replanted with low growing trees and not left bare.

We also had a blitz on overhead wires, both telephone and electricity, particularly in the villages where they were most unsightly. It was easy to persuade those officials who were keen photographers and I approached them with the argument that their lines prevented good photographs being taken. I only wish road surveyors would have the same sensitivity when siting their traffic signs.

Advertising Hoardings

One of my first actions was to challenge the fifteen groups of general advertising hoardings which disfigured the main roads through the County and were a particular anathema to me. All the hoardings were removed except for a group at Longniddry station which remain there to this day. The appeal had been heard by a part-time Reporter from the west of Scotland appointed by the Secretary of State. He would not accept my argument that these hoardings diminished the character of Longniddry which we were trying to promote as a good residential area. He said that hoardings were a normal and acceptable adjunct to any railway station, as they are through much of Britain. However, the A1 was cleared of hoardings and few will now remember how disfiguring they were in the open countryside.

Performance

Each year we provided the Committee with an analysis of the planning applications received by categories of use and of those approved or refused. It gave the average length of time taken to determine them, together with a reconciliation table of applications withdrawn or lapsed or awaiting decision at the end of the year. By statute, an applicant was allowed to appeal to the Secretary of State if his application had not been determined within 8 weeks of its submission. Our average times improved over the years from 5.2 weeks to 4 weeks but our percentage of refusals fell from 13% to 7.5%. This I worried about, thinking the Department was getting soft, until I realised that the number approved as submitted was also increasing, as a result of architects and builders policing themselves. Not wanting to waste time by arguing with us, they submitted plans they knew from prior consultation we would recommend for approval. In practice they were doing our job for us. However, I told my staff that I did not expect the refusal rate to fall below 7% and we raised our standard to achieve this—for instance asking for real stone in place of precast, bowed dormers in place of square ones.

Recording System

In about 1965 we had to abandon Sir Frank Mears' progress sheets as they were becoming so crowded, so dog-eared and so undecipherable. As the staff was growing in numbers and changing we had to have a more foolproof system which took account of all the special zonings and considerations arising from previous decisions. We therefore adopted a system pioneered by Tom Clark, an officer of the Ministry of Town and Country Planning in Reading, which consisted of a series of transparent overlays arranged numerically by their map reference so that a glance through the transparencies showed the zoning, the sites of specisl scientific interest, tree preservation orders, the road widening schemes, the structural dangers, adjoining consents and refusals. This was more time-consuming for the draughtsmen to prepare but for many years was the basis of our information system. It is still operational in East Lothian and has been adapted into a computerised system.

Annual Coach Tours

The opportunity occurred in the mid 1960s, when the East Lothian Water Board was regionalised into the Edinburgh and Lothian Water Board, to take over the slot for the annual Water Board outing. This was an eagerly anticipated event when councillors were taken on a tour of the water works, and thoroughly tested the water for its quality as a blend with whisky and, no doubt, other spiritous liquids. I never attended one of these exclusive outings but the accounts of them were tremendous. I thought that it would raise the status of planning to lay on something similiar for the Committee members and invite guests from adjoining Authorites, the Scottish Development Department, the universities, amenity and professional bodies to join us. The bus left County Buildings at 10 o'clock in the morning and we gave them a good lunch in an hotel, continuing the tour until about 5 o'clock when we always managed to arrange for some body or institution to provide refreshments. I tried to get them all back to County Buildings by 7 p.m., more sober and wiser than on the Water Board outings which had customarily ended at midnight. These planning tours were all themed with a booklet giving plans and details of the sites visited. They gave me the opportunity to stop the bus and comment on some of the development as realised on the ground, ribbing them on the poor results where they had not accepted our advice and congratulating everyone where things had turned out well. I could do this, being in sole charge of the microphone and because of the general bonhomie engendered on the coach. It was something that I could never have got away with in the Council Chamber or on an official site visit. I think that the Councillors all appreciated these frank off the record comments and began to be more fully aware of what we were going on about. Councillor Bell of West Lothian who later became Vice-Convener of the Lothian Regional Council once told me that he and his colleagues never knew what planning was about until they had been on a Tindall Tour. Certainly, things got easier after these tours and they were keenly looked forward to year by year. I must have conducted nine or ten of them and the ratepayers had no reason to grudge the Councillors this "jolly" which paid such high dividends in making the planning system more visible and more understandable to them, and led to better decisons.

The tours I remember were "Development Control in the Eastern Half of the County" 1968, "New Industries" 1969, "Countryside Projects" 1970, "Town Centre Developments" 1971, "Developments in the Western Half of the County" 1972, "Environmental Improvements" 1973.

One Billion Pounds of Development 1979

I also led the Lothian Regional Council on a similiar tour of major developments in East Lothian in 1979. I was astonished to realise that these involved the expenditure of over £1,000,000,000 and was equally delighted to realise that we had or were able to fit these massive schemes into the landscape of East Lothian without major damage. Most of these large projects, such as the Torness Nuclear Power Station, the north quarry of the Dunbar Cement Works, the Tranent Bypass, Meadowmill, Blindwells open-cast site and the Markle roadstone quarry have already been remembered in previous chapters but there are two that deserve mention here.

Open-cast Coal Working

The Blindwells open-cast coal workings was the development with the greatest potential for damage and the Councillors were staggered when they saw the extent of it. As has already been mentioned the rationale for its conditional planning consent was firstly, that deposits of shallow coal would have been sterilised by the construction of the Tranent Bypass. Secondly, the extraction of the shallow seams, which had been worked in the old days by bell-pits and stoop and room, would eliminate the need for special measures to construct a solid base for the Bypass, so reducing its costs which was essential as it only just met the economic criteria. There was also the argument that these shallow coals were "sweeter", having less sulphur content, than the deep mined coal and when mixed, could reduce the atmospheric pollution from Cockenzie Power Station. The counter arguments were the waste of good agricultural land, the horrible appearance of the rock heaps removed to get at the coal, and the dust and noise involved in the transport of coal by lorry within the site. All these concerns were squared by planning conditions. The Board had to appoint a clerk of works to look after the top-soil and the soil-parent material so that they could be replaced without the loss of too much organic material. No contractor appreciated that top-soil should be treated like a housewife treats pastry. It should not be worked when it was too wet or too dry and so it was important that the clerk of works controlled the programme of removal and restoration. The peripheral heaps had to be left with a flat level profile at all times, the hours of working were laid down and it was a requirement that a rail siding was constructed to transport all coals off site by train. These conditions have been honoured; and it appears to be a tidy operation from the outside and at sufficient distance from the towns and main roads not to impinge too much. It was a great improvement on the "Mountains of the Moon" landscape that the same contractors had created in Northumberland. After initial teething troubles, it never caused much offence and permission was later given to extend it eastwards into the planned but rather decayed landscape of St Germains, but here again a condition to replant this planned landscape was imposed by the District Council.

Fourth Natural Gas Pipeline

The other proposal was the laying of the fourth natural gas pipeline from St Fergus in Aberdeenshire to Bishop Auckland in County Durham. The previous three pipelines had all crossed the Forth at Blackness and passed through West Lothian but there was inadequate room at various pinch points for a fourth, due partly to lack of foresight. Elie, on the Fife coast, to Gullane was the next shortest sea crossing. The pipeline needed a soft beach landfall and a site for a pumping station using Rolls Royce aero jet engines. The route of the line would impose significant constraints on future developments. A line was jointly selected up the west edge of the Archerfield Estate, near Dirleton and the pumping station sited well away from the coast in a corner of the former East Fortune Airfield. A crossing of the River Tyne was chosen at Nether Hailes. Restoration conditions were imposed and now there is little sign on the surface, except where the service access track passes through heather. Again we tried to get the waste heat from the pumping engines used beneficially for crop production in the small holdings round East Fortune and again we failed. Waste management was not yet in fashion.

15

THE SCOTTISH SCENE AND BEYOND

Planning Research • Delegation to Russia 1953
Japan 1964 • The English Job Circuit • Census Planning
Ordnance Survey • Scottish Study Groups
Town and Country Planning Summer School
Conference Handbook 1965 • Countryside in 1970, Study Group Nine
OBE Award • National Trust for Scotland • Professional Bodies
Reorganisation of Local Government in Scotland 1975
Director of Physical Planning, Lothian Regional Council

Planning Research

For some years after my appointment to East Lothian I continued my involvement with the Royal Town Planning Institute in London where I was the Vice-Chairman of the Research Committee. I organised two national conferences—one for urban research workers and another for rural research workers. These aimed at drawing into the planning process the increasing number of academics and research institutes who were outside the professional structure of planning practice, and at making professional planners more familiar with the process and results of research. I was also the Institute's Board Member on the Planning and Transport Research and Computation Company Ltd. until its bankruptcy in 1975. This company played an important part, with its annual four-day meetings and its consultancy work, in introducing statistical and computing disciplines into the planning process. I must confess I never really understood computing and East Lothian's computer was mainly used to churn out our monthly pay cheques. But I was anxious that computers should be used to resolve the many social and statistical problems that were beginning to obsess planners in the larger authorities. The link between planning and transportation was also very important as the great American studies, predicting the volumetric traffic needs of, say, 2020 were worked backwards to measures that should be taken now. I was always sceptical of this approach considering that effort should be put into analysing and relieving existing traffic pressures with an eye to the long term needs. The American-based studies seldom got beyond the production of massive volumes. These were a great worry to us as working off their assumptions, their logic was unassailable. Although the British practitioners took a more pragmatic view, Edinburgh suffered from several studies of this type which cost a lot and resulted in very little action.

Delegation to Russia 1953

In 1953 Mary and I were invited by the Anglo-Soviet Society of Great Britain to join their first delegation of architects and planners to Russia. This was after Stalin's death and when Malenkov was in power. The Russians made no professional distinction between architects and town planners and had many man and wife working couples whom Mary and I were intended to match. However, Mary was then pregnant and was advised not to travel. Indeed we had a most exhausting three weeks itinerary. We flew to Moscow, Stalingrad, Erivan in Armenia, Kiev and Leningrad, returning by train to Moscow. It was a high powered delegation including Berthold Lubetkin, our maestro from Peterlee days, F R S Yorke, Frank Yerbury, Cecil Handiside, John Berger, Douglas Alan and Nares Craig from the Building Research Station, my chum from Cambridge days. We were greatly welcomed and vastly over-entertained in the local "Houses of Architects" which were funded not by the subscriptions of members as in this country but by a small percentage on the jobs they carried out. The hospitality was such that we had to arrange for two of the delegation to miss out on the dinner each evening so that they would be able to carry out all the formal duties and make the speeches the next day. Amongst my deepest impressions was the splendid restoration work, for restoration's sake, being carried out by the Russians to honour the skill of the Russian craftsmen. Our only reservation was that this seemed to apply only to palaces of the Czars and some churches and monasteries, and not to the attractive eighteenth century quarters of wooden houses of the ordinary people which had got a bad reputation due to overcrowding on the scale of one family to each room. Their new work was also very strange to us. This was presented in 6m long fully rendered drawings of the great fourteen to eighteen storey terraces, squares and crescents that they were building in mass brick work. I remember asking: "Where was the kindergarten?" and they pointed to the fourth storey where it was imbedded in the classical facade. This of course was quite contrary to the best British practice where a nursery school would have been a delightful building in the garden at the rear.

I was greatly struck by Charles Cameron's work for Catherine the Great and took many photographs that were later used in an Arts

Plate CXV   Cameron's Art Gallery, St Petersburg

I was very pleased with this photograph, taken in 1953, of this splendid airy gallery just restored after the war. To the right is the enclosed picture gallery and it is all perched on a high ground floor storeroom, overlooking the great park at Tsarkoe Selo.

Council exhibition and by Isobel Rae in her book entitled *"Charles Cameron, Architect to the Court of Russia"* 1971. Nares Craig has reminded me I was always last back on the coach and that I seemed to be the one who always had spare film, black and white, as we did not trust the Russians not to develop the films before we left and at that time they had very poor colour film processing. We were the first delegation allowed to take photographs in post-war Russia, but that did not keep us entirely out of trouble. I took my pictures with an old Leica given to me at Tansweg prisoners' camp by Hans, my interpreter/driver who in civil life had been a press photographer. I got special consent from the East Lothian County Council to go on this trip and thereafter my political leanings, which local government officers were not supposed to show, were the subject of comment which stayed with me the rest of my time in East Lothian.

Japan 1964

This opinion was slightly modified by special leave granted me in 1964 to attend with Mary the Conference of the International Union of Landscape Architects in Japan, the model of post-war capitalism. We extended this trip by stopping off in Delhi on our way out and in heavenly Kashmir on our way home. The locals quipped that there would be a flood of pagoda roofs in the County after this trip and indeed I was always keen to have finials placed on roofs. However I could not get Bermaline to rebuild the pagoda roof over the Maltings in Haddington which still badly needs one.

The English Job Circuit

After the production and approval of the Development Plan in 1955, I applied for a number of jobs with larger English authorities as I did not feel very secure in East Lothian. I was short-listed for the County Planning Officer's job in Nottinghamshire and in Cambridgeshire, which I would dearly liked to have had. I was not successful in any but no doubt if I had continued I would eventually have got an English County as it was the same people who appeared on the short lists and one by one they were getting the jobs.

By the 1960s East Lothian was settling down to implement their Development Plan. Shaken by the closure of the coal mines and the decline in agricultural employment, we were entering a phase that the Scottish Development Department called, for want of a better name "Development Planning". Our family of three were growing up in a good environment, we were settled into our fine old house at Ford and making a grand garden, so my enthusiasm for the job round faded and we stayed put, immersing ourselves further in the Scottish scene.

Census Planning

One of the first tasks I undertook for the Scottish Branch of the Royal Town Planning Institute was to beard the Registrar General in his den in West Register House. It was the only time I have seen a fire screen being used as he protected his face from the heat of the large coal fire he had burning in his office grate.

The purpose of my visit was to try and persuade him that he should instruct the local registrars to consult their local planning authorities when drawing up the enumerators' districts for the 1961 Census. Traditionally these had been carried over from Census to Census and if a new housing area had been built this was sliced into the walking route. It had got to the situation where, for instance in Haddington, an enumerator's district started in, say, the north side of Market Street and then deviated up Newton Port to include the new housing scheme and then came back to include a bit more of Market Street. What planners needed was information on homogeneous areas, such as those living on both sides of Market Street, and of those within the housing estates, private or public, built at a similar time. The Registrar General, being an intelligent man, understood exactly what town planners were asking for, but being lazy refused to do anything and left it to us to try locally with our registrars. I managed to persuade most of mine by giving them a copy of an updated Ordnance Survey map, which they had never had before and greatly simplified their work.

Ordnance Survey

Another task I undertook was to represent Scottish planners on one of the Ordnance Survey advisory panels and I did it so long that finally it became my turn to chair it.

I had several objectives. First, that they should produce blank maps of the sea so that we could produce nice squared-off wall maps—important as so many Scottish counties had long coastlines. This they did eventually. Another objective was to get them to show buildings of architectural or historic interest by a different stipple on their large scale maps. The maps showed some public buildings that way which was hardly necessary. It would have been a great help to surveyors or lawyers when using these maps for property transactions, if they had a visual warning that the buildings were listed by the Secretary of State, rather than finding out in a written note on the title deeds at a later stage when the property deal had been concluded. This I never achieved, but still believe it is very desirable.

A more fundamental issue arose when I was Chairman and this was the question of the privatisation of the Ordnance Survey which we with others organisations were able to modify to an agency status. Otherwise there would have been little prospect of maintaining up to date the national archive of large scale maps, especially in the rural areas where there was only a slow sale of the maps. The Committee, again with others, helped save the 2 1/2 inch to the mile maps, the so called 'Pathfinder' series, which are the essential map for walkers and countryside recreation and for much rural planning. This representative function meant annual trips to Southampton and an annual conference in Scotland.

Scottish Study Groups

In 1956 I inaugurated a series of ten annual three-day study groups for practising planners in Scotland under the auspices of the Scottish Branch of the Royal Town Planning Institute but entirely self-financing. Practising planners were still very thin on the ground and many were unqualified. We seldom met because of the long distances involved, and when we did, we discussed Institute matters, such as the winter lecture programmes, not professional practice matters. So Tom Lyon, who was head of the planning school at the Royal College of Science and Technology in Glasgow (the precursor of Strathclyde University), and I conceived the idea of these groups where we could meet, present and discuss our planning problems. Tom, a great Geddesian with a fine Glaswegian sense of humour, was the academic tutor and provided the crits, and I was responsible for the organisation. We always shared a room together and arranged the next day's work long into the night. Each year we studied a different theme and invited some distinguished person to come to the group to introduce the subject. Professor Sir Robert Matthew was at the first one. The themes and places where the groups were held were as follows:

1956—The Redevelopment of Historic Burghs—Stirling
1957—Planning and Agriculture—St Andrews
1958—Housing Layout—St Andrews
1959—Development Control—Dunbar
1960—Review of Development Plans—Newbattle Abbey
1961—Recreation and Tourist Facilities—Braemar
1962—Private Housing Development—North Berwick
1963—Redevelopment of Central Areas—Dundee
1964—The Attraction of Industry—St Andrews

The 1956 Study Group was held over a weekend but this debarred planners from the Islands, who then were not allowed to work or travel on a Sunday. So we ran the later ones mid-week in some cheap accommodation, staying in hotels during their start-up week or in university hostels during the Easter vacation. Perhaps the most memorable was the Braemar Study Group which as well as planners, included representatives from other tourist and countryside organisations. At its conclusion we drafted a submission to the Scottish Development Department which became the substance of their Circular 2/1962. This laid down what the Secretary of State expected local authorities to do for tourism and the opening up of the Scottish countryside to the public. The Local Government and Countryside Act 1962 contained the additional powers which we had asked for. Equally important was the building up of friendships and understanding between all those bodies with interests in tourism and the countryside, and showing them the advantages of working through the local planning authorities. By 1964 I had had enough and Tom Lyon was dead, so I passed responsibility for running the study groups onto the Edinburgh University Department of Planning. It effectively killed them off by turning them into a lecture course, the last thing that senior planners were prepared to take.

Town and Country Planning Summer School

I and Professor Gerald Smart, who was then in Hampshire, tried to introduce similar presentations of work into the Town and Country Planning Summer School run each year under the auspices of the Royal Town Planning Institute. At the time the proceedings had got into rather a rut with main papers usually given by non-planners, followed by discussion groups on these papers and afternoon subject sessions where the lecturer repeated his yarn to different audiences. Gerald Smart and I felt all this was dealing with aspirations and not actual achievements/failures on the ground. The good talkers shone but one felt that they were not the achievers—too much aspiration, too little reality. The Council members who ran the Summer School for many years enjoyed their free evenings for reminiscences and relaxation. But there were many young 'scholars' like us who had few memories, were keen improve our practice, and to meet with others facing similar problems and learn how they were coping with them, and to talk things through to a conclusion. So evening sessions were introduced, but as they could not be structured in advance and depended on scholars bringing along their own work, they also degenerated into lecture courses—more words without conclusions, and one did not learn what one's colleagues were achieving. At this stage I ceased going to the Summer Schools, which I confess was naughty, although I continued to participate in the School when it was held in St Andrew's University.

Conference Handbook 1965

I was never one for attending annual conferences and the County Council were not prepared to fund attendances outwith Scotland. But when the Town Planning Institute held their Annual Conference in Edinburgh for the first time in 1965, Mary and I produced and edited a conference handbook which was a great innovation. It stated boldly that it was produced to illustrate the distinctive aspects of Town and Country Planning in Scotland and what had been achieved by the Scottish planning authorities. There were fourteen contributors to the handbook and twenty plates. It was published by Edinburgh Pictorial Ltd whose proprietor and managing director, Mr Cummings, lived in Haddington. It was financed by the advertisements and became a feature of all subsequent annual conferences held in different towns in Britain. It gave more reality to these conferences which had tended to be more a record of aspirations than of actualities and paid little regard to the regional characteristics apart from the routine coach tours. Mr Cummings continued to publish them even when the conferences were in the south of England; a good friend.

Countryside in 1970, Study Group 9

Under the auspices of the Duke of Edinburgh and the drive of Reggie Boote, twelve Study Groups were set up to review the situation of the 'Countryside in 1970'. Study Group Nine: Countryside: Planning and Development in Scotland was chaired by Professor Robert Grieve and he asked me to be the Convener Secretary. The County Council allowed me to have every Thursday off to carry out this task. I set up the 'countryside table' in the east window of the dining room at Ford, where I prepared the papers for the seven meetings of Study Group Nine held in St Andrew's House. The Group considered 53 papers of which I wrote seven on such subjects as: *"The Main Considerations peculiar to or of particular significance to Scotland"*, and *"Public Land Ownership in Scotland"*. The latter revealed for the first time that 2,062,420 acres, an eighth of Scotland's 19,000,000 acres, were state owned. The map I prepared kept getting mislaid and was often found displayed in the Secretary of State's, Willie Ross', room in St Andrew's House. It also revealed that 50% of the land in the Loch Lomond Trossachs Direction Order (428 square miles) was publicly owned as well as 20% of the Cairngorm area (180 sq miles). This, my Paper argued, should take the heat out of the resistance by the private landowners to the setting up of National Parks. But it was not to be. Other papers I wrote were entitled: *"The Peak District National Park, its Budget and Achievement"*, and *"Canadian National Parks and the*

Plate CXVI   **State-owned Land in Scotland**

I assembled this map for Study Group Nine. It was the first time that such a map had been prepared as records were kept departmentally. State-owned land, being one ninth of the land area of Scotland, could be used to great effect, but isn't. The Crown foreshore is largely used to finance the Crown Estate Commission. In 1998 we still await National Parks in Scotland, fifty years after the Ramsay Report identified the five Designated Areas, also shown on the map.

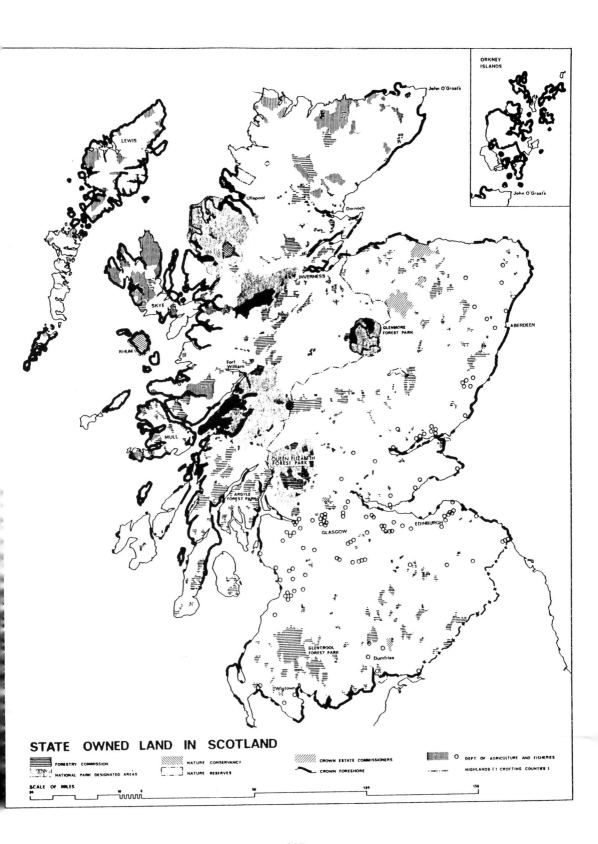

STATE OWNED LAND IN SCOTLAND

FORESTRY COMMISSION	NATURE CONSERVANCY	CROWN ESTATE COMMISSIONERS	DEPT OF AGRICULTURE AND FISHERIES
NATIONAL PARK DESIGNATED AREAS	NATURE RESERVES	CROWN FORESHORE	HIGHLANDS (7 CROFTING COUNTIES)

SCALE OF MILES

ORKNEY
ISLANDS

John O'Groat's

John O'Groat's

LEWIS

Ullapool

Dornoch

INVERNESS

ABERDEEN

SKYE

GLENMORE
FOREST PARK

RHUM

Fort
William

MULL

QUEEN ELIZABETH
FOREST PARK

EDINBURGH

ARGYLE
FOREST PARK

GLASGOW

GLENTROOL
FOREST PARK

Dumfries

Wigtown

Department of Recreation and Conservation, British Columbia". More papers were contributed by members of the Group and other people who I invited to cover the questions of Access, National Parks, Multi-purpose landuse, Case studies and the Agencies.

The report had six chapters: a Statement of Special Considerations peculiar to Scotland, the Forces of Change, the Reorientation of Attitudes, Examples Examined and the Question of Agency. It had an appendix containing an authoritative definition of the Law of Trespass in Scotland, finally laying to rest the myth that there is no trespass in Scotland, and a very full abstract of statistics. The report of Study Group Nine ended up by recommending a new agency, The Countryside Commission for Scotland. After approbation at the conference in 1965, our report was circulated by the Government as a White Paper as the Scottish Office stated that they could not better it! It resulted in the Countryside (Scotland) Act 1970 and the setting up of the Countryside Commission for Scotland.

I was disappointed that I did not get the job of Director of the Countryside Commission when it was advertised. I have always thought that John Foster from the Peak District National Park, who got the job, did not make the most of the opportunity that we had created, but, no doubt, the civil service kept him and the Commission on a very tight rein. I would not have been happy under those circumstances.

O.B.E.Award

In the Queen's Birthday Honours of 1969 Bob Grieve got a knighthood and I got an OBE. Bob's, was very much deserved, having assumed successfully the arduous job of being the first Chairman of the Highland and Islands Development Board, a difficult transfer to the political sphere after a long and most distinguished career as a civil servant. I hastened to congratulate him and he, in his reply, said how nice it was that we were honoured in the same list.

How it came about seems to have been as follows. Some one must have put forward my name during the spring of 1969. I never learnt who it was. Lord Hughes, then the Minister in charge of Local Government and Housing at St Andrew's House wrote to the County Clerk saying he would like to be shown the planning work going on in the County. A date was arranged when, fulfilling a previous engagement, I was away overnight in Fife lecturing to the North-east Fife Preservation Society in Anstruther and taking the morning to advise them on some of their projects. So it was left to the County Clerk and Graham Duncan to conduct Lord Hughes round the County in the morning. I joined the party for lunch in Dunbar and escorted them back through North Berwick and along the coast ending up I remember at Prestongrange where our way-out proposal for a coal mining industry heritage site was taking shape. Lord Hughes left us there giving me a cordial invitation to meet him any time in the House of Commons, which I regret I never took up.

It was in May when I received a letter, in confidence, from No 10 Downing Street on blue embossed paper saying that the Prime Minister had in mind submitting my name to the Queen with the recommendation that I should be appointed an Officer of the Order of the British Empire and asking for my assurance that this would be agreeable to me. I was very doubtful whether this was in fact the case, as I was generally opposed to the honours system and I knew that it would lead to a great deal of jealousy amongst my colleagues in Haddington. However, on the other side of the argument, I recalled the old soldier's quip that an OBE was an officer's 'gong' for "other's bloody effort" as opposed to the soldier's MBE for "my bloody effort", and so I owed it to my staff to accept it—they certainly thought so. It was also a recommendation from Harold Wilson, whom I greatly admired, and further it was a recognition of the achievements and status of planning officers that they were beginning to be recommended for decorations.

Maurice Taylor, the County Planning Officer of Fife was the first and Frank Bracewell of the Central Region was a later recipient. Knighthoods and decorations had usually been reserved in local government for the Town Clerks of the four cities and Chief Constables. Mary also rightly pointed out that it would do no harm on my curriculum vitae, when we all lost our jobs had to apply for new posts after the reorganisation of local government in 1975; and said she thought it would please our right wing friends! And so I replied that it would be agreeable to me. When the award was published on the Queen's Birthday no attribution was made, I was just noted as the County Planning Officer for East Lothian and so I still do not know why I got it. It certainly made life quite difficult in County Buildings, Haddington, as several of my colleagues were very jealous, but I received a very large dossier of congratulatory letters from many people whom I greatly respected.

National Trust for Scotland

I spent some eighteen years on the Council of the National Trust for Scotland mostly representing the Royal Town Planning Institute, but for three years as an elected member. The NTS held quarterly meetings of the Council which included rural landowners and their connections. I considered it my duty to represent the urban man and speak and vote accordingly. I had three lines that I banged on about whenever I got the chance. Firstly, the NTS should acquire more countryside and coastal properties rather than castles and mansion houses. They gibbed at the acquisition of forty thousand acres of Knoydart which became available once the idea of the tank firing range had been abandoned by Michael Heseltine, then Minister of Defence. As the John Muir Trust has shown, wild land has a special place in people's hearts. The NTS has since acquired Upper Glen Affric and the 90,000 acres of the Mar Lodge Estate. Secondly, the NTS should widen the range of properties in their portfolio by acquiring urban properties, both domestic and industrial. In my time they acquired the Tenement Flat in Glasgow and the Printing Works in Innerleithen and the both have proved extremely popular but have not led to any large industrial acquisition such as Lady Victoria Colliery. Thirdly, I was very critical of the fact that the NTS had no architecturally qualified staff to look after their properties, which seemed to be at the mercy of amateurs and land agents and to be dominated by tourist considerations. Year by year their properties assume the appearance of film sets or museums, without the authentic ring of history. There are lavish new curtains and carpets when money should have been spent on rhones and down pipes. Dry rot outbreaks were bewailed as unexpected misfortunes rather than the result of negligence. I am glad to say that now they get private architects to carry out quinquennial inspections but there is still no staff architect to see that their recommendations are carried through into the annual budgets and work programmes. A curious situation in a body who has in its care some of the finest buildings in Scotland.

Professional Bodies

I also served on the Executive of the Scottish Branch of the Royal Town Planning Institute and in due course became its Chairman from 1965 to 1967. I established with Jack Baillie, the County Planning Officer for Midlothian, the County Planning Officers' Society so that planners could have an advisory role in the Convention of Scottish Local Authorities and, incidentally, campaign for a rise in their rather meagre salaries. These were way below those of the County Road Surveyors, despite the fact that most chief planning officers had dual qualifications or were university graduates in addition to their professional qualifications, as in my case. Planners also undertook a wider range of duties, much in the public eye. I am glad to say that this campaign was fruitful in that the Regional Authorities put Planning Officers on a par with Directors of Education and above those single function officers such as Architects, Directors of Drainage, Highways, etc. I do not remember anything notable about these representational jobs, just more paper and more committee meetings.

Reorganisation of Local Government in Scotland 1975

The Labour Government set up a Royal Commission, under Lord Wheatley, to study the reorganisation of local government in Scotland.

In 1966 I found myself involved in three submissions of evidence to the Royal Commission: my personal views, the views of the Regional Studies Association and the views of the Royal Town Planning Institute. I am glad to say that they differed more in form and detail than in principle, but it caused me some embarrassment when I was invited to give oral evidence wearing three different hats. I have my personal submission here before me as I write and it is typed on foolscap paper which was still then in use in Haddington County Buildings.

My paper, after analysing the faults of the pre-1975 system: the lack of regional planning, the small size of the typical Scottish county and the parochial attitudes of the burgh councils, put forward the proposal for three regional planning commissions. One would cover the Highlands and Islands and north-east Scotland, which share the same interests in the development of their natural resources and multi-purpose rural developments. The second would cover the industrial central belt of Scotland to end the duality of Edinburgh and Glasgow, attract new industries to replace the old heavy industries and act as a kind of economic land-bridge between America and Europe. It would be on a scale that could rival the industrial regions of Europe such as Amsterdam/Rotterdam and the Ruhr. The third region would cover the Borders and Dumfries and Galloway and ideally land on both sides of the basins of both the River Tweed and the Solway Firth. I advocated that these three regional planning commissions should be composed of people both nominated by the Secretary of State and representatives of the local authorities. They would represent the coming together of both central and local government and the public and private sectors, drawing their finance from precepts on the local authorities, grants from central government and, for their investment functions, direct from the Scottish Office. The Planning Commission would control and finance all the development of the infrastructure services: electricity, transportation, water supply, drainage, etc., the location of industrial sites and new large-scale investment in urban growth—matters which are still largely outwith the democratic control.

The next level of local government would be some eleven or thirteen most-purpose elected authorities formed by amalgamating the small counties and the four cities. This tier would carry out all the local services, as at present. They would be large enough to provide cost-efficient services. The third tier would be local consultative councils, based on the market towns and their spheres of influence, having responsibility for all the minutiae of local government and the management of housing. They would inherit the traditions and dignities of the Scottish burghs.

This was a slightly different proposal from the Geddesian concept of valley units, which was advocated by the Scottish Branch of the

Royal Town Planning Institute and adopted later by the Government with some modification. The outcome was eleven directly elected regional councils controlling the basic services of structure planning, education, transportation, social work, water and drainage, fire and police. Below them, District Councils dealt with local planning, development control, implementation, housing, public health, recreation and related matters.

The procedure of this review was the complete opposite to the reform of local government in 1996, which has been pushed through by Conservative political dogma without any Royal Commission or proper examination of how successfully the 1975 system had worked. It reverted to a system of small all purpose counties and cities, with scarcely any acknowledgement of regional planning, no control over the many government quangos which dictate the spread of investment, and no vision of how Scotland could rise to the challenge of the twenty first century.

Director of Physical Planning, Lothian Regional Council

Fortunately Scotland did get twenty years of regional government and I was delighted to be selected as Director of Physical Planning by the Lothian Regional Council, enabling me to play a role that I had always wanted since my days at Cambridge. I was more suited by education and temperament to this new job than to the minutiae of architectural and nature conservation that filled much of my life as County Planning Officer in East Lothian. It was only having married an architect and moving in her circles that enabled me to find satisfaction in that role. I was also very pleased that Graham Duncan, my deputy, succeeded me as Director of Planning for East Lothian District and could carry on with the policy and attitudes which had been our hallmark.

16

CHAPTER SIXTEEN

My Two Offices • With Love • My Staff
A Cast-iron Souvenir • My Colleagues and their Secretaries
Regional Planning
Lothian Building Preservation Trust.

My Two Offices

On the 4th May 1975, I visited my office in Haddington to clear my desk. It was a nice room on the second floor of the technical block, facing west with a view out over old pantiled roofs to the fields beyond the town. It was painted my favourite "shit-brown" colour, as it was rudely called. There was a one inch to the mile O.S. map of the County pasted on the conference table, and on one wall hung a large oil painting of the Gairloch by the Victorian academician Horatio McCulloch. It was one of many I had rescued from the attics of the County Buildings and persuaded the County Council to have valued and restored and hung throughout the Buildings. There was a long bookcase with a number of conversation pieces on the top: a piece of driftwood mounted in an striving posture, a present from Otto Kaltenborn of Tanberg; various smooth beach rocks from the County's shoreline; a fisherman's glass float; and an old iron spearhead found in the River Tyne near Haddington.

I had been spending at least half my time in a very different office in Edinburgh. This was vast, the former office of Edinburgh's Chief Constable in the old Police Headquarters above the Burgh Police Court. I renamed it No 1 Parliament Square. It had an Adam's fireplace and two large windows from which I could see the Mercat Cross, the east end of St Giles Cathedral, the Parliament Buildings of the High Court and, across the High Street, the City Chambers. On entering the doorway I had to pass through a motley crowd of citizens who were being marshalled by our door keeper as witnesses for the Burgh Court. I really felt I was at the heart of things, a truly Geddesian situation.

With Love

Mid-morning on my last day as County Planning Officer my Haddington staff came in and presented me with a Goxhill clay non-interlocking pantile inscribed simply "To FPT with love from" and sixteen signatures; George McNeil's and three rangers' were absent. Later they presented me with a set of 12 table mats, being the reproduction at half size of the 12 conservation village boards we had erected in 1975. They were useful talking points between serving up dishes at our supper parties.

What a change from the gallant four who started off with me in 1950—Neroli Wilkins, planning assistant, a New Zealander, George Alexander and John McNeil, technicians and Joyce Sheerin, typist. By 1975 we had a development budget of £3 million and our influence stretched into every corner of the County. It was, of course, empire building but it had to be fought for from a very tight fisted Council.

My Staff

The sixteen were:

Graham Duncan, my depute since 1972 and an architect planner who saved me from many a pitfall and got me out of those I fell into. He was in charge of all the architecture we were putting on the ground. He succeeded me in Haddington and later became the City Planning Officer in Edinburgh.

Liz Thomas, a planner "pure and simple" who worked on the Development Plan and later moved to Midlothian. She then married and lived at Castle Eden near Peterlee where my planning career had started, and is now with Brighton City Council.

David Thompson, a geographer planner who also worked on the Development Plan and now has the Depute job in Dumfries and Galloway.

Jim Henry, a geologist planner, a Haddington boy who was the only one who came with me to the Regional Council despite "all the love".

Jim Farquhar, the Falkirk 'bairn' who worked so well in development control and kept our flag flying when I and Graham had gone.

Christine Crichton, a planner from genteel Edinburgh.

"Big Jim" Carnegie, our industrial officer who came from Irvine New Town and was big in every way.

Ian Fullerton, our landscape officer from Dundee Parks Department, who knew his own mind.

George McNeil, an engineer planner, a local lad from Musselburgh who took charge of our environmental rehabilitation and other projects, and subsequently became Director of Planning in West Lothian. A splendid operator.

Jim McCall, another local lad from Elphinstone, a former Coal Board surveyor who worked with George on our rehabilitation projects.

Archie Mathieson, our countryside ranger, without compare.

Richard Digby, a young fair-haired keen ranger.

Plate CXVII Graham Duncan—Architect Planner

He came to East Lothian in 1967 after a spell in Singapore, but he was an Edinburgh boy, married to Helen, an Edinburgh girl, and they had two Haddington boys. He left East Lothian District Council to be Director of Planning in the City of Edinburgh and retired in 1996.

Margaret Morrison who headed the drawing office and produced many of our fine pamphlets.

Kate Denholm and Helen Robertson, both married ladies, who shared a draughtsman's job working from the same drawing board and even on the same drawing with great charm.

Roderick McLean, a trainee planner who now works in Fife.

Betty Shand, my long suffering secretary and organist at the parish church.

Elaine Mason, a typist.

I remembered other staff who had made outstanding contributions and then moved on:

John Reid, a very talented man who could succeed at most things, had two spells with us and eventually landed up as Development Officer for the Falkland Islands after that war.

Ian Becker, an architect planner in the early days who was responsible for the design of Prestonpans Civic Square and laid the foundations for a very happy office.

Richard Adams, our first industrial officer, whose life work is to support the poor of the Indian subcontinent through his TEAR organisation as has already been mentioned.

Russell Turner, a geographer planner who was the backbone of the development plan section and provided, as well as the methodology for much of our survey work, a baby-sitting service for us and for the Duncans who lived on the same floor as he did of Mitchell's Close. He later became Assistant Director of the Countryside Commission for Scotland and received an OBE for his efforts.

Hamish Macdonald, a surveyor/draughtsman who produced splendid drawings and became a planner in Midlothian.

Nora McLaughlan, my secretary, but that is not a very good job description, as my department, like the others, was kept running by these capable women. She served a long time with us, then left to have children, and subsequently returned to run the County Clerk's department and was a great ally in the right place.

What a happy crowd and I think it was true that we were all a little in love with each other.

A Cast-iron Souvenir

At lunch time that day I thought a roof tile, however subscribed, was not quite adequate as a keep-sake of my East Lothian days and I remembered that Mr Leslie the auctioneer, furniture restorer and remover, had acquired the eight cast-iron finials that had proudly surmounted the columns that guided the rise and fall of the gas tank at the Haddington Gas Works. He had one left and I asked him the cost: "£12" he said and I quickly asked "delivered ?" to which he assented. Over the weekend I rapidly built a stone plinth in our garden at Ford and the next Monday it came trundling across the lawn on a piano trolley. I was at work in Edinburgh but Mary steadfastly insisted that it must be delivered onto the plinth, despite its weight and the men's

Plate CXVIII My Cast-iron Souvenir

This finial was one of eight that graced the framework for the rise and fall gas-holder in Haddington. It now graces a corner of my garden at Ford, backed by a large leaved ivy and embraced by a cotoneaster. It is surprising how few of our visitors can guess its origins even though every town once had a gas-holder.

protests that the cement was still green. There it remains to this day, a constant reminder of happy days and high endeavour.

My Colleagues and their Secretaries

In the afternoon I went round to say good-bye to my colleagues in County Buildings where I had a few friends and admirers. George Russell, the County Treasurer; Jimmy Gibson, the County Sanitary Inspector who was awarded an MBE on his retirement; and David Lyle, the assistant County Clerk, who serviced the Planning Committee and later became Secretary to the Scottish Development Agency. I had always made a point of getting on well with the secretaries in all departments. They were all local women and good relations with them ensured that our papers kept moving even when we failed to click with their chiefs. I remember Molly Dodds and Nan Wallace, successively County Clerk's secretaries; Miss Storey, architect's department, and May Laidlaw, public health, to use their maiden names because until the mid sixties they were always dismissed on marriage.

Regional Planning

As I went the rounds I asked what they thought I should do in my new job which the local paper had described as "Planning Supremo" of the Lothian Region. "Make the Region a little like East Lothian" they said and this I tried to do. But it was a very different world I was entering. It was not dealing with real people from all walks of life and with real projects on the ground but with fellow bureaucrats. We all behaved like actors representing our own departments, endlessly rearranging words on paper and repetitive meetings. However the Lothian Region Structure Plan, approved in 1978, postulated a period of consolidation with no green field sites for building beyond those which already had planning consent. This conferred on them a land value the Regional Council could not afford to buy back. Consolidation meant strengthening the life of all communities, making up deficiencies such as old folk's housing and other educational and health service provisions, filling up gap sites, clearing dereliction and promoting prosperity. A fine data base was built up on the capacities and needs of all the towns and villages in terms of services. Thus through the Thatcher years we were able to reduce the demand for new infrastructure by utilising this spare capacity.

We finally settled the City Bypass controversy by determining its line, linking up the M8, M9 and the A1, and it was built section by section. We set about measures to make the road traffic fit the City and not the City fit the traffic as was then the orthodoxy and abandoned the Inner Ring Road.

To get out in the countryside and do something visible we

Plate CXIX   Mavisbank House, Loanhead
(a) 1987   (b) 1724, Model

(a) Mavisbank is the first and perhaps the finest of William Adam's houses, 1724. It became a matter of great concern for me in the Lothian Regional Council and later, as Director of the Lothian Building Preservation Trust, I saved it from demolition.

(b) Model made by Simon Montgomery showing the House as designed with its attractive semi-domed roof and a row of 22 chimneys coming up through the centre of the building. It represents my unfinished business but now rests squarely in the Secretary of State for Scotland's court.

launched the Central Scotland Woodlands Project in 1980, the first of the new forest proposals in the United Kingdom. We established, with the Department of Leisure and Recreation, the Regional Park organisation for the Pentland Hills. I had also recruited a Land Rehabilitation Unit which dealt with the backlog of industrial dereliction and other environmental projects to the tune of a million pounds a year.

I volunteered to take over responsibility for dealing with the gypsy problem which none of my colleagues would touch. It gave us equal measures of fun and frustration. Eventually we built them a well-equipped permanent site at the former Craigmillar rail yard. I was also the Regional Council's representative involved in preparing the comprehensive plan for Craigmillar by the Craigmillar Festival Society under their inspired Director, Helen Crummy. Craigmillar was a deprived pre-war housing estate to the south-east of Edinburgh which was the first to obtain funding through the European Social Fund. It was my task to certify that the money was well spent. Thus I kept in touch with real people and got real satisfaction.

Lothian Building Preservation Trust

Finally, on retirement from the Lothian Regional Council in March 1983, I was asked to become the unpaid Director of the Lothian Building Preservation Trust with the self-imposed task of keeping an eye on all historic buildings at risk in Lothian and acting as an "agency of last resort". The Trust restored three groups of buildings: Broxmouth South Lodge and Gateway, near Dunbar; 1-5 London Road, Dalkeith; and Bankton House, Prestonpans. It saved Mavisbank House, Loanhead, from demolition in dramatic circumstances on the night of 26 March 1987 and prepared a feasibility study which persuaded Historic Scotland to declare it an Ancient Monument and the Government to agree to acquire and restore it.

I retired from the Trust in January 1996 at the age of 77 and settled down to write these Memoirs of the Halcyon Days of Town Planning. They were truly pioneering days when there was more construction than there has ever been and, with the disasters of the thirties still in mind, great public support for planning. It was a time when one could stretch the limits of planning to cover all aspects of the environment in a truly Geddesian way embracing Folk-Work-Place. It is for others to judge whether I left East Lothian a more contented, prosperous and beautiful place than I found it. Adieu.

INDEX

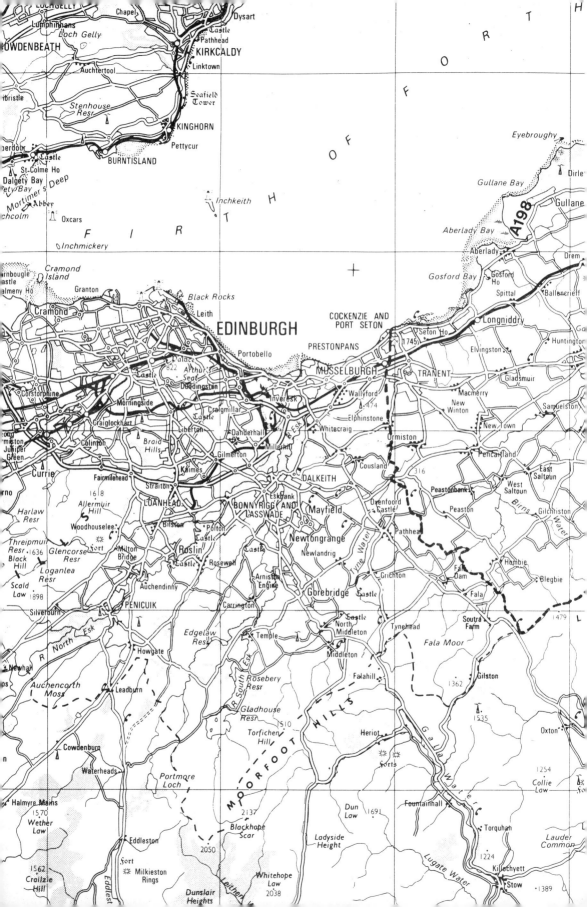